HOLY LAND
IN MAPS

Edited by Ariel Tishby

The Israel Museum, Jerusalem

RIZZOLI
NEW YORK

The Israel Museum, Jerusalem

Holy Land In Maps

Published in conjunction with the exhibition
*On the Map: Cartographic Images
of the Holy Land*

Rena (Fisch) and Robert Lewin Gallery
Hildegard and Simon Rothschild Foundation
(Switzerland) Gallery
Nathan Cummings 20th Century Art Building
Fall—Winter 2001/2

Curator-in-charge: Meira Perry-Lehmann
Curator: Ariel Tishby
Exhibition design: Rivka Myers

Editors: Vivianne Barsky and Evelyn Katrak
English translations: Idan Yaron, Timna Seligman,
David Maisel, Esther Boreda, Almuth Lessing
Book design: Stephanie & Ruti Design, Jerusalem
Typesetting: Esther Rosenfeld, Yael Golan
Printed in China

Israel Museum catalogue no. 459
ISBN 965-278-269-6

Exhibition and catalogue made possible by the donors
to the Israel Museum 2001 Exhibition Fund —
Ruth and Leon Davidoff, Paris and Mexico City;
Hanno D. Mott, New York; The Nash Family Foundation,
New York — and its Share 2000 Program

The book draws on the Noman Bier Section for Maps of
the Holy Land in the Department of Prints and
Drawings at the Israel Museum, and on selected maps
from major public and private collections in Israel and
abroad.

**Books are to be returned on or before
the last date below.**

Exhibition
CATALOGUE

LIBREX —

WITHDRAWN

List of Contributors

M. B.   Prof. Moshe Brawer, Tel Aviv University

S. C.   Shai Cohen, The Hebrew University of Jerusalem

D. G.   Dr. Dov Gavish, The Hebrew University of Jerusalem

S. G.   Dr. Shimon Gibson, The British Institute of Archaeology, Jerusalem

H. G.   Dr. Haim Goren, Academic College, Tel Hai

N. K.   Prof. Naftali Kadmon, The Hebrew University of Jerusalem

M. L.-R.   Dr. Milka Levy-Rubin, The Hebrew University of Jerusalem

R. R.   Prof. Rehav Rubin, The Hebrew University of Jerusalem

R. S.   Prof. Rudolf Schmidt, International Coronelli Society, Vienna

T. S.   Tamar Sofer, The Hebrew University of Jerusalem

A. T.   Ariel Tishby, The Israel Museum, Jerusalem

Y. T.   Prof. Yoram Tsafrir, The Hebrew University of Jerusalem

Contents

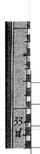

Foreword

In the history of cartography, maps of the Land of Israel are a continuous presence, reflecting nearly every period from antiquity to the present day. It is with pride and pleasure that the Israel Museum produces an exhibition and book which offer its audience a comprehensive presentation of cartographic depictions of the Holy Land and of Jerusalem, from a 6th-century mosaic map to contemporary satellite images. These maps document the changes in religious, scientific, and artistic thought which have taken place over the last two millennia.

The common feature of old maps of the Land of Israel derives from their essential purpose: to make concrete the events described in the Holy Scriptures, through what was known as "sacred geography." Initially these maps were historical in nature rather than practical, and they provided cartographers with an opportunity to experiment artistically with techniques, styles, designs, and cartographic symbols. From the end of the 18th century, however, with advances in scientific methods and a greater number of researchers and visitors actually in the region, maps took on a more functional role and began also to document local demographic changes.

Like the Israel Museum itself, mapmaking and its history are by their nature multidisciplinary. This is reflected in the variety of fields represented in this exhibition and book: historical geography, cartography and the history of cartography, archaeology, and the history of art. And we are indebted to the scholars who contributed their breadth of knowledge to illuminate our subject. We offer our profound thanks to Norman and Frieda Bier of London, who, continuing their long-standing tradition of generosity to the Museum, created the Section for Maps of the Holy Land in the Department of Prints and Drawings. The Biers, together with Karl and Li Handler, Vienna, and Teddy and Tamar Kollek, Jerusalem, also provided many of the maps that today are the backbone of our collection. We are likewise grateful to the lenders to the exhibition, including the Gross family, Tel Aviv; Isaac Einhorn, Tel Aviv; Zalman Enav, Tel Aviv; the Moldovan family, New York; Rudolf Schmidt, Vienna; Dr. Richard Cleave, Nicosia; the Wajntraub family, Jerusalem; the British Library, London; and the Jewish National and University Library, Jerusalem. The exhibition and catalogue were made possible through the essential generosity of the donors to the Israel Museum's 2001 Exhibition Fund and its Share 2000 Program.

Finally, we acknowledge most gratefully the initiative, enthusiasm, and dedication of Ariel Tishby, editor of this volume and curator of the exhibition it accompanies, who worked together with a committed team of Israel Museum staff to realize this project with all of the rich fullness it deserves.

James S. Snyder
Anne and Jerome Fisher Director
The Israel Museum, Jerusalem

Introduction

Many definitions for the term "map" have been proposed in the past. Today, the more accepted ones seem to be those that are broadly encompassing — witness that given by Harley and Woodward in the first volume of their *History of Cartography* (1987): "Maps are graphic representations that facilitate a spatial understanding of things, concepts, conditions, processes, or events in the human world."[1] A more concise yet wider definition is that of Robinson and Petchenik: "A map is the representation of the milieu."[2] The term "milieu" here denotes surroundings in the widest sense — not just the topographic "surface," but everything connected to the way a map reflects a worldview.

Maps thus constitute spatial configurations of places of human meaning and content.[3] In this organization of space, the central factor is not the morphology or geometric structure of the forms in the described area, but the "story" behind them.

This aspect is very conspicuous in antique maps and those describing pilgrimage to the Land of Israel. The phrase "Holy Land" evokes both the earthly and the sublime. Typical of the convergence of cultural coordinates with geographical ones is the search for the "center of the world." Even in the age of scientifically measured maps, the backdrop of national confrontation over the same "homeland" renders any map of this area an object of loaded symbolism and importance. Because the Land of Israel, more than any other part of the world, has been continuously mapped through history, these maps act

also as a summary of the story of mapping in general.[4] The Swiss humanist Joachim von Watt (Vadianus) (1484–1551) maintained that real science can contribute greatly to real religion. It follows that without geographical knowledge, it is not possible to grasp fully either the events or the sites where they occurred as described in the Holy Scriptures. The present volume, then, reflects cultural history as well: science, art, and religion.

There is no decisive scientific proof that maps existed in the Land of Israel in prehistoric and ancient times. But in the opinion of the archaeologist Shimon Gibson their absence results from the inevitable gap between the modern concept of "map" and the possible depiction of their environment by local inhabitants during early periods. Certain archaeological finds, such as petroglyphs incised with indecipherable lines and markings, were eventually identified as possible maps. An intriguing example is the Bronze Age (about 5000-years-old) stone with a circumference of about 5 m found in 1978 in a cave close to Petra in Jordan; another is the group of standing stones found in the Golan Heights, made by wandering Christians (Ghassanids) during the Byzantine period, and incised with lines and shapes that seem to represent roads and water sources.[5]

Biblical texts provide detailed geographical descriptions and perhaps hint at the use of maps during biblical times. Not only is the Bible replete with the names and locations of sites, but measuring lines were apparently already used in

issue unt cuis. e mut
unt gir tres cuis
e destrut in deni
meemer.

kiut v hõ merta nře
seignur a cruclfier
Ananie ki baptiza
seit poil: le baptiza.

Hic coñisantur opti
mi mcatores q an
tps machometi
meuru dm
mcatoru
coluert.

gernam diminucio
ru valet dno suo
cordie qngeras
libras argñti.

Ci
rma

Tute ceste terre ki gi't est eriche est en la seignurie des sarrazins. E entres les autres Sap
poissantz imeint li ueuz de la muntainne. co est a sau li suuerins de hautz assis. ki por
tent les cuteus e ocient cestui dur il cumandemet delur suuereint. E cele obedience co dient
les sauuera.

Hic si procul usus borea
manet uetus de
monte.

Hic habundant cameli bubali
mulis e asini quibz utuntur
institores int orientales
e occidentales insme
antes.

Le cimetere
seit nicholas v hõ
entere les mortz

La tur asaudite

La porte par
le moldn de

ochia dom
mori mos
est de tur renunice est
north e nord. cest de
re v il ia priarche e
nice. E est de acre a
neos.

le chastel le rei de acre.

LA
VILE
DE ACRE

lospital
mans.

la tur de

este espate sestent
uir deuers le
orthz ardant ki
uunte usbilc
antioche.
ut ia tur la
duine numee
et citez e uile
hasteus ause
en la meillur
ur ki esta
ce e tyrus. est
ere coz sidon.

Co est le burg ki est apele mir misard la por te de us
si est la tur le plus baliue de engloise. seint nicholas

La tur de pisanz

Ceste cite ki ore est apele acre
ia apelec cholomaida. Ele est
rance e resiu as tuz crestiens t
la terre seinte uut e remend
pur les sucurs ke le a de la me
li uent de tute europe e de tut
isles ken la mer sut e crestien

la maisun del
hospital seit joha

Doui militia eccc
st lazari q st
bello
pam
bu

Ceste uile uaut a sun
seignur chescun
an cinquite
mile liure
dargent.

Le tem
ple.

Matthew Paris,
ca. 1195–1259
Map of the Holy Land (detail)
St. Albans, England, ca. 1252
Manuscript on vellum
ca. 350x255 mm
The British Library, London
Royal MS14C VII, fol. 4v

those times: "I lifted up mine eyes again, and looked, and behold a man with a measuring line in his hand. Then said I, Whither goest thou? And he said unto me, To measure Jerusalem, to see what is the breadth thereof, and what is the length thereof" (Zech. 2:1–2).

The Bible later served European mapmakers as the basic source for their historical maps of the Land of Israel. To this were added many other descriptions — those by the first Greek explorers such as Poseidonios (2nd century BCE), to Josephus Flavius, to Hieronymous (Jerome), to Eusebius, who wrote the Onomastikon in the first half of the 4th century. A list of sites mentioned in the Bible, it was written with the help of local Jewish inhabitants who added information on interpretations of Jewish traditions.[6] The Madaba Map (see p. 66) was apparently based on the Onomastikon. If there were maps preceding it, their orientation was probably to the east, as in the Madaba Map and as in later European maps. Among the Semitic peoples, orientation was principally to the east, the rising sun being founded in biblical language (as in the Book of Joshua), with the east described as "forward" (kadima), and the west as "behind" or "toward the sea" (referring to "the Great Sea" — i.e., the Mediterranean.[7]

Especially noteworthy as an early map and a source for other maps is the Book of Jubilees, dated mid-2nd century and written against the backdrop of the fight against Hellenism. Fragments of the original were found in the Qumran caves. The complete text exists in an Ethiopian translation. It covers the history of the world and the people of Israel, from the Creation to the Exodus. The eighth chapter describes the division of the world among Noah's sons and differs from Genesis 10. In-depth research has concluded that the book relates not only to the intellectual or verbal image of the world but also to an actual map.[8] The Christian so-called T-in-O maps of the Middle Ages may in fact be based on the tradition whose source lies in the Book of Jubilees, according to which the world was divided among Noah's three sons.

Over the generations, the Land of Israel has attracted numerous travelers, visitors, and pilgrims of all three monotheistic religions, many of whom wrote descriptions of their journey, thus adding to our knowledge about the country. Information accumulated from these various descriptions directly influenced maps of the Land of Israel. The historical geography of Jerusalem also allows us to understand the numerous changes that took place in this city. A prime example is the archaeological explorations that revealed the Cardo, a street in Jerusalem, using the first original map — the Madaba Map — as a guide.

Just as the history of culture is reflected in, or can even be mapped with the help of various maps throughout history, so can the history of science.[9] The profession of measurement and mapping — known as geodesy — is as old as days. Up until the end of the Middle Ages the main systems of measurement were based on astronomical observation, geometry, and mechanical devices. The measuring of time, at first by means of sand and water clocks and sun dials, and

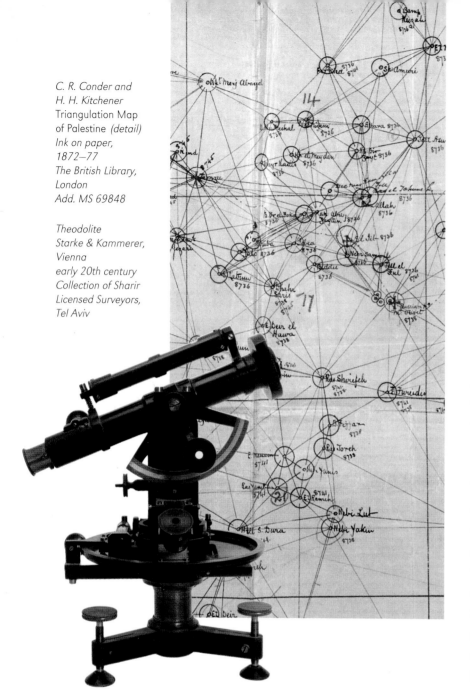

the length of the sides were calculated, and using this system, called triangulation, national grids were created that were combined into an international grid. Thus the way was paved for scientific measurement. The combining of photographic technology and the measuring of distance through radio waves and laser rays allowed for a precision previously unknown. The use of satellite imaging, of computerized geographic information systems (GIS), as well as navigation and determining location via satellite (GPS — global positioning system), attests to the incredible advances humanity has made since the first attempts to map the world and, specifically, the Land of Israel.

The contents of this book were to a large extent determined by the fact that it accompanies the exhibition *On the Map: Cartographic Images of the Holy Land* at The Israel Museum, Jerusalem. The majority of maps in the book are featured in the exhibition, allowing visitors to survey firsthand the historical survey of maps of the Land of Israel. Most of the maps come from the Museum's permanent collections, especially the Norman Bier Section for Maps of the Holy Land.

later by means of mechanical clocks, served in measuring the world's circumference and determining the placement of the equator. The theodolite, a complex instrument that measures horizontal and vertical angles, was apparently invented in the 16th century and was refined through developments in optics and fine mechanics. By measuring the distance between two points giving the basis of an imaginary triangle, and measuring two angles of the triangle,

I would like to express my deep appreciation to Professor Norman Bier of London, who donated over 130 important maps to the Museum. Through his generosity the Section for Maps of the Holy Land was established, and as a result the book and exhibition were able to take off.

I owe a great debt of gratitude to Professor Naftali Kadmon and Professor Rehav Rubin of The Hebrew

University, Jerusalem, who, apart from their major contributions to this book, accompanied the dual project from its early beginnings and aided me with vital information.

Special thanks are due to Helen Laor, widow of the eminent collector of Holy Land maps, Eran Laor, and to Shoshana Klein, Curator of the Eran Laor Cartographic Collection at the Jewish National and University Library, Jerusalem, for years of professional advice; and also to Dr. Shimon Gibson of the British Archaeological Institute in Jerusalem, Dr. Joseph Forrai, Chief Scientist at the Survey of Israel, Dr. Adolfo Roitman, Curator of the Shrine of the Book at the Israel Museum, and Dr. Itai Meiraz, for the important articles they made available to me, deepening and enriching my knowledge of the subject. I am likewise grateful to Professor Avigdor Poseq and Professor Moshe Barash of the Hebrew University of Jerusalem's Department of Art History for their sound advice and constructive criticism. The book would of course not have been realized without the dedication of the translators and editors. A particular word of gratitude to Vivianne Barsky and Evelyn Katrak, who devoted many months to the project.

Within the Museum I wish to thank Meira Perry-Lehmann, Michael Bromberg Senior Curator of the Department of Prints and Drawings, for her encouragement of the founding of the Map Section; Yigal Zalmona, Chief Curator-at-Large, Suzanne Landau, Chief Curator for the Arts, and Judith Spitzer, Managing Editor of Art Wing Publications, for their involvement and support throughout; Rita Gans, General Manager of Israel Museum Products,

Ltd., for her vision and patience in seeing the book through its production; Timna Seligman, Assistant Curator in the Department of Israel Art, for her invaluable work, cheer, and stamina; as well as curators Dr. Rika Gonen, Dr. Iris Fishof, Na'ama Brosh, and Debby Hershman for their wise counsel; and all the other members of the Museum staff who had a hand in the project. Finally, I wish to acknowledge the important contributions of Museum volunteers Ruth Mittelmann and Tamar Aviad.

A. T.

1. J. B. Harley and D. Woodward, eds., *The History of Cartography*, vol. 1 (Chicago, 1987).

2. A. H. Robinson and B. B. Petchenik, *The Nature of Maps* (Chicago, 1976), p. 16.

3. I. Meiraz, "Pilgrim's Maps," lecture in the series *Mediterranean Maps*, initiated by Tel Aviv University and Mishkenot Sha'ananim, Jerusalem, June 1999.

4. I. Schattner, *A Map of the Land of Israel and Its History* (Jerusalem, 1951), p. 13 (in Hebrew).

5. C. Dauphin and S. Gibson, "Ancient Settlements in Their Landscapes: The Results of Ten Years of Survey on the Golan Heights (1978–1988)," *Bulletin of the Anglo-Israel Archaeological Society* 12 1992–93, pp. 7–31.

6. S. Klein, *A History of the Survey of the Land of Israel in Hebrew and General Literature* (Jerusalem, 1937) (in Hebrew).

7. M. Harel, "Geographic Orientation and Its Use in Biblical Maps," in *Israel — People and Land* 19 (Tel Aviv, 1984), pp. 157–67 (in Hebrew).

8. F. Schmidt, "Jewish Representations of the Inhabited Earth during the Hellenistic and Roman Periods," in *Greece and Rome in Eretz Israel*, ed. A. Rasner, U. Rappaport, and J. Fuks (Jerusalem, 1990), pp. 119–34.

9. I thank Dr. Joseph Forrai, Chief Scientist at the Survey of Israel, for summarizing this subject for the present book.

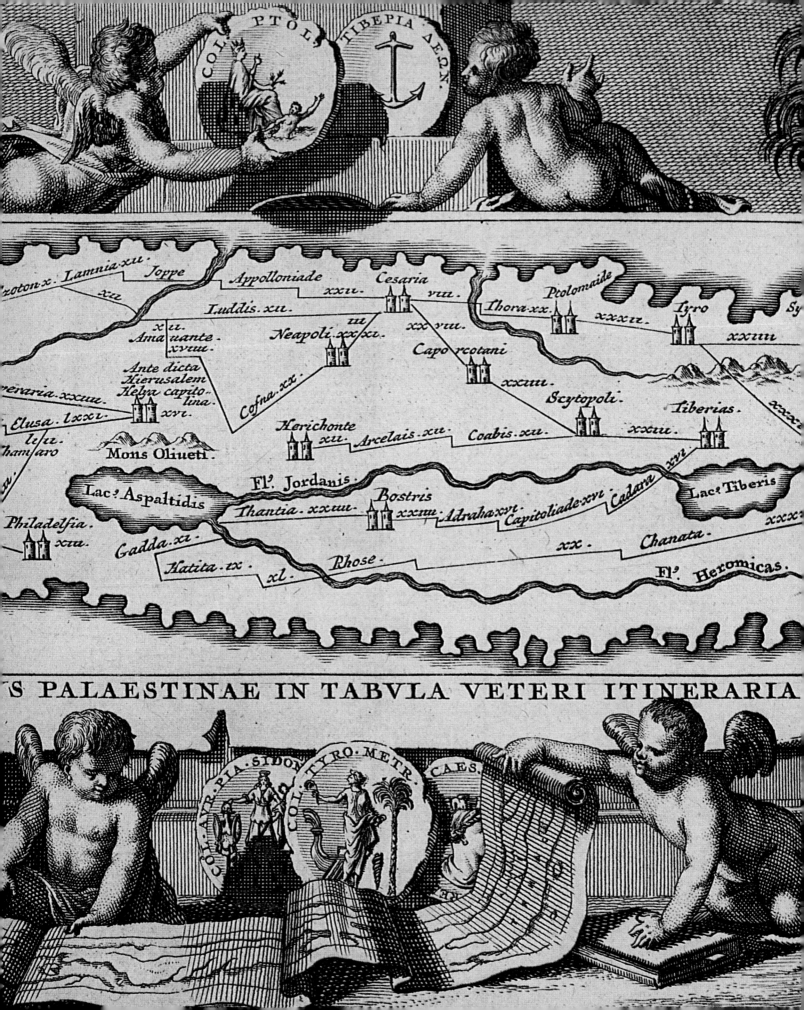

The Holy Land in Maps:
From Stone Mosaic to Satellite Image
Naftali Kadmon

The Dawn of Mapping and Maps of Antiquity

Israel does not constitute the subject of the oldest known maps; this distinction belongs to ancient Mesopotamia, where maps were inscribed in clay some 4,500 years ago. But the Holy Land undoubtedly boasts the longest unbroken chain of graphic representations in the world.

A geographical map is a graphic presentation, usually flat or plane, which shows the Earth as well as phenomena — whether real or imaginary — on its surface. But this descriptive function is performed also by a picture such as a landscape drawing. The primary distinction between a map and a picture lies in the fact that maps chiefly make use of formal symbolization. While the artist's eye sees whatever it sees at a more or less horizontal angle, from within the landscape, as it were, the classical map depicts the Earth from above, either vertically or obliquely. The first significant step in man's endeavors to map the Earth lay in elevating the viewing angle to a point from which the mapper regards the world from above — albeit in his mind's eye only, since this viewpoint was not attained until the first practical aerial conveyance was invented — namely, the Mongolfier brothers' hot air balloon in 1783. Moreover, maps can display phenomena not only on the Earth's surface but also below it, such as tectonics, or above it, e.g., high-level meteorological data. In the past, cartography — the science, art, and technology of maps and mapmaking — dealt only with the planet on which we live. Today, cartographers also map other heavenly bodies, and even the moons of distant planets and asteroids.

"Primitive" and ephemeral maps were drawn in the sand already at the dawn of human communication; later came Mesopotamian clay maps, the first permanent or "hard copy" maps. Cartography evolved as a discipline generating formal products both in East Asia and in Europe, particularly in the domain of Greek classical culture. Since Israel belongs chiefly to the sphere of influence of Western culture and technology, the present article will deal only with the history and background that created the maps of our country. Cartographic research in the Western World originated in ancient Greece as an integral part of history and cosmology. Before long geographers (who did not at first apply this title to themselves) began to produce maps of regions described in their writings, whether terrestrial-continental or maritime. This approach, however, required new and original intellectual tools that had been unavailable to their predecessors. What, then, distinguishes the two modes of graphic expression, the verbal and the cartographic? Whereas a verbal text is one-dimensional, to be followed strictly word by word, a map is two-dimensional and hence able to display each place and every spatially distributed phenomenon according to its location on the globe, in both latitude and longitude. The third dimension, altitude, is then superimposed graphically. If we refer to the globe it is because the Earth is a spheroidal or globular body. I shall, therefore, briefly describe the history of the transition from globe to plane surface.

Already in the 3rd century BCE the Greeks were aware that the Earth is not a flat plate but a spherical body, although maps describing it had to be produced on a flat surface, e.g., on a sheet (chartis in Greek, hence "chart") of papyrus or vellum and later of paper. This realization gave rise to the cartographic sub-discipline of map projections.

A map projection is a mathematical procedure of transferring points, lines, and areas from the spherical surface of the Earth (or a globe representing it) onto the plane of the map sheet. Such a transformation always generates distortions in the map, which no amount of research throughout two millennia has been able to eliminate. The first person to collect the cartographic body of knowledge of his era (adding much of his own) was Klaudios Ptolemaios of Alexandria (Claudius Ptolemaeus in Latin, and known in English as Ptolemy) in the 2nd century. He did this in his important treatise *Geographiki Yphigisis* (Instruction in describing the Earth), usually referred to as Ptolemy's *Geographia* or *Cosmographia*, which was still used by Christopher Columbus some 1,300 years later. Ptolemy appended 26 maps to his treatise and included a list of over 8,100 named places in the world, each defined by a pair of coordinates — latitude and longitude. Ptolemy's original maps were lost, but the verbal text reached later generations intact. The maps were reproduced in the Renaissance (14th and 15th centuries), on the basis of medieval copies and with the aid of the list of coordinates. Ptolemy based much of his work on information from earlier sources; it was very precise (in terms of his era) for the heartland of Western culture in and around the Mediterranean basin, but precision of location as well as of content decreased with distance from these regions. Israel appears in relative detail in the fourth part of the map of Asia (*Quarta Asiae Tabula*), being represented by some 30 points designated by coordinates.[1] The map was oriented to the north, like the rest of Ptolemy's maps.

It must be stressed that all extant maps of Ptolemy are reproductions or copies that underwent numerous changes. Speaking of reproductions, a most interesting map discovered in the early 16th century should be mentioned. Today referred to by the name of the German humanist who first published it — *Tabula Peutingeriana*, or Peutinger's map — it was made in the 12th or 13th century but was apparently copied from a Roman road map of the mid-4th century. This map shows in great detail the network of paved interurban roads throughout the Roman Empire, including the main roads in Palestine. We find three significant innovations in the Peutinger Map. First, it makes use of a system of "conventional signs" or symbols representing the degrees of importance of the various sites appearing in the map. Second, road distances between cities, towns, and other road stations are indicated in Roman miles, thus predating modern road maps. Third, since the map was designed for traveling it was drawn on a vellum scroll, with the outlines of the Roman Empire compressed in a north-south direction. This compression was achieved by representing the seas, in particular the Mediterranean and Black seas, as only narrow bands of water, the rationale behind this idea being that there are no paved roads at sea! No reference is made to the sphericity of the earth. This innovative approach to the problem of map projections — distorting the landforms in order to depict a particular theme or subject — was forgotten until a computerized projection with geometrical and topological properties resembling those of the Peutinger Map was invented in Israel in the later

20th century.[2] The original Peutinger Map is kept in the Austrian National Library in Vienna; the Eran Laor Cartographic Collection in the Jewish and National University Library in Jerusalem has an exact full-size facsimile.[3]

Medieval Maps

The oldest extant map of Israel that is not a reproduction is the so-called Madaba Map of the 6th century.[4] A large stone mosaic constituting the floor of a Byzantine church in the town of Madaba, Jordan, this map, too, is a topological representation: it conserves relative directions but not geometrical — i.e., measured — distances.

Roughly, the greater the distance between any given site and Jerusalem, the map's physical and spiritual center, the smaller its relative distance in the map. In present-day terms: map scale decreases with distance from map center. Cities of importance are shown in the mosaic by pictures covering a large area. The Madaba Map thus serves as an early example of a cartographic product whose guiding principle is the relative importance of a place and not only its geometric location. This subjective topological approach stands in contradistinction to Ptolemy's geometrical precision. Moreover, the Madaba Map combines two directions of viewing the Earth: in general, the terrain is shown as seen from above, but cities and towns are depicted either horizontally or obliquely. Many tourist maps today employ a similar approach. In the representation of

cases are imaginary or symbolic. Among the most numerous are the so-called *Orbis Terrarum* maps,[5] some of which show the earth in the form of a letter T inscribed within the letter O. The T represents the main water bodies of the ancient world: the Mediterranean Sea as the vertical stroke, and the rivers Tanais (Don) and Nile as its horizontal bar. The letter O stands for the Mare Oceanum, the world ocean surrounding all land areas. These graphics are therefore also referred to as T-in-O maps. The three land sectors between the T and the O usually represent the three known continents: Asia (top), Africa (right), and Europe (left), which in some of these maps are designated by the names of Noah's three sons: Shem, Ham, and Japhet, respectively. In the center of some of these maps appears Jerusalem, the Holy Land (Terra Sancta) or Paradise. Other imaginary maps depict the world in a form representing the artist's mental picture of the biblical stories, sometimes with mythological or other fantastic creatures surrounding it. Two fine examples of this genre, centered on Jerusalem and framed by a garland of mythological creatures, are the Ebstorf Map in Germany and the Hereford Map in England, both originating in the 13th century and measuring some 3 m in diameter. The later (1585) clover-leaf map by Henricus (Heinrich) Bünting[6] also comes under the category of symbolic-imaginary maps.

the *cardo maximus* (the main Roman longitudinal thoroughfare) in Jerusalem and some other places, the columns are shown "folded" to the outside of the street, which itself is shown vertically from above. One finds a similar device used in the Mesopotamian clay maps mentioned earlier.

It was noted above that maps can also represent imaginary phenomena. On the one hand one finds among the medieval graphic products included under the term "maps" depictions of countries — and even of the entire world — whose outlines in many

In the 14th century, toward the end of the medieval era, maps of increasing accuracy, used in maritime navigation, were being developed. These are characterized by a net of straight radial direction lines — so-called rhumb lines or loxodromes, as distinct from geographical lines of latitude and longitude — that radiate from wind roses placed throughout the map in order to assist with navigation. Collectively these maps are known as portolans . An excellent example is the Catalan Atlas of ca. 1375.[7]

North or South, East or West – The Orientation of Maps

The orientation of maps of the Holy Land is in itself an interesting topic. "Orientation" refers to the point of the compass found at the top of the map, this also being the direction in which most names in the map can be read. The majority of ancient maps were directed toward the east; in fact, the term "orientation" is derived from oriens (Latin for "east"). Thus in the Madaba Map the regions east of the Jordan are shown at the top, while the river itself flows from left (north) to right (south), parallel to the upper map border. As far as we know, Ptolemy was the first to point his maps to the north, i.e., toward the only star — Stella Polaris, the pole star — known not to change its position in relation to the Earth.

During the Middle Ages "scientific" cartography as formulated by Ptolemy was forgotten, and maps of the world and of the Holy Land produced in Christian Europe were again oriented to the east. In later editions of Ptolemy's *Geographia* Israel even appears twice: once in the *Quarta Asiae Tabula* pointing northward, and once truly oriented — i.e., pointing to the east — in one of the maps grouped under the term *tabulae modernae* (new maps). In the 16th and 17th centuries one finds other orientations — namely, to the west, northwest, southwest, southeast, etc. An interesting case is Erhard Reuwich's map of the Holy Land in Bernhard von Breydenbach's book of 1486 describing his pilgrimage.[8] The country is shown directed eastward, but Jerusalem appears in near-photographic detail rotated by 180 degrees, as seen from the Mount of Olives westward, because this direction offers the best view of the Holy City.

Until the Zionist revival in the 20th century, the Arabs, unlike Christian mapmakers, never mapped the Holy Land or Palestine as a separate geographical or political entity but only as part of ash-Sham — Syria. In Arabic or Muslim maps of the Mediterranean region from the 10th to the 12th centuries, which in theory should have been oriented toward Mecca or at least southward, the four cardinal directions north, south, east, and west are indicated in Arabic in the four corners of the map, so that in effect these maps are directed toward the southwest. But the large world map by Muhammad Idrisi from the middle of the 12th century is indeed directed toward the south.[9] (See, e.g., the facsimile of sheet no. 25 showing Syria and one of its parts, Palestine.) In the course of time the northward orientation of maps was accepted as an international standard. Today, however, some maps of Israel are again pointing in different directions, especially north-northwest, because the "oblique" coastline then lies more or less parallel to the rectangular map frame (resulting in a saving of paper).

Invention of Printing; The Atlas

The invention of printing from movable type was undoubtedly the most decisive innovation in the history of maps and mapmaking.

To the best of our knowledge, Ptolemy, in the 2nd century, was the first to include in his *Geographia* a world map divided into a number of smaller regional maps, each showing several countries. Muhammad Idrisi, too, divided his world map into 70 small map sheets. Only later reproductions of these hand-drawn maps have survived. Volumes of maps showing the world divided into separate sheets were produced mainly after the invention of the printing press.

Printing from engraved or carved wooden blocks was practiced already in the Middle Ages. But the printing of texts from individual leaden letters, which could be used over and again, was invented by Johann Gensfleisch, better known as Johannes Gutenberg, in about 1445. The first volume he produced, between 1450 and 1455, was the Bible in Latin. Already in 1475 the verbal text of Ptolemy's *Geographia* was printed in Vicenza. Two years later, in Bologna, the maps were printed for the first time, in effect as an addition to the verbal text and the list of coordinates.

Two of the earliest printed maps were made by Lucas Brandis de Schass in 1475 and published in an instructive book for acolytes.[10] The first is a world map centered on Jerusalem, the second a map of the Holy Land.

The earliest printed collection of maps, each describing a specific country and bound together in book form, was produced by the great Dutch cartographer and publisher Abraham Ortelius and given the name *Theatrum Orbis Terrarum* — "stage of the circle of countries" — i.e., the world. One of its innovations was that Ortelius, as chief editor, listed all the cartographers and geographers responsible for the individual maps of the *Theatrum*. Folio 51 of the *Theatrum's* 1570 edition carries the heading "Palaestina vel Terra Sancta" (Palestine or the Holy Land), with the subheading *"Nova descriptio auctore Tilemanno Stella Sigenensis"* (i.e., New description by Tilemann Stella of Sigen [today Siegen, Germany]).

The specific term "atlas" for a book of maps was coined by the important cartographer Gerhard Kremer, better known by his Latin name Gerardus Mercator, in the mid-16th century.[11] In Greek mythology, Atlas was one of the Titans, son of Iapetus and the nymph Clymene; his brother was Prometheus, creator of man. One version has Atlas revolting against Zeus, for which he was condemned to carry the heavens on his shoulders. The mountain range in northwest Africa was named after him. But Atlas was also the name of a legendary king of Mauretania, a patron of the sciences and an expert at globemaking, whom Mercator wished to honor.

A geographical atlas is characteristically composed of maps of different scales, bound together in identical-sheet format. Today, atlases are classified as general world atlases, regional or national, and thematic atlases. The most comprehensive one covering the Holy Land is the 20th-century *Atlas of Israel* (see below).

From Sphere to Plane: Map Projections since the Renaissance

Cartographic projections constitute a further subject to be dealt with here. Development of this important sub-discipline of cartography began in Greece and it, too, was lost or forgotten during antiquity and until the rediscovery of Ptolemy's work in the late Middle Ages. Only the 16th century saw experiments in representing the Earth with the aid of new projections, differing from those devised and used by Ptolemy. It should be stressed that no projection exists — or can be devised in theory — that transfers forms from the surface of a globe onto a plane without causing distortions of direction and/or

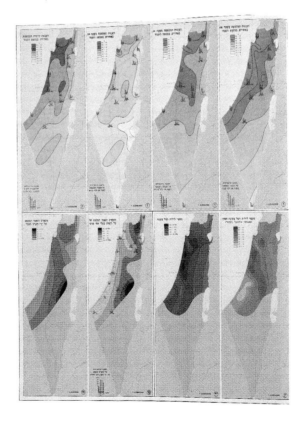

Climatic maps of Israel, Atlas of Israel, Survey of Israel, first edition, Tel Aviv, 1956

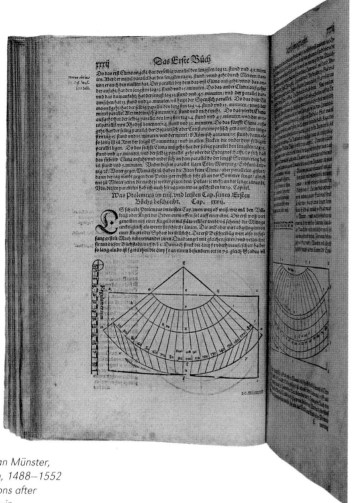

distance.[12] One of the prime innovators in the field of map projections was Gerardus Mercator, who invented the cylindrical projection named after him that still serves navigation today. Mercator also produced a map of the Holy Land with Sinai and the Nile Delta, directed to the northwest. In the 17th and 18th centuries maps of Israel were drawn on various projections, mostly conic-normal (in which the projection surface of the map is tangential to a parallel of latitude) or cylindrical-normal (tangential to the equator). Later, transverse cylindrical projections were devised, in which the map's projection surface is tangential to a meridian of longitude. Such transverse cylindrical projections

were used by British cartographers in mapping not only the British Isles but also some of Britain's colonies. British mapmakers were also the first to survey and cover the Holy Land "from Dan to Beersheba" with a series of topographic maps based entirely on field surveys and a specific projection, which were very accurate for their time. This work, performed mainly between 1872 and 1877,[13] resulted in the great Map of Western Palestine referred to in short as the PEF (the London-based Palestine Exploration Fund) map. Napoleon Bonaparte's expeditionary army had earlier mapped parts of Western Palestine during its 1798—99 Egyptian campaign. However, this map, often referred to as Jacotin's map (after the chief surveying military engineer), was of reasonable accuracy and precision only in those restricted areas, chiefly in the coastal plain, traversed by the French army.[14]

During World War I the two opposing armies — the Turks and Germans on one side, the British and Anzac (Australian and New Zealand Army Corps) forces on the other — produced original topographic maps. German survey units mapped the country before and during the retreat of the Turkish army and the German air force units. The British and Dominion forces surveyed and mapped it while advancing from the Suez Canal to the northeast. In both cases the resulting maps were on a larger scale and more detailed than anything achieved previously. The German maps were on a scale of 1:50,000 and, in the area of central Palestine, on the even larger scale of 1:25,000; the British maps were on a scale of

1:40,000.[15] The German air force took numerous aerial photos of this country, but the British were the first, in 1917, to employ air photos in mapping. The British 1:40,000 scale map served as a partial basis for the 1:100,000-scale topographic maps produced by the British Mandate authority of Palestine in the 1930s and '40s. The Mandatory Survey of Palestine also produced 1:20,000 topographic maps.

Place Names in Maps of the Holy Land; Hebrew Maps

No region in the world can claim a longer unbroken line of maps than today's Israel; the list of name revisions resulting from political, administrative, and linguistic-phonetic changes is correspondingly extensive. A place name is a living organism. It is born, attains maturity, changes, dies, and is often reborn — as exemplified by many ancient names in Israel.[16] The place with the longest list of name changes throughout its history is Jerusalem. The names appear variously in maps produced in different countries, by different cultures, and in different periods. Among the "official" appellations are Urshm (?) in ancient Egyptian records, Jebus, Zion, Yerushalem, Hierosolyma (Greek), Aelia Capitolina (under Roman rule after 135 CE), Bayt al-Maqdas or Muqaddas, al-Quds, and Urshalim (Arabic), Qods Sharif (under Turkish rule), Jerusalem (under British administration), and finally, again Yerushalayim. In addition, different languages use different exonyms for the capital, such as Jérusalem (French), Jerusalen (Spanish), Gerusalemme (Italian),

and Erusaremu (Japanese). The name of the country itself underwent changes reflecting its history, as also encountered in maps. Among these are Canaan, Yehuda, Yisra'el, Greco-Roman Judaea and Palaestina (from Philistia), Arabic Falastin (as part of ash-Sham, Syria), the Crusader Kingdom of Jerusalem, British Mandatory Palestine, and again Yisra'el, Israel. Maps from the Renaissance and the Reformation carry such names as Terra Sancta, Palaestina, Israel, Judaea, and even das heilig Jüdischland, the Holy Jewish Land.

In this context, mention should be made of the earliest Hebrew maps.[17] Among these we find schematic topological graphics used by religious authorities, chiefly in the Middle Ages, to explain and illustrate laws of the Torah, the Mishnah, and the

Sebastian Münster, after Ptolemy Table of place names, detail from Terra Sancta XXIII Nova Tabula, from Ptolemy's Geographia, Basel, 1545 The Israel Museum, Jerusalem Gift of Karl and Li Handler, Vienna

Talmud. Some of these quasi-maps were composed of straight lines serving as demarcations between the tribes of Israel as well as representing coastal and river lines. Later geographical-historical maps were mostly copied from the work of Christian cartographers in Europe, with place names inserted in Hebrew. The apparently oldest printed map in Hebrew, dating from the mid-16th century, was discovered in Zurich not long ago.[18] In the 1920s and '30s a number of Hebrew maps were produced, based on surveys by the Survey of Palestine, the mapping authority of Mandatory Palestine, which employed some Jewish surveyors and cartographers. Only after the State of Israel was founded in 1948 were Hebrew maps produced from original land surveys by cartographers of the national mapping authority, the Survey of Israel, based in Tel Aviv.

Diagrammatic representation of a photoflight in the brochure Aerial Survey Cameras and Accessories, *ZEISS, Oberkochen, Germany*

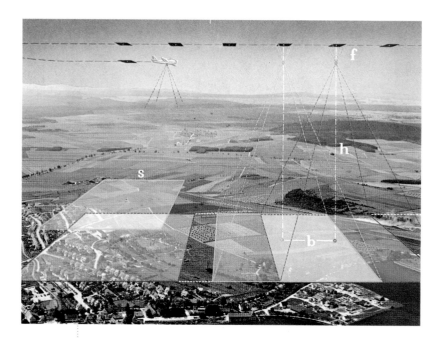

Aerial Photographs, Computer Maps, and Satellite Images

The State of Israel inherited the British Mandate's topographic maps and, as an initial stage, translated these English maps into Hebrew, at first in bilingual editions. As a second stage, Hebrew-only maps were published, later also maps with Hebrew (and other) names transliterated into Latin script. The Survey of Israel was the first cartographic establishment to map the entire country, from Metulla in the north to Eilat in the south, on a scale of 1:50,000, employing photogrammetry — i.e., planimetrically corrected mapping from aerial photographs. An important mapping project was the *Atlas of Israel*, produced between 1956 and 1964, the large-size national research atlas containing 720 individual thematic maps in its first, Hebrew, edition. An updated English edition was published in 1970, and a bilingual (Hebrew-English) one in 1982, followed in 1994 by a small version for schools. Work on the *Atlas of Israel* gave rise to the development of thematic mapping in Israel. Whereas the first division of cartography, known as topographic mapping, chiefly describes land surface configuration, the second, thematic cartography, consists of maps depicting the physical, social, economic, political, and historical geography of the area — exclusive of pure topography.

The history of cartography does not end with the 19th century or even the 20th, as maintained by some writers. Recent developments in mapmaking should therefore be mentioned. Among these are digital (computer-generated) maps, and maps derived from satellite images. Digital mapping was introduced when cadastal (land ownership) maps were made shortly after the introduction of digital computers by the national mapping authority. Today the Survey of Israel produces all new topographic maps and town plans with the aid of computerized so-called geographic information systems (GIS) based on a national database. Satellite-based global positioning systems (GPS) provide for high-precision definition of location. These methods partly replace triangulation and trilateration — earthbound surveying methods using optical instruments.

Since the 1970s the planet Earth has been circled by American (followed by Russian and French) mapping satellites that scan its surface. The digital scans are transmitted "in real time" to ground stations, where they are converted to graphic images on the computer screen or as "hard copy" on paper. The Survey of Israel produces satellite maps from scanned data transmitted by the French *Spot* satellites. The satellite images and maps, being composed of tiny graphic units, pixels (a contraction of "picture elements"), return us to the oldest map of our country — namely, the Madaba mosaic map, which is composed of millions of small colored stone cubes, or tesserae. While technology strides ever forward, the cartography of Israel thus closes a historical circle.

1. *Quarta Asiae Tabula*, in Claudius Ptolemaeus, *Cosmographia* Leonardus Holle (Ulm, 1482).

2. N. Kadmon and E. Shlomi, "A Polyfocal Projection for Statistical Surfaces," *The Cartographic Journal* (London) 1 (1987), pp. 36–41.

3. *Tabula Peutingeriana. Codex Vindobonensis* 324. Complete facsimile of the original (Graz, 1976). See also J. Elster and

N. Kadmon, "Tabula Peutingeriana," *Atlas of Israel*, sheet I/2 (Jerusalem and Amsterdam, 1970).

4. The *Madaba Mosaic Map*, with introduction and commentary by Michael Avi-Yonah (Jerusalem, 1956).

5. L. Bagrow, *History of Cartography*, revised and enlarged by R. A. Skelton (London, 1964), pp. 41–43.

6. Henricus Bünting, *Itinerarium Sacrae Scripturae, das ist ein Reisebuch über die gantze heilige Schrifft* (sic!) (Helmstadt, 1585).

7. *El Atlas Catalan do Cresques Abraham, primera edición con su tradución al Castellano en el sexto centenario de su realización, 1375–1975* (Barcelona, 1975).

8. Bernhard von Breydenbach, *Peregrinatio in Terram Sanctam* (Mainz, 1486). See also J. Elster and N. Kadmon, "Bernhard von Breitenbach's Map," *Atlas of Israel*, sheet 1/2.

9. K. Miller, *Mappae Arabicae — Arabische Welt- und Länderkarten*, vol. 1, no. 2: *Die Weltkarte des Idrisi vom Jahr 1154* (Stuttgart, 1926).

10. Lucas Brandis de Schass, *Rudimentum Novitiorum, sive Chronicarum Historiarum Epitome* (Lübeck, 1475).

11. Gerardus Mercator, *Atlas, sive Cosmographicae Meditationes de Fabrica Mundi et Fabrica Figura* (Duisburg, 1595).

12. D. H. Maling, *Coordinate Systems and Map Projections* (Oxford, 1992).

13. C. R. Condor and H. H. Kitchener, *Map of Western Palestine in 26 Sheets, from Surveys Conducted for the Committee of the Palestine Exploration Fund 1872–1877* (London, 1880). See also J. Elster and N. Kadmon, "Map of the Palestine Exploration Fund," *Atlas of Israel*, sheet I/5.

14. *Carte topographique de l'Égypte et de plusieurs parties des pays limitrophes*, composed by M. Jacotin, Paris, 1818. See also J. Elster, "Jacotin's map," *Atlas of Israel*, sheet I/4.

15. D. Amiran, "Topographic Maps of Palestine from World War I," *Eretz Israel, Archaeological and Geographical Studies*, vol. 2 (Jerusalem, 1954), pp. 33–40 (in Hebrew).

16. N. Kadmon, Toponymy: *The Lore, Laws and Language of Geographical Names* (New York, 2000), p. 169.

17. Z. Vilnay, *Hebrew Maps of the Holy Land: A Research in Hebrew Cartography* (Jerusalem, 1944) (in Hebrew); E. and G. Waintraub, *Hebrew Maps of the Holy Land* (Vienna, 1992).

18. Hans Jakob Haag, "Die vermutlich älteste bekannte Hebräische Holzschnittkarte des Heiligen Landes (um 1560); "Israels Auszug aus Ägypten in der Sicht Raschis," *Cartographica Helvetica* 4 (1991).

From Center of the World to Modern City: Maps of Jerusalem through the Ages

Rehav Rubin

Introduction

For hundreds of years Jerusalem's special status has attracted pilgrims of the three monotheistic religions to the city. Many left behind written impressions of their travels, and these works include a significant number of graphic studies of the city: maps and views, panoramic scenes, and depictions of buildings and sites, as well as fanciful images drawing on tradition and events from the Holy Scriptures. Additional graphic representations were set into mosaic floors and murals or were incorporated in illustrations of the Scriptures, biblical commentaries, historical chronicles, and the like. These were usually drawn on parchment or paper and were very few in number. However, once the printing press was invented they became increasingly common.[1]

Most of the ancient maps were not intended to guide travelers or to serve any other practical purpose. They were regarded rather as a means of communication, transmitting information, viewpoints, ideas and, in the case of Jerusalem, conveying the sanctity of the city and its centrality in the eyes of the faithful. The attempt here is to focus on some major features — the content as well as the graphic forms — that characterize these works, to which we will give the comprehensive title "Ancient Maps of Jerusalem."

To facilitate discussion, a distinction is made between maps made before the invention of the printing press and those produced later.

Mapmaking before the Invention of the Printing Press

Early Maps

The first geographic recording of Jerusalem as a city and crossroads — under its Roman name, Aelia Capitolina — appears on a map drawn during the Roman rule of Palestine, now known as the Peutinger Map. A superb 6th-century mosaic floor map at Madaba, Jordan, depicts the Holy Land, including the Nile Delta, the Mediterranean coast, part of the Negev, parts of Transjordan, and central Israel from Beersheba to Nablus.[2] In its center is a detailed graphic description of Jerusalem with its walls, gates, streets, and buildings.

Jerusalem in the Madaba mosaic map, 6th century

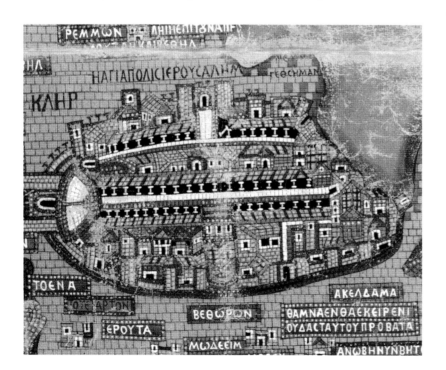

Other depictions of Jerusalem from the Byzantine period have come down to us as well. In mosaic, a second one was found in Jordan,[3] and others adorn the churches of Santa Maria Maggiore and Santa Pudenciana in Rome and San Vitale in Ravenna. In addition, Byzantine maps are found in illuminated manuscripts.[4] However, in all these depictions the walled city of Jerusalem is portrayed schematically — as an idea rather than as the geographic image of a place.

Not a single map of the city remains from the next period, the 7th to 12th centuries, when Jerusalem was under Muslim rule. However, it was during this period that the cartographic perception of Jerusalem as the center of the world was consolidated. This perception is particularly salient in the model recurring in the so-called T-in-O maps, according to their full Latin name *Orbis Terrarum* as well as to their graphic form. These maps depict the world as a circle whose apex points east, with Asia in the top part, Europe at the lower left part, and Africa in the lower right. A T-shaped area of water separates the continents. The leg of the T is the Mediterranean, at top right is the Nile, at top left the Don. In some maps Jerusalem was thus placed at the center of the world, and theological perception and cartographic realization thus came to complement each other.[5]

This viewpoint is represented in maps spanning hundreds of years. It is still seen in Henricus (Heinrich) Bünting's 16th-century map, which portrays the world as a clover leaf (the symbol of his hometown, Hanover), with Jerusalem as the center of the world[6] — and this in spite of the fact that a fourth continent, America, also appears in his map, as do the British Isles and Scandinavia.

In the summer of 1099, following the Crusader conquest, Jerusalem once more became a Christian city and for some ninety years was the capital of the Crusader Kingdom. A large number of churches were erected, pilgrim traffic increased, and descriptions and maps of the city proliferated. Some fifteen maps of Jerusalem made during the Crusader period have been preserved in manuscripts, some from the period itself and others copies in the 13th and 14th centuries. They are named after the places where they were found: the London Map, the Brussels Map, the Paris Map, the Hague Map, the Copenhagen Map, the Uppsala Map, etc. The majority depict Jerusalem as a circle, with the main streets intersecting to form the shape of a cross. It would appear that the T-in-O maps of the world inspired the designers of these maps of Jerusalem.[7]

Two square maps of the city are also known. One is the Montpellier Map, probably drawn in the 12th century, of which a 14th-century copy remains. The map depicts the city and its walls in the form of a square with five gates. Only two buildings are drawn within the square: the Church of the Holy Sepulchre and the Church of Santa Maria Latina. Other sites within and outside the city are mentioned in lists that do not indicate their location in the city. This

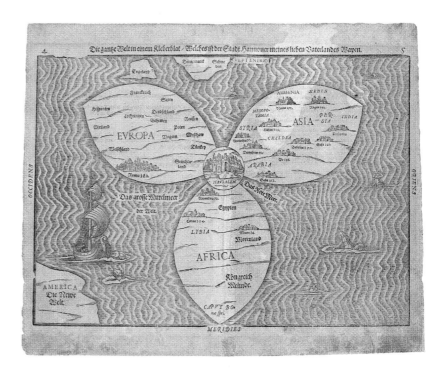

map is highly schematic; it lacks detail and shows very little of the city. It is doubtful that the person who drew it had firsthand knowledge of Jerusalem, yet he seems to have relied on generally reliable sources, particularly as regards data relating to the Crusader siege of the city.

The other square map is the Cambrai Map, dating from the 12th century, which depicts the walled city as a diamond shape. From the many details, some of which are of secondary importance, it is clear that of all the Crusader cartographers, the one who drew up the Cambrai Map was most familiar with Jerusalem and most adept at selecting his sources; he may even have relied on his own eyes.

Heinrich Bünting,
German, 1546–1606
The Whole World in a
Clover Leaf
Woodcut, 1581
The Israel Museum,
Jerusalem
Gift of Tamar and
Teddy Kollek, Jerusalem

Later Maps in Manuscripts

Four maps in manuscripts of the period from the fall of the Crusader Kingdom to the first appearance of printed maps are known. These four — Marino Sanuto's map, the map appended to the manuscript written by Burchard of Mount Sion, the one attributed to the German pilgrim Sebald Rieter, and that included in the Ptolemaic atlas — all represent in different ways some of the features that typify the maps of Jerusalem.

Sanuto's was one of four maps included in his book, published at the beginning of the 14th century, urging the Christian world to embark on a new Crusade.[8] It depicts Jerusalem realistically and in detail; however, the walls stand intact even though it is well known that those walls were destroyed by the Ayyubids as far back as 1219.

The map in Burchard's manuscript[9] makes no reference to the city as it looked in those days, but rather portrays it in an imaginary way using the names of gates and towers mentioned in the Scriptures. It is interesting to note that the map features an internal wall named the "the Ancient Wall" to justify the discrepancy between the knowledge that Jesus was crucified beyond the city walls and the fact that the Holy Sepulchre — the site of the crucifixion — is in the center of the city.

The map drawn by Sebald Rieter is characteristic of pilgrim maps, a style that would blossom as printing

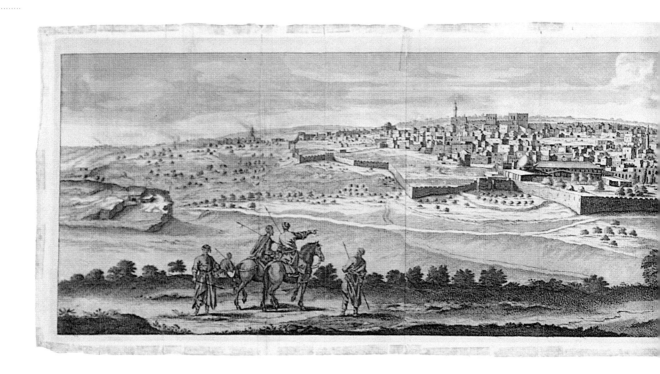

developed. Like most of these, the Rieter map portrays the city as viewed from the top of the Mount of Olives, the traditional observation point.[10] The Temple Mount and its mosques and the Holy Sepulchre are enhanced, with the facade of the church rotated so that it appears to face east even though it actually faces south and can barely be seen from the Mount of Olives. Close by the Holy Sepulchre, Jesus can be seen carrying the cross, as though pilgrims could have seen the crucifixion with their own eyes. This may be an early testimony to the development of the Via Dolorosa tradition. Both here and in Ptolemy's map[11] the city wall is shown destroyed and broken through in a number of places, as was in fact the case.

Printed Maps

In the mid-15th century, the first printed book — the Gutenberg Bible — was published in Germany. Shortly afterward, in the last two decades of that century, maps too began to be printed, including maps of Jerusalem. The printing of maps was a long and complicated process. The map had first to be drawn and then transferred to a printing block. Initially the blocks were produced as woodcuts, but later on copper plates were developed. After being printed, some were hand-painted. The printing of maps greatly increased their dissemination. Between the end of the 15th century — when Jerusalem maps first appeared in print — and the publication of maps compiled on the basis of exact

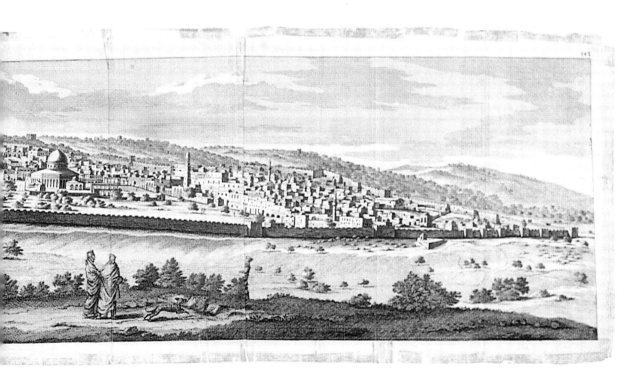

Cornelis de Bruyn, Dutch, 1652–1726 Panoramic View of Jerusalem *Etching, 1698* The Wajntraub Family Collection, Jerusalem

measurements in the 19th century, hundreds of maps of the city were printed. It is therefore not possible to present them in detail here, and only some of their general characteristics can be outlined.

Jerusalem between Fantasy and Reality

Some of the maps of Jerusalem were made by travelers who visited the city and drew it according to their impressions. These maps are not accurate by modern standards, although they are based on reality. The city and its buildings look as they did in true life, and viewers can learn a lot about the city's appearance. Their characteristic realism is exemplified in the two maps shown here: Francisco Quaresmius's map, which provides a slanted bird's-eye view of the city, and Cornelius de Bruyn's panorama, a horizontal vista. Both look out over the city from the Mount of Olives toward the west.

Born in Italy in 1583, Francisco Quaresmius was a Franciscan friar who spent many years serving in the East. During his service he got to know Jerusalem well and even acted as head of the Franciscan order in the city, a post entitled "Custodian of the Holy Places (Custos)." Upon terminating his service he returned to Europe and wrote a comprehensive book on the Holy Land, including in it a detailed map of Jerusalem.[12] The map, depicting the city from a Christian viewpoint, was intended for pilgrims and their Franciscan guides. The map's key mentions 115 sites and buildings in Jerusalem and its close environs — most of them sacred to Christianity.

The Dutch 17th-century landscapist Cornelius de Bruyn, wandered throughout the East for many years and recorded its scenery. Upon returning to his native Holland he published his impressions and drawings in a comprehensive book that was translated into several other European languages.[13] In his description of Jerusalem, de Bruyn tells of climbing to the top of the Mount of Olives, accompanied by Franciscan friars, to draw the city from there. All gave the appearance of taking their leisure at the site so as to hide from the distrustful Turkish governor and his men their true intention of depicting the city.

De Bruyn's long and narrow view of Jerusalem portrays with quasi-photographic accuracy the city as seen from the top of the Mount of Olives looking westward. The minute detail and the beauty of the panorama were the reasons this view of Jerusalem came to be copied over and over by numerous authors, and several books on Jerusalem up to the 19th century carry versions of it.

However, among the many maps of Jerusalem a significant number were originally created with absolutely no connection to the actual geography of the city. They were conceived of as images based on the Scriptures, on descriptions offered by Josephus Flavius, and on other writings. Their captions often relate to Jesus' Jerusalem, to biblical Jerusalem, etc.

Of these maps the richest and most detailed is the one made by Christian van Adrichom. Born in Delft in the 16th century, Adrichom worked for most of

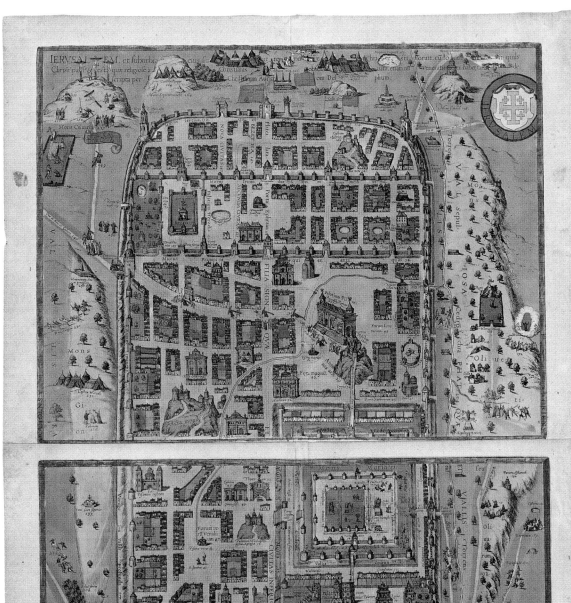

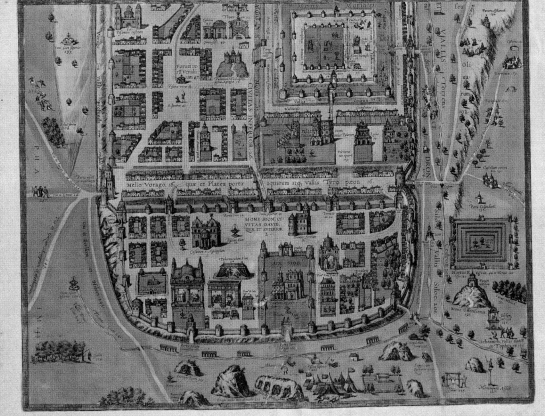

*Frans Hogenberg,
Flemish,
1535–1590,
after Christian van
Adrichom, Dutch,
1533–1585*
Imaginary Plan of
Ancient Jerusalem
and Its Suburbs at
the Time of
Jesus Christ
*Hand-colored
etching on 2
sheets joined
together,* 1590
*The Israel Museum,
Jerusalem
Gift of Karl and
Li Handler, Vienna*

his life in Cologne, and produced a large map (505x735 mm) of Jerusalem in the days of Jesus.[14] On this map, he included more than 280 sites, each numbered. The numbers refer the reader to an accompanying booklet containing a text and a miniature drawing on the tradition of each event depicted. The long list of sites, which include some dating back to the days of kings David and Solomon and up to the destruction of the Second Temple, testifies to Adrichom's outstanding proficiency in the Scriptures. They include the palaces of the kings of Jerusalem — David and Solomon; the Hasmonean monarchs, Herod, Berenice, and Agrippa — scattered throughout the city; the Temple with its walls and gates, courtyards and chambers, and the high priest facing the altar of the incense, between the candelabra and the table carrying the shewbread; the camps of the various armies that besieged Jerusalem; and of course the events relating to the life of Jesus, from his entry into Jerusalem (Palm Sunday) until his crucifixion, resurrection, and ascension.

Another example of fictitious maps is a pair of views of Jerusalem depicting Nebuchadnezzar's siege and the conquest of the city as told in the Bible (2 Kings 25). This pair of depictions was incorporated into an extensive exegesis that included a large number of illustrations and was printed by Calmet, a French Benedictine friar and professor of theology who lived at the beginning of the 18th century.[15]

The first view presented Nebuchadnezzar's siege, the second the wall being broken down and the city being conquered. The two depict the outline of the city identically, although the second shows the scene closer up and in greater detail. This depiction is not even remotely connected to geographic reality; it divides the city into two areas separated by an internal wall: on the right, a magnificent building, probably the king's palace, can be clearly seen; on the left, the Temple is the most prominent structure. This pair of views teaches us nothing about the city's history or geography, or even about the Babylonian war. The regiments of the Babylonian army are presented anachronistically bearing standards, with the infantry standing apart from the cavalry troops — a division attesting rather to Calmet's knowledge of European armies. Even the siege towers and war machines look more like medieval weapons of war than those of biblical times. Nevertheless, the entire display is extremely picturesque and attractive to look at.

A third example, interesting in particular for its highlighting of the complexity of the relation between reality and fiction, and between history and anachronism, is a map entitled "The Destruction of Jerusalem" (Destruccio Hierosolime) printed in H. Schedel's book in 1493.[16] The map does not in fact portray the destruction of Jerusalem. The Temple — captioned "Te[m]plu[m] Sa[l]omo[n]is" — can be seen ablaze in the foreground, and the city wall is broken through in several places. However, the Temple resembles the Dome of the Rock, which was built by the Muslims. Use of the term "Templum Salomonis" is also anachronistic, as this is a Crusader appellation. In the center of Jerusalem two magnificent buildings stand out, completely intact, as if the city had not been destroyed at all. One is called "Calvarie," the other "Sepulchr[um] Dom[ini]." In reality, the two buildings were never separate; the Holy Sepulchre always included the site of Jesus' crucifixion and his burial place. It could be claimed that the presentation of the Holy Sepulchre, standing intact, was the fruit of Christian ideology aspiring to present Christianity's victory over Judaism and the realization of Jesus' prophecy of the destruction of the Temple (Matt. 24:1–3). However, alongside the Holy Sepulchre is a minaret crowned by a crescent, reflecting the reality of Jerusalem in the 15th century and emphasizing Islamic rule over the city at that time. This map, then, does not differentiate or distinguish among different issues and events, combining the Temple's destruction with sections of the cityscape borrowed by the artist from the various graphic sources available to him. One of these may have been Sebald Rieter's map mentioned above.

The Development and Copying of Jerusalem Maps

Even today, cartography often relies on earlier maps, which may be copied and their information and graphic forms restored. This is particularly true of early maps of Jerusalem. Moreover, since travel to the Holy Land was lengthy, costly, and dangerous, even cartographers of realistic maps often made do with copying an existing map rather than travel as far as Jerusalem to see it firsthand. And as for the fictitious maps, it was only natural that from the moment a mode of depicting the city became "sanctioned" due to the author's status, that mode

was copied over and over. Research on Jerusalem maps reveals that certain graphic models recur with great frequency. These maps could therefore be classified into groups or families defined by their similarity of form. In addition, after an initial classification and on the basis of the date the maps were printed, each group could be sorted according to its development — like a kind of family tree.[17]

Bernhard von Breydenbach visited the Holy Land in 1483 accompanied by an artist,[18] and in his book he included a map of the Holy Land with a detailed description of Jerusalem at its center. This description was copied by Stephano du Perac and by Claudio Duchetti. Duchetti's map, in turn, was reprinted by Henricus van Schoel and by Ioannis Orlandis.[19] An additional copy of Breydenbach's version was printed by Matthias Merian,[20] and it served as the basis for a long chain of copies that continued until the mid-18th century and included maps by Jansson, Haffner, Aveline, Leopold, Seutter, Daumont, and many others.[21]

Another interesting example is the map of A. de Angelis, printed at the end of the 16th century, which served as the basis for several copies and was then lost. However, some of the maps that copied it, in particular those of Bernardino Amico and Johannes Zuallardo, themselves became famous and were copied time and again. It was only when a rare copy of the original de Angelis map[22] was discovered some years ago that its great influence on maps copied from it, and on others copied in turn from them, could be appraised.[23]

Jerusalem's sanctity, particularly to Christian Europeans, prompted the production of numerous maps presenting the city as it was perceived by the pilgrims, emphasizing in particular the holy places. Among the many maps that present Jerusalem in this way are some that give us a glimpse of the world of the pilgrims. These maps — in particular those of the Catholics de Angelis, Quaresmius, and De Pierre and that of the Greek Orthodox Chrysantos — merit the appellation "pilgrim maps," due to two outstanding features. First, they are drawn in great detail — de Angelis's map lists 90 sites in its legend, Quaresmius's records 115, and De Pierre's and Chrysantos's maps mention no fewer than 170 sites in the city and its surroundings. Second, these maps were created by members of religious orders who sheltered and cared for the pilgrims, guided them around the holy places, and fostered the concept of Jerusalem as a city holy to Christianity. The maps marked the various pilgrim routes in the city and its environs. But they were intended as well for Christians unable to undertake pilgrimages — those remaining at home in Europe, for whom the contemplation of the sites depicted in the maps served as a kind of vicarious pilgrimage.

A study of these maps raises several questions:

a. How did the pilgrims see the city and its inhabitants? An analysis of the maps reveals that they put great emphasis on the holy places, restricting references to Muslim rule and to the presence of Jews and Arabs in Jerusalem. Even the detailed maps make hardly any mention of the city's markets, its rulers, its mosques, its synagogues, or the daily life of its inhabitants.

b. How did the different Christian communities relate to one another? A comparison between a map drawn by a Catholic Franciscan friar and one by a Greek Orthodox monk is instructive. The Franciscans only reluctantly recorded the Orthodox presence and Greek dominance in numerous churches. Chrysantos, in contrast, mentioned all the Greek monasteries, even the small ones hardly known to most of Jerusalem's present-day inhabitants; he paid particular attention to the monasteries in the Judean desert inhabited during the Byzantine period by famous monks who were later canonized — Euthymios, Sabas, and Theodosius.

c. How were pilgrimages organized? From the order in which the sites were described in the maps, it is quite obvious that pilgrimages proceeded along set routes, as they still do today. The pilgrims entered the city by Jaffa Gate and visited the Church of the Holy Sepulchre. The itinerary included visits to several places of worship:

1. the Via Dolorosa;
2. from Mount Zion to the Hinnom Valley;
3. the Monastery of Saint Simon, the Monastery of the Cross, and Ein Kerem;

NOVÆ IEROSOLYMÆ ET LOCORVM CIRCVMIACENTIVM ACCVRATA IMAGO

Anonymous,
after Francisco
Quaresmius, French,
active in Jerusalem
first half of
17th century
An Accurate View of
Modern Jerusalem
and Its Surroundings
Etching, ca. 1640
The Israel Museum,
Jerusalem

4. Bethlehem and Hebron, sometimes with the addition of a visit to the desert monasteries; and 5. from the Mount of Olives to Bethany (Azariah) to Jericho and the site of the Baptism on the River Jordan.

The Greek Orthodox provided another type of guide apart from maps — a booklet for pilgrims containing drawings of the holy places.

From Drawn to Surveyed Maps

As mentioned above, most maps of Jerusalem produced between the invention of printing and the development of mapmaking based on field measurements and geometrical calculations were artistically drawn. The content of some was entirely imaginary; others presented the city more realistically. In both types, however, the artistic

c. a gradual transition from panoramic sketches and slanted bird's-eye views, which presented the city from a horizontal perspective — usually from the top of the Mount of Olives — to a vertical bird's-eye view;

d. the development of methods to describe the topographical relief — from free panoramic drawings, to drawings in perspective, followed by the use of shading and hachuring culminating in the development of the system of contour lines customarily used in modern topographical cartography; and, finally,

e. an increasing trend toward orienting the maps to the north rather than to the east.

element of freehand drawing remained central to their graphic nature. Toward the end of the 16th century a new, rather scientific trend developed in the maps depicting Jerusalem. The evolution of this trend was long and gradual, spanning the 16th to 18th centuries, and initially it did not bring about the disappearance or even a decrease in the production and circulation of the artisticgraphic maps. It can be characterized by five major developments:[24]

a. a growing reliance on signs, letters, and numbers to indicate buildings, sites, and details in the landscape;

b. a concomitant lessening interest in graphic artistry reflected also in the disappearance of magnificent cartouches, human forms, etc. in the map margins;

Accompanying the above features in the margins of the maps, as illustrative elements, were numerical linear scales, compasses, and compass roses. However, it was only at the beginning of the 19th century that maps of Jerusalem relying on the exact directional measurement of distance and height, as well as on trigonometric calculations, began to appear.

The earliest map to turn away from the picturesque and opt for a clear linear sketch is probably that of Zuallardo (Zuallart), a Flemish pilgrim who traveled to the Holy Land and visited Jerusalem in 1586. This map was first published in his book in 1587 and was later reprinted.[25] It is of small format (90x120 mm) and marks the locations of the sites with minuscule letters that refer the reader to a key at the bottom of the map.

The first map to present the city from a vertical bird's-eye view was included in a book by a French nobleman, Baron Louis des Hayes, who served as a diplomat at the court of King Louis XIII and went on a pilgrimage to the East in 1621 on a diplomatic mission.[26] This angle of depiction was extremely innovative in the scientific cartography of Jerusalem; even in Europe it represented a new trend. In addition, the map was reliable and the topography surrounding the city was depicted in the then fashionable style.

The continuation of this scientific trend can be observed in a map by Jean Doubdan[27] — the first in which the topography was displayed in shading — as well as in maps by Pococke, Shaw, d'Anville, Chateaubriand, and others.[28]

However, in spite of innovations in design and various cartographic developments, the maps still contained many inaccuracies in depicting the natural landscape and the built-up areas of Jerusalem and its environs. Compiled by devout pilgrims, they continued to present mainly the Christian tradition, and in this respect they hardly differ from the artistic pilgrim maps.

Although these maps were still not based on measurements and calculations, in using a scientific approach they paved the way for the first measured maps, which appeared in the course of the 19th century. Since the development of measured maps of Jerusalem has been researched and expounded upon elsewhere,[29] only the first such map, forming a link between unmeasured scientific maps and precisely measured ones, is presented here.

This map was made in 1818 by Franz Wilhelm Sieber, a doctor of medicine and naturalist.[30] A native of Prague, Sieber was particularly interested in botany, and on his travels throughout Europe, Asia, and Africa he gathered plants that he later exhibited in Europe. During a visit to Jerusalem he spent three weeks collecting topographic data and measuring 200 sites in the city. The map he compiled on the basis of these data came to be highly praised by scholars of geography and researchers of the Holy Land.

Sieber's map faces east and features Jerusalem and its environs from the Mamilla Pool in the west to the top of the Mount of Olives in the east, and from the Mount of Evil Counsel (Abu Tor) in the south to north of the Damascus Gate. The topography around the city is indicated with shading and hachuring; it includes arable fields, in particular on its northern side, surrounded by stone walls. In the city itself only streets and buildings are marked. A considerable area of the map, particularly north and east of the city, shows open land devoid of construction. Important buildings are depicted in greater detail and provided with captions: the Temple Mount and its mosques, the Holy Sepulchre, the Citadel, the Latin Monastery, the Armenian Quarter, the Jewish Quarter with its Sephardic synagogues, etc. Much attention is given to the Kidron and Hinnom valleys, although the name given to the latter, "the Valley of the Gihon or Refaim," is of course anachronistic and misleading.

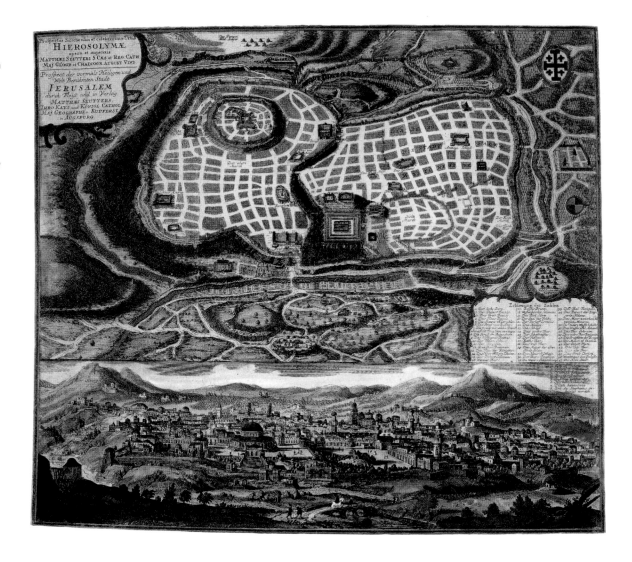

In the map's margins are six boxes of different sizes. The title of the map, its author, date, place of printing, etc., are stated in the one at the top. The box centered below features an arrow indicating the north and a linear scale. A third box, to the right, features a plan of the Holy Sepulchre, and three of the map's corners bear a box containing a reduced map of Jerusalem. These served as partial references for Sieber.

Sieber's map marks a breakthrough in the history of Jerusalem cartography. Whereas the maps by his predecessors, Popocke, Chateaubriand, and d'Anvillee, represent the scientific world of earlier centuries, his is the first map of Jerusalem to be based on measurements and trigonometric calculations, leading the way to the measured, precise mapping of the city that became the norm by the mid-19th century.

1. See E. Laor, *Maps of the Holy Land: A Cartobibliography of Printed Maps 1475–1900* (New York and Amsterdam, 1986); K. Nebenzahl, *Maps of the Holy Land* (New York, 1986); R. Rubin, *Image and Reality: Jerusalem in Maps and Views* (Jerusalem, 1999).

2. P. Palmer and H. Guthe, *Die Mosaikkarte von Madeba* (Leipzig, 1906); M. Avi-Yonah, *The Madaba Mosaic Map* (Jerusalem, 1954).

3. M. Piccirillo, "The Mosaic at Umm er-Rasas in Jordan," *Biblical Archaeologist* 51, no. 4 (1988), pp. 208–13.

4. B. Kühnel, *From the Earthly to the Heavenly Jerusalem: Representations of the Holy City in Christian Art of the First Millennium* (Rome, 1987).

5. D. Woodward, "Medieval Mappaemundi," in *History of Cartography*, vol. 1, ed. B. J. Harley and D. Woodward (Chicago, 1987), pp. 286–370.

6. H. Bünting, *Itinerarium et chronicon ecclesiasticum totuis sacrae scriptorae* (Helmstadt, 1585; first edition 1581).

7. M. Levy, "The Medieval Maps of Jerusalem," in *Sefer Yerushalayim: the Crusader and Ayyubid Period, 1099–1255*, ed. Joshua Prawer and Haggai Ben Shammai (Jerusalem, 1991), pp. 418–506 (in Hebrew); M. Levy-Rubin, "The Rediscovery of the Uppsala Map of Crusader Jerusalem," *Zeitschrift des Deutschen Palästina-Vereins* 111 (1995), pp. 162–67; R. Simek, "Hierusalem civitas famosissima," *Codices Manuscripti* 12 (1992), pp. 121–51.

8. M. Sanudo, "Secrets for True Crusaders," translated by A. Stewart, *Palestine Pilgrims Texts Society* XIV, part III (London, 1896); Marino Sanudo, *Liber secretorum fidelium crucis*, ed. Bongars (Hanover, 1611; rep. Jerusalem, 1972).

9. Levy (n. 7, above).

10. R. Röhricht and H. Meisner, ed., *Das Reisebuch der Familie Rieter*, Bibliothek des Literarischen Vereins in Stuttgart 168 (Tübingen, 1884).

11. Levy (n. 7, above).

12. Francisco Quaresmius, *Historica theologica et moralis Terrae Sanctae* (Antwerp, 1639).

13. C. de Bruyn, *Reizen van Cornelis de Bruyn door de vermaardste deelen van Klein Asia . . .* (Delft, 1698); C. de Bruyn, *A Voyage to the Levant . . .* (London, 1702).

14. C. Adrichom, *Jerusalem et suburbia eius, sicut tempore Christi floruit* (Cologne, 1584).

15. A. Calmet, *Dictionarium historicum chronologicum geographicum et literarium Bibliorum* (Paris, 1722).

16. H. Schedel, *Liber chronicarum* (Nuremberg, 1493).

17. R. Rubin, "Original Maps and Their Copies: Carto-Genealogy of the Early Printed Maps of Jerusalem," *Eretz Israel* 22 (David Amiram Volume) (Jerusalem, 1991), pp. 166–83 (in Hebrew).

18. Bernhard von Breydenbach, *Peregrinatio in Terram Sanctam* (Mainz, 1486).

19. C. Duchetti, *Hierusalem* (Venice, ca. 1570); S. Du Perac, *Hierusalem* (Rome, ca. 1570); H. van Schoel, *Hierusalem* (ca. 1600); *Orlandis* (Rome, 1602). See also Laor (n. 1, above), pp 147–48. On van Schoel, see also R. V. Tooley, *Tooley's Dictionary of Mapmakers* (New York, 1979), p. 568.

20. M. Merian, *Ierusalem* (Frankfurt am Main, ca. 1645).

21. J. Jansson, *Ierusalem Turcis Cusembareich, Nazareth, Ramma* (Amsterdam, 1657), Laor (n. 1, above), p. 153, no. 1050; J. C. Haffner, *Hierosolyma Ierusalem* (Augsburg, ca. 1720), Laor, p. 15, no. 1030; P. R. Aveline, *Jérusalem comme elle est à présent* (ca. 1723), Laor, p. 13, no. 947; J. C. Leopold, *Hierosolyma Jerusalem*, (Augsburg, 1730), Laor, p. 155, no. 1066; M. Seutter, "Prospectus sancta olim et celeberrimae urbis Hierosylme," from his Grosser *Atlas* (Augsburg, 1734), Laor, p. 164, no. 1130; Daumont, *Ierusalem comme elle est à présent* (Paris, ca. 1780), Laor, p. 145, no. 1003.

22. A. Moldovan, "The Lost De-Angelis Map of Jerusalem, 1578," *The Map Collector* 24 (1983), pp. 17–29.

23. R. Rubin, "The De-Angelis Map of Jerusalem (1578) and Its Copies," *Cathedra* 52 (1989), pp. 100–111 (in Hebrew).

24. R. Rubin, "From Pictorial to Scientific Maps of Jerusalem," *Cathedra* 75 (1995), pp. 55–68 (in Hebrew).

25. G. Zuallardo, *Il devotissimo viaggio di Gerusalemme* (Rome, 1587), map of Jerusalem on p. 131.

26. *Voiage de Levant, fait par le commandement du Roy en l'année 1621 par le Sr. D.C.* (Paris, 1629). See also, Louis Hayes, *Nouvelle Biographie Générale*, vol. 23 (Paris, 1858), pp. 661–62.

27. M. I. Doubdan, *Le Voyage de la Terre Sainte* (Paris, 1666), map of Jerusalem between pp. 172 and 173. See also Jean Doubdan, *Nouvelle Biographie Générale*, vol. 14 (Paris, 1858), p. 671.

28. R. Pococke, *A Description of the East and Some Other Countries*, vols. 1–2 (London, 1743–45); "Richard, L. Pococke," in *The Dictionary of National Biography*, vol. 16, ed. S. and S. Lee (Oxford, 1921–22), pp. 12–14; T. Shaw, *Travels or Observations Relating to Several Parts of Barbary and the Levant* (Oxford, 1738); the map is found only in the second edition (London, 1757), between pp. 276 and 277; J. B. d'Anvillee, *Plan de la Ville de Jérusalem Ancient et Moderne* (Paris, 1747); F. A. de Chateaubriand, *Itinéraire de Paris à Jérusalem . . .* (Paris, 1811).

29. Y. Ben-Arieh, "The Catherwood Map of Jerusalem," *The Quarterly Journal of the Library of Congress* 31 (1974), pp. 150–60.

30. T. W. Sieber, *Karte von Jerusalem, und seiner naechsten Umgebungen, geometrisch aufgenommen* (Prague, 1818).

Between Art And Science: Artistic and Aesthetic Aspects of Mapmaking[1]

Ariel Tishby

Representation and Abstraction

The Latin term *imago mundi* — the "form (or image) of the world" — hints at the complex nature of the science of mapmaking or cartography. It embraces both the representative aspect of cartography — which at the same time reflects the mapmaker's outlook — and its artistic, pictorial aspect. "In all but the most narrow definitions of a 'work of art,' it can readily be seen that art and science have coexisted throughout the history of map-making," observed the well-known cartographic historian David Woodward.[2] In this essay I will point out a number of points of convergence between art and mapmaking.

In defining a map as a fusion of art and science,[3] many people view the "art" component as applying only to the decorative features of early maps. These features were not always purely decorative, however. For example, the cartouches or decorative frames that appear in the margins of Netherlandish maps of the 16th and 17th centuries contain not only artistic elements but important information — such as the title of the map, the names of the patron, the cartographer, and the publisher, the scale, and the date. They are also replete with cherubs, sailing ships, sea monsters, etc., and it was in these that people saw the chief artistic value of the old maps.

However, apart from this narrow perspective there is also a broader connection between mapmaking and the artistic representation of the world around us. Maps, like other means of depicting the visual universe, including painting, constitute an abstract and schematic representation of reality.

The language of cartography, like written language, has an alphabet, a vocabulary, a syntax, and a grammar. The "alphabet" includes the wide range of symbols and agreed signs developed over the centuries;[4] the "vocabulary" encompasses an array of lines and underlinings of varying thickness and density to indicate physical features, as well as

that in 1989 the scholar and cartographic expert Arthur Robinson noted: "To capture the essence of a landscape requires that the components be blended graphically so as to have an iconic quality, a unique sense of place and character. This aspect of topographical mapping is rather like portrait painting in that the objective is to produce an image blending feature and expression that conveys the essence of a personality."[6]

All maps, including modern ordinance maps, being necessarily both selective and generalizing, inevitably present a partial and hence arbitrary picture of reality, and are designed with a certain objective in mind. Jorge Luis Borges captured well the absurdity of aspiring to a full representation of reality: "In this kingdom, the art of cartography attained such a state of perfection that a map of one region of the country could be spread over a whole city and a map of the kingdom could be spread over a region of the country. In the fullness of time, the cartographic academies brought out a map of the kingdom whose scale was that of the kingdom, and it corresponded exactly, precisely . . . Succeeding generations abandoned it to the ravages of the sun and the winter weather [trans. D. M.]."[7]

In *How to Lie with Maps*, the geographer Mark Monmonier declared: "There's no escape from the cartographic paradox: to present a useful and truthful picture, an accurate map must tell white lies."[8]

Maps, like works of art, are also a powerful means of relaying messages through cultural symbols.

disparate methods of representing aquatic elements like rivers and lakes. Moreover, from the dawn of mapmaking, various types of shading have been used to give form to the relief.[5] Yet shading and highlighting are clearly artistic techniques.

Further points that cartography has in common with drawing and painting include scale and distance, concepts of space, projection and perspective, viewpoint, line, form, color, texture, contour and script.

One approach to maps is from an aesthetic standpoint, relating to their beauty and style. There is in any case a great similarity between the stylistic rendering of space and material features in the maps of a given period and the stylistic qualities of paintings of the same period.

Mapmaking, like painting, reflects a cultural interpretation of milieu. It is therefore not surprising

Many an old map is a visual résumé of the knowledge and outlook of its maker. In addition to the limited function of conveying geographical information, maps, as works of art in all respects, contain many layers of iconographic meaning.

Maps indeed reflect the culture in which they were created. They are a powerful means of communication that allows for the expression of messages of a religious, political, or economic nature. Sometimes hidden within the symbols, the cartouches, and the written text — or even in the colors and points of emphasis — these messages generally transcend the geographical significance of the map. They often serve political interests or the ambitions of those in power, and in this sense they are geographic-historical documents with strong didactic aims and purposes.

Geo-graphia – "Writing the World"

The systematic investigation of the structure of the world, at least in Western culture, began with Greek philosophy. The concern of philosophy was originally with "the study of the world, cosmology and cosmogony,"[9] and mapmaking was linked to this concern. Anaximander of Miletus (6th century BCE) is regarded as the first to have drawn a map of the inhabited world (the *Oikumene*). The literal meaning of the Greek word geo-graphia is "writing the world." Although archaeology has not revealed the existence of graphic "maps" in the days of the Bible, their use is perhaps hinted at in the Book of Joshua:

"Joshua charged them that went to describe the land . . ." (18:8).

The 2nd-century Alexandrian scholar Claudius Ptolemaeus (Ptolemy), at the beginning of his great work *Geographia* or *Cosmographia*, drew an interesting distinction between "chorography" (the description or mapping of a certain area) and "geography": "The end of chorography," he elucidated, "is to deal separately with a part of the whole, as if one were to paint only the eye or ear by itself. The task of geography is to survey the whole

Petrus Plancius
Geography of
the Exodus
(detail)

in its just proportion, as one would the entire head."[10] In this analogy, Ptolemy draws attention to one of the major points in common between art and cartography: the comprehensive nature of the undertaking, which limits and determines how one represents and what is represented; both entail the representation of a three-dimensional — not to say multidimensional — reality on a circumscribed surface.

In the thousand years of the Middle Ages, the period between the Roman era and the beginning of the Renaissance, there does not seem to have been a separate term to denote "geography." It has been suggested that this area of knowledge was replaced at that time by "scraps of science and pseudo-science, biblical dogmas, travelers' tales, philosophers' conjectures and mythological imaginings."[11] Where scientific development is concerned, this time span has been called "the great interval." Art was enlisted in support of the teachings of the Church: maps were "Christianized" and became increasingly schematic. The American historian Daniel Boorstin has called medieval maps of the world "pious caricatures" whose sole aim was to serve as a guide to the principles of the Christian faith. The scholar of the history of geography Isaac Schattner, speaking of mediaeval maps, did not hesitate to categorize them as "primitive," even if he did not regard them as wholly "useless productions, without value or consequence for the development of cartography."[12]

Maps of the world in the tradition of Beatus of Liebana, which went back to the 8th century — and gave centrality to the Land of Israel — were first and foremost apocalyptic commentaries and descriptions of the apostles' activities and their extensive travels to spread Christianity. Such examples the Ebstorf Map or the Hereford *mappa mundi* (which served as a large altar painting in the local cathedral) — both dating from the end of the 13th century — typified the projection of a religious-historical worldview onto a geographical framework, with a stress on the spiritual rather than the material reality. They sought to give concrete expression to the physical identity between the world, man, and God. The Ebstorf Map expressed the concept of unity between the microcosm and the macrocosm — the *Corpus Domini* — in which Jerusalem was both the navel of the world and the center of redemption (the Zodiac expresses a similar idea of a parallelism between the cosmos, the astrological signs, and the human body). Medieval art did not seek to give an accurate rendering of nature but used it to convey a religious conceptual message based on the principles of faith. But it should be pointed out that toward the end of the period in which maps served as altar paintings in churches, relatively accurate portolan charts were being used for practical navigational purposes. Many of the maps were in essence paintings (e.g., those of Matthew Paris and William Wey). Maps of the Holy Land were of particular importance, and much of the geographical data they contained was based on reality (see the Madaba Map, the Crusader maps of Jerusalem, and the Sanuto–Vesconte maps).

In contrast to the situation in the Christian world, geography, optics, and astronomy, among other sciences, flourished in the Muslim world in the Middle Ages. The writings of Ptolemy were translated into Arabic in the 9th century and were also preserved in the Greek Orthodox monasteries in the east. At the same time, the early Muslim maps appear to have been strongly influenced by the abstract-geometric decorative style of Muslim art (see p. 128).

Although modern scholarship tends to blur the line of transition from the Middle Ages to the Renaissance, the 15th century saw a rapid and radical change of approach in the domain of cartography.[13] The major change resided in the liberation from the trammels of ecclesiastical dogma, making man and the world the center of interest and endeavoring to give a "true and accurate" account of nature. The translation of Ptolemy's *Geographia* from the Greek into Latin in Florence in 1406, coupled with the revival of interest in classical Greek and Roman language and literature at the end of the 14th century, contributed greatly to this change of approach and to the dissemination of old-new methods of mapping based on measurement and mathematical projections. This process was contemporary with the teachings on perspective and the artistic theories of Brunelleschi and Alberti.

The scientific revolution — directly inspired by the Copernican revolution as well as by Mercator, Galileo, Kepler, and Newton — ended the narrow conception of the universe that placed the Earth at its center, bringing about far-reaching changes in the mapping of the world. Simultaneous with these changes were the voyages of exploration and the discovery of new continents, providing new and up-to-date information on the structure of the Earth. The great discoveries made between 1490 and 1520 played a decisive role both in the development of the sciences — above all in mathematics — and in the spiritual development of Europeans; the former philosophical vision of the world had now become anachronistic. The new science sought to formulate claims subject to empirical proof concerning the real world and abandoned the abstract scholastic theories of qualities and essences, derived from the attempt to create a synthesis between philosophy and Christian doctrine.

The Renaissance forged a close connection between art and mapmaking, many of the professional cartographers being painters as well.[14] Pieter Breughel, Albrecht Dürer, Jacopo de Barbari, and Leonardo da Vinci all engaged enthusiastically in the production of maps. In one of his notebooks, Leonardo wrote: "The eye is the master of astronomy. It creates cosmography. It counsels and corrects all human arts. The eye carries men to different parts of the world. It is the prince of mathematics. It has created architecture and perspective and divine painting. It has discovered navigation."[15]

The rise of landscape painting played a major role in this process of bringing painting and mapmaking together. Enthusiasm about noble landscapes and the forces of nature is already to be found in the writings of Dante, Boccacio, and Petrarch. The last-mentioned, one of the forerunners of the Italian Renaissance, was known as a first-class geographer and cartographer.[16] The images of cities in Schedel's and Münster's cosmographies or in the atlas of Braun and Hogenberg, for instance (see p. 146), were usually presented from a "bird's-eye" view and were a good example of the blurring of boundaries between landscape painting and mapmaking. This viewpoint was used in maps before it was adopted in landscape paintings. Apart from drawing and embellishing maps and producing globes, the artist Albrecht Dürer wrote an essay on the measurement of the Earth and perfected the technique of engraving, which was immediately adopted by mapmakers. The points that maps and prints had in common (the same media — woodcut and engraving — and even the same publishing houses) also had the effect of bringing artists and cartographers together. The painter Lucas Cranach the Elder, for example, made a map of the Holy Land, the only complete extant copy of which is discussed in the present volume (see p. 82).

The collaboration between cartographers and artists is envinced in the explicitly pictorial and decorative features introduced into maps and in the custom of filling uncharted areas with pictures. There were also illustrations of historical events in the geographical areas in which they took place and especially of biblical scenes in the Holy Land. This tradition, which had its roots in the Middle Ages, acquired new forms of expression, giving rise to a sort of coexistence: mapping aimed at fidelity and exactitude; art reflected the style of the time and place in which the map was produced. The "fantastic" maps of the Middle Ages, like the maps of the Renaissance and Baroque periods or such "cartographic curiosities" as Bünting's maps (Europe in the form of a queen, Asia in the form of Pegasus, or a map of the world in the form of a clover leaf with Jerusalem at its center), have to be judged within their own cultural context.[17] These cartographic curiosities "were not the product of defective geographical knowledge but were metaphors in all respects." The belief of the High Renaissance artists that maps were a microcosm of the macrocosm resembled the mediaeval view, but reflected the mood of a new period, "the discovery of the world and of man," as the historian Jakob Burckhardt termed it.[18]

John Speed, English, 1552–1629
Canaan . . .
Engraving, 1595, detail of cartouche showing Adam and Eve, after Albrecht Dürer
The Jewish National and University Library, Jerusalem
The Eran Laor Cartographic Collection

In addition to the collaboration between cartographers and artists, there was a great deal of eclecticism and uninhibited quotation in the decorative elements of maps.[19] For instance, Dürer's Adam and Eve are incorporated in John Speed's map (see p. 100), and the decorative frame surrounding the cartouches of Ortelius are generally taken from the prints of Jacob Floris or Hans Vredeman de Vries. The source of the well-wrought medallions in Ortelius's map *Abraham's Journeys* is Maerten de Vos's illustrations and the extraordinarily artistic maps of the painter Plancius — i. e., David Vinckboons.

Cartography flourished in 17th-century Holland, and there was a close connection between Dutch painting and this "mapping impulse."[20] The Dutch were among the first to produce maps to display on the walls of houses — presumably as a kind of status symbol indicative of the householder's education. It is possible that they also expressed certain political or social points of view. Thus the large maps hanging on interior walls in the paintings of Vermeer not only represent a situation in which they are considered art objects, but also constitute part of the complex and allusive iconography of the paintings as a whole. His *Art of Painting* (ca. 1670) is a good example. This domestic-allegorical scene depicts the artist in his studio painting Clio, the Muse of history, and hanging on the wall is a large map. It may be that the map in this picture expresses longing for a different political situation in Holland, and that the painting as a whole suggests the hope of a military victory over France.

The "Myth" of the Scientific Map

Although modern scientific maps rely on highly sophisticated measuring techniques and have dispensed with many of the earlier decorative elements, they still require aesthetic design. In the words of Arthur Robinson: "Even the most rigorously-prepared, accurate, large scale topographical map is an artistic creation."[21]

Moreover, even scientific mapmaking can present reality in a selective, symbolic, and arbitrary manner. Like any representation of reality, the use of scale, projections, and recognized signs and symbols demands generalization and simplification; and even "accurate" maps inevitably convey an interpretive and biased view of their subject matter.

On the face of it, the more "scientific" map-making has become, the more the artistic elements have disappeared, in the effort to be "accurate" rather than aesthetic or picturesque. But the distinction between these spheres is by no means simple or obvious. The geographer J. B. Harley maintains: "Maps are never value-free images. . . . Once the ubiquity of symbolism is acknowledged, the traditional discontinuity accepted by map historians between a 'decorative' phase and a 'scientific' phase of mapping can be recognized as a myth."[22]

Since the 1980s, scholars of art history have shown increasing interest in maps, while cartographic scholars have evinced a greater interest in art.

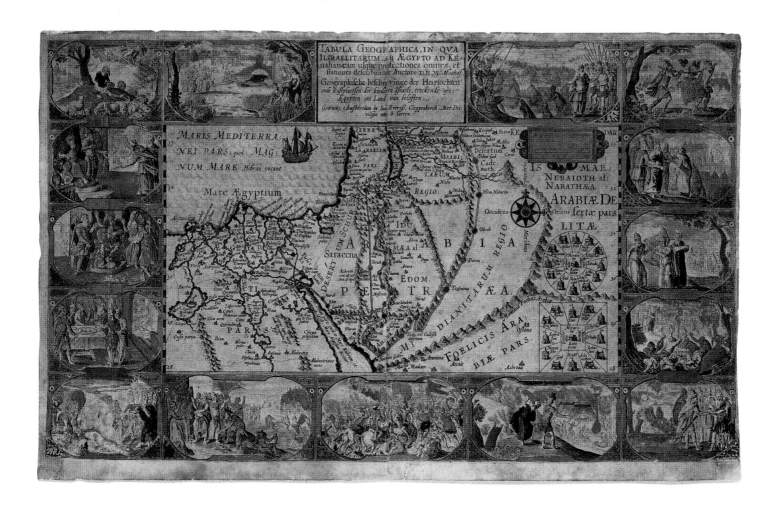

*Petrus Plancius,
Flemish, 1552—1622
Geography of the
Exodus, adaptation by
D. R. M. Mathes
Hand-colored
engraving, ca. 1600,
from a Dutch Bible
Collection of Isaac
Einhorn, Tel Aviv*

Contemporary notions about "reading texts" have brought us back to the literal meaning of the word "geography." They have given us a new approach to the concept of "writing the world" and shown that maps are a kind of text that can be read on different levels and can therefore be said, in the scientific discourse, to be "intertextual."[23]

Representations of landscape, whether in art or in maps, are not an imitation of reality but a product of their cultural environment. A map is not a concise summation of the objective universe but a stringing together of ideas existing in a cultural-political context. "Deconstructive analysis" — taking apart the map — obliges us to read between the lines of the "text" and uncover the hidden contradictions within the visual image.[24] For, as E. H. Gombrich reminds us in *Art and Illusion*, every visual representation is based on conventions and on a schematic infrastructure found within the soul of the creative person.[25]

1. David Woodward concludes his introduction to the collection of articles he edited with these words: "If we can show that the role of art in cartography runs far deeper than the decorative and the ornamental, and if we can induce others to plumb these depths, this book will have achieved its aim" (David Woodward, ed., *Art and Cartography* [Chicago, 1987]). (This book has served as a major source of facts and inspiration for the present article.)

2. Ibid., p. 2.

3. "Cartography is the art and the science of making maps and charts." ("Mapping and Surveying," *The New Encyclopedia Britannica [Macropedia]*, vol. 11 [1974], p. 470).

4. A. G. Hodgkiss, *Understanding Maps: A Systematic History of Their Use and Development* (Folkestone, Kent, 1981), p. 25.

5. R. Meyers "How Do You Draw a Mountain on a Map," *Mishkafayim* 27 (October 1996), pp. 66–67 (in Hebrew).

6. A. H. Robinson, "Cartography as an Art," in *Cartography: Past, Present, and Future*, ed. D. W. Rhind and D. R. F. Taylor (London and New York, 1989), pp. 91–102.

7. Jorge Luis Borges, *Del Rigor en la ciencia* (On the precision of science), in *El Hacedor, Ovras Completa 1923–1972* (Buenos Aires, 1974), p. 847.

8. M. Monmonier, *How to Lie with Maps* (Chicago, 1991).

9. S. Shkolnikov, *The History of Greek Philosophy: The Proto-Socrateans* (Tel Aviv, 1981), p. 2 (in Hebrew). The meaning of the word "cosmos" is "order" or "harmonious order," and the research of this order is a prime scientific topic.

10. Ptolemy's Geographia, which arrived in Western Europe at the beginning of the Renaissance, was seen by artists of the time as an authentic essay. S. Y. Edgerton, quoted in the introduction "From Mental Matrix to *Mappamundi* to Christian Empire: The Heritage of Ptolemaic Cartography in the Renaissance," in *Art and Cartography*, ed. David Woodward (Chicago, 1987); the quotation is on p. 14.

11. D. Boorstin, *The Discoverers* (New York, 1983), p. 100.

12. I. Schattner, *A Map of Eretz-Israel and Its History* (Jerusalem, 1951), pp. 60ff (in Hebrew).

13. D. Woodward, "Maps and the Rationalization of Geographic Space," in *Circa 1492* (Washington, D.C., 1992), p. 83.

14. R. Rees, "Historical Links between Cartography and Art," *Geographical Review* 70 (1980), p. 62. See also E. Oberhummer, "Leonardo da Vinci and the Art of the Renaissance in Relation to Geography," *The Geographical Journal* 33 (1909), pp. 540–69.

15. S. Y. Edgerton, Jr., *The Renaissance Rediscovery of Linear Perspective* (New York, 1975), pp. 91–92.

16. J. Burckhardt, *The Culture of the Italian Renaissance*, (Jerusalem, 1949), p. 226 (in Hebrew).

17. G. Hill, *Cartographic Curiosities* (London, 1978).

18. J. Burckhardt, *The Culture of the Italian Renaissance* (Jerusalem, 1949), pp. 215ff (in Hebrew).

19. J. F. Hejbroek and M. Schapelouman, ed., *Kunst in Kaart, Decorative Aspecten van de Cartografie* (Utrecht, 1989), pp. 31, 68–70. Today this preoccupation is very common, among international, Israeli, and Palestinian artists alike, such as Jasper Johns, Joshua Neustein, Michael Sgan-Cohen, and Mona Hatoum to mention only a few.

20. S. Alpers, "The Mapping Impulse in Dutch Art," in *The Art of Describing: Dutch Art in the Seventeenth Century* (Chicago, 1983), pp. 119–95.

21. A. H. Robinson, "Cartography as an Art," in Cartography: *Past, Present, and Future*, ed. D. W. Rhind and D. R. F. Taylor (London, 1989), pp. 91–102.

22. J. B. Harley, "Maps, Knowledge, and Power," in *The Iconography of Landscape: Essays on the Symbolic Representation, Design and Use of Past Environments*, ed. D. Cosgrove and S. Daniels (Cambridge, 1988), pp. 279, 301.

23. T. J. Barnes and J. Duncan, ed., Writing Worlds, Discourse, *Text and Metaphor in the Representation of Landscape* (London and New York, 1992).

24. J. B. Harley, "Deconstructing the Map," in *Writing Worlds, Discourse, Text and Metaphor in the Representation of Landscape*, ed. T. J. Barnes and J. Duncan (London, 1992), pp. 231–53.

25. E. H. Gombrich, *Art and Illusion: A Study in the Psychology of Pictorial Representation* (Washington, D.C., 1960).

Early World Maps

Richard of Haldingham,
English, active ca. 1260–1305
*Descriptio Orosii de
Ornesta Mundi*
(Description of the world
according to Orosius de
Ornesta), ca. 1285
Manuscript on vellum,
1660x1360 mm
Hereford Cathedral, England

At the end of antiquity there were two main traditions of representing the world in maps. One was intended to meet practical and governmental needs, the other developed through more abstract, scientific thinking.

The only map surviving from the practical tradition is that known as *Tabula Peutingeriana*, or the Peutinger Map, a long, narrow scroll presenting the Roman world, with the Mediterranean Sea — Mare Nostrum — as its main axis.

However, some information in Roman literature points to the preparation of world maps intended for practical use at an earlier date in the Roman Empire. Julius Caesar ordered a survey of the world and sent four geographers, Greek in origin, to carry out this task; but it seems to have been completed only in the reign of Augustus, who ordered his right-hand man Marcus Agrippa to draw a map of the world. This map, apparently the prototype of all medieval world maps of the type of the Hereford Map (see below), was prominently displayed in Rome.

The second, theoretical tradition of mapmaking derives from the Greek and Hellenistic culture. Scholars were in dispute about the shape of the world, and their renderings therefore vary. Eratosthenes determined already in the third century BCE that the world is round and succeeded in arriving at a reasonable estimate of the circumference of the globe. He followed his predecessor Dicaearchus in establishing a system of longitudinal and latitudinal lines, with the main latitude passing through the straits of Gibraltar, and the main longitude through Rhodes. Thus was established the concept of dividing the world into a network of latitudes and longitudes. This concept became the foundation for the famous *Geographia* of Claudius Ptolemaeus (Ptolemy) of Alexandria (CE 90—168). It included a long list of place names, together with their position according to a system of coordinates, and supposedly provided the basis for the drawing of a world map or a series of world maps; none of them, however, have survived. Other Greek scholars, among them Orosius and Macrobius, continued during the 4th and 5th centuries to develop these concepts, but of their work no maps have come down to us, only written texts.

Copies of maps derived from these early notions survive from the late Roman period and beginning of the Middle Ages, depicting the world as a circle surrounded by an endless ocean. Two main methods were used in these maps to describe the settled world, the *Oikumene*. One method, founded on the work of Macrobius in the 5th century, divides the world into seven parallel strips according to climatic zones. The second method, on which the so-called T-in-O maps are based, portrays the world

as a round disk oriented toward the east: Asia is at the top, Europe at lower left, Africa at lower right, and a T-shaped body of water divides the continents. The stem of the T is the Mediterranean Sea, the right-hand part of its head is the Nile, and the left-hand part is the Don. This graphic portrayal appears in the encyclopedic work by Isidore of Seville (ca. 560–636), *Etymologiae*. This very popular pattern, which appears in 660 manuscripts, continued until the end of the Middle Ages. The portrayal of the world in these schematic maps points not to an ignorance of the realistic geographical pattern but to a preference for a schematic symbol over a known reality.

Between the 11th and 12th centuries a new type of world maps — the *mappaemundi* — appeared in Europe, reaching its peak in the 13th and 14th centuries. Though based on the T-in-O pattern, these maps were very detailed and rich in geographical information, partly real and partly legendary. They drew on the Bible and on the classical works of Strabo, Plinius, Augustinus, Orosius, and Hieronymous. Most famous among them are the 13th-century Ebstorf Map, destroyed during World War II and existing in facsimile only; the diminutive mid-13th century Psalter Map of England; and a large map drawn on parchment by Richard of Haldingham around 1290 and kept in Hereford Cathedral, in England.

All of these world maps emphasize the hegemony of Christianity in the world. Henry of Mainz's map of the late 12th century is bordered by the four Evangelists. In the Ebstorf Map, the largest and most impressive of these maps, the world is actually the body of Christ: his head is above the Garden of Eden, his arms embrace the map on either side, and his legs appear below. In the Psalter Map, Jesus looks on from the position of the Pantocrator (the almighty ruler), holding in his hand a T-in-O-shaped globe. Finally, in the Hereford Map, a Day of Judgment scene appears at the top.

These maps are unique in that they bring together the world of religious symbols, folklore, and encyclopedist scientific knowledge in the areas of geography and cosmology that spread after the renaissance of the 12th century. Thus the Hereford Map depicts the Exodus, the sin of the Golden Calf, the wanderings of the Children of Israel in the desert, and other scenes in Sinai; Saint Augustine in his episcopal seat in Hippo, North Africa; and the Nile Delta, according to classical sources, in Egypt. Many animals are also described on the basis of information from classical sources. For example, legendary and folkloric elements appear in Africa, where strange races of humans are portrayed, some with one eye and one leg, some four-legged, and some whose faces are set in their chests.

An interesting development occurs in world maps during the 12th century, following the Crusades, when Jerusalem begins to occupy a central position. In the earlier world maps Jerusalem is shown as similar in size to other sites and appears in the upper right-hand part of the circle — as in Sir Robert Cotton's map of the 11th century, in the map attached to Isidore of Seville's work of the 12th century, in the map by Henry of Mainz of the late 12th century, and even in the Vercelli Map of the early 13th century. In the Psalter, Hereford, and Ebstorf maps, however, Jerusalem occupies a place of honor in the center of the map, representing the biblical tradition according to which Jerusalem is the navel of the world (Ezek. 5:5). This tradition did not end even after the fall of the Crusader Kingdom at the end of the 13th century; in the 14th century Ranulf Higden still drew a world map of this type highlighting Jerusalem at its center.

It is interesting to note that as late as the end of the Middle Ages — after the discovery of America, when Europe was engaged in the great expeditions and the geographical discovery of a wide world — the tradition of world maps preferring cartographic symbolism over geographic reality still prevailed. A significant expression of this trend may be seen in the maps printed at the end of the 15th century in Henricus (Heinrich) Bünting's book *Itinerarium* . . ., depicting Asia as a galloping winged horse, Europe as a queen, etc.

Bünting included in his book a map entitled "The whole world in the shape of a clover leaf, the symbol of our beloved city of Hanover." Indeed, the map depicts the three continents as a three-leaf clover; its center is Jerusalem, and the oceans surround it. This map points to the tension between form, content, and geographic knowledge. On the one hand, the map itself attests that Bünting knew of the discovery of America: outside the three-leaf clover England, Scandinavia, and the New World are depicted as islands in a vast ocean. On the other hand, notwithstanding geographical knowledge, the author preferred the artistic form of the clover leaf, with Jerusalem at the center of an Old World that included only three continents. Here the clover-leaf form is the reverse of the T-in-O pattern: the bodies of water form the letter T and dry land fills most of the circle.

This world map brings together two phenomena — the preference for symbol over reality and the centrality of Jerusalem — taking them to their peak, as well as to their end. A short time later such maps disappeared, and realistic mapping based on expeditions, geometric calculations, and eventually also surveys became the mainstay of cartography.

M.L.-R. R.R.

H. Bünting, *Itinerarium et Chronicon Ecclesiasticum Totius Sacrae Scriptoriae* (Helmstadt, 1585).

P. D. A. Harvey, *Mappa Mundi, the Hereford World Map* (Hereford, 1996).

N. J. W. Thrower, *Maps and Man* (Englewood Cliffs, N.J., 1972).

D. Woodward, "Medieval Mappaemundi," in *History of Cartography*, vol. 1, ed. J. B. Harley and D. Woodward (Chicago, 1987), pp. 286–370.

The Peutinger Map

Conrad Peutinger, German,
1465–1547
*Tabula itineraria ex illustri
Peutingerorum bibliotheca . . .*
(The Peutinger Map),
detail including Palestine,
segments VI and VII
Engraving, 1653,
2050x515 mm (complete map)
Composed of 8 segments
on 4 sheets
From J. Janssonius and
G. Hornius, *Accuratissima orbis
antiqui delineatio,*
Amsterdam, 1653
The Israel Museum, Jerusalem
Gift of Norman and
Frieda Bier, London

Produced sometime around the year 1200, lost, and rediscovered in 1506, this unique manuscript map is, for several reasons, one of the highlights of world cartography. Known as the *Tabula Peutingeriana*, it was belatedly named after the city librarian and archivist of Augsburg (Germany), Conrad Peutinger, who undertook the first steps to publish it in the 16th century. (*Tabula Peutingeriana* is often erroneously translated as "Peutinger's Table," whereas the Latin *tabula* also means "map.") The Peutinger Map, which today resides in Vienna's National Library, was preserved in the form of a parchment scroll some twenty times longer than its width of ca. 32 cm — and was clearly intended for travel. When first examined it was found — judging primarily by the 3,500 place names and stepped red lines — to constitute a road map of the entire Roman Empire. Its contents — but not its date of production — point to the mid-4th century, about the year CE 365. The map was later cut up into twelve segments and mounted flat for display. The westernmost segment, which may have included data about the map's author and its date, was lost.

The Peutinger Map presents its viewer — and in the past its user — with three innovations prefiguring modern mapmaking. One of these was lost for some 600 years or — if one accepts the 4th century as the map's true date of origin — for some 1,400 years, while another was reformulated only some 25 years ago. It is the first map known to have employed a consistent system of "conventional signs" — size-graded symbols indicating the relative importance of the places represented. Second, in

strict deviation from Greek mapping theory and practice as formulated by Ptolemy (see p. 70), it did not delineate the Roman world (roughly twice as long in longitude as it was wide in latitude) on a geometrical map projection as prescribed by Ptolemy, which would have preserved correct relative distances or true angular measures, i.e., directions. Instead it severely compressed all south-north distances, mainly by rendering the seas as narrow wavy bands (there being no roads on the sea). This led to deliberate deformations, enabling the entire empire to be drawn on a long, narrow scroll. The Peutinger Map thus departs from the Greek geometrical graphic presentation, which primarily strives for locational precision, adopting a strictly topological method that only conserves contiguity. While in general, following Ptolemy, it is "oriented" to the north, most north-south lines had to be turned so as to run right-to-left. This has been mistakenly described by some writers as leading from east to west. The method of deliberate deformation was forgotten, and only in 1978 was a mathematical and computerized projection invented and published by two Israeli cartographers, enabling such purpose-dictated deformations in thematic maps to be produced formally.

The third innovation relates to the representation of the network of paved Roman roads throughout the empire — drawn as straight lines, with "steps" at cities, towns, and other road stations (e.g., those serving the *veridus*, the Imperial mail). On each such road segment its length appears in Roman miles (*milia passuum* — a thousand [double] steps).

Totaled, these distances in the map amount to some 100,000 km. Only in modern cartography does one find a similar system for indicating distances in road maps, where little "flags" replace the steps in the Peutinger Map. Here, in contrast to the map background, real distances are strictly adhered to — within the limitations of contemporary instrumentation and methods.

The map segment showing Palestine includes all important cities, indicated by their Roman names, and the roads joining them — remnants of which are still recognizable today — throughout the Holy Land. In accordance with the topological principle mentioned above, the country, including the Mediterranean coastline and the River Jordan, stretches from right (local north) to left (local south). In addition to the cities, the rivers Jordan and Heromicas (Yarmuk) are named as well as the Dead Sea (Lacus Asphaltidis), the Sea of Galilee (L. Tiberis) and the Mount of Olives. Near the latter appears the inscription "Formerly called Jerusalem, [now] Aelia Capitolina"; and in Sinai, "The desert in which the Children of Israel wandered for forty years led by Moses" and "Where they accepted the Law on Mount Sinai."

N. K.

Die Peutingersche Tafel, published by Konrad Miller with an explanatory text (Stuttgart, 1962).

Tabula Peutingeriana. Codex Vindobonensis 324, facsimile of the original map, with commentary by Ekkehard Weber (Graz, 1976).

O. A. Dilke "Itineries and Geographical Maps in the Early and Late Roman Empires," in *The History of Cartography*, vol. 1, ed. J. B. Harley and D. Woodward (Chicago and London, 1987), pp. 234–42.

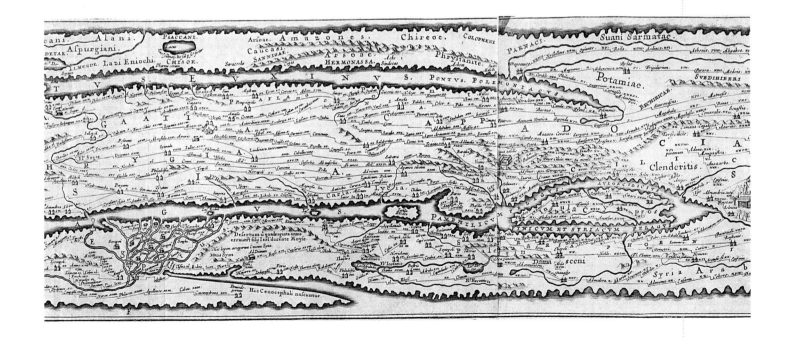

The Geographical Atlas

An atlas is a collection of maps showing the topographic and demographic characteristics of all or some of the world's surface. With its roots in early classical culture, the atlas has evolved and changed over the centuries, reflecting ongoing scientific, technological, social, and political developments, to its present range of content and form.

The term "atlas" derives from the Greek mythological figure who carried the world on his shoulders. It is commonly assumed that the first cartographic work that can be considered an "atlas" is the treatise by the Greek scholar and cartographer Claudius Ptolemaeus (Ptolemy), who lived in 2nd century CE Alexandria. This work contained a series of maps of the expanses of the Earth as known to him. The maps were frequently copied over the next 1,400 years, and the copiers, many of them Christian monks incorporated "improvements" — corrections and additions, but also many errors. Up to the mid-15th century all compilations of maps were hand drawn, greatly limiting the number of copies in a given collection, so that only single maps have been preserved to reach contemporary map collections.

In the late 15th century and even more so in the 16th, collections of single-sheet maps of the known world, or parts of it — those that were later to be collated into what is now defined as an atlas — were produced in a number of centers in western Europe. One of the most prominent contained about 60 maps prepared by the Italian cartographer Batista Agnese in the mid-16th century. Many cartographic historians tend to recognize the collection of maps by the Flemish cartographer Abraham Ortelius, who

was guided by Gerardus Mercator, as the first atlas. This collection was bound as a book that at the outset contained 53 maps, among them maps of the Holy Land, and was published in 1570 under the title *Theatrum Orbis Terrarum* (Stage of the circle of countries). In this "atlas" Ortelius put together maps by 87 mapmakers, and it evinces a remarkable lack of consistency in content and form of cartographic expression. During the same period, in Rome, Antonio Lafreri compiled and published an atlas containing 142 maps of the known world.

Gerardus Mercator, a Fleming of German extraction who was one of the most prominent geographers and cartographers of the Renaissance, was the first to use the word "atlas" in the title of a collection of maps — in this case a set he had compiled that included a map of the Holy Land: *Atlas sive Cosmographicae Meditationes de Fabrica Mundi* (Atlas or cosmographic meditations on the structure of the world). This atlas, published in 1595, functioned as a de facto manual for the many atlases compiled in the 17th century.

With the expanding knowledge of regions and countries supplied by travelers and explorers, the maps in the numerous atlases published in Western Europe became increasingly sophisticated. They also benefited from the artistic boom of the time, becoming enriched with hand-colored maps and highly aesthetic renderings, by the best artists, of biblical and mythological events, characters, sites, and landscapes. In addition, they were improved by developments of cartographic methods and printing techniques. Apart from those representing the Holy

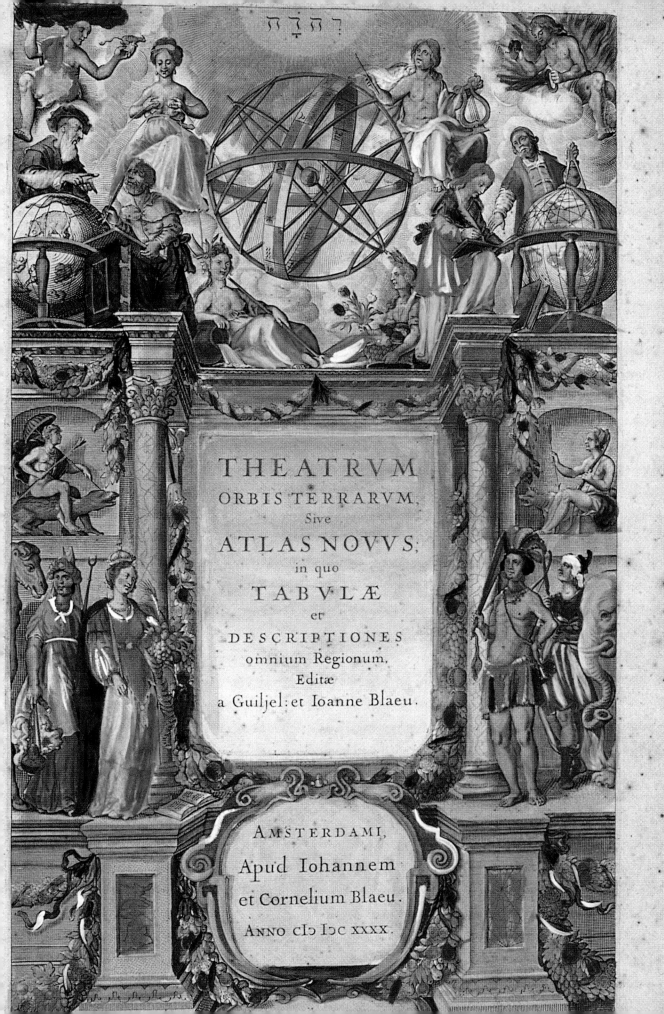

THEATRVM
ORBIS TERRARVM,
Sive
ATLAS NOVVS,
in quo
TABVLÆ
et
DESCRIPTIONES
omnium Regionum.
Editæ
a Guiljel: et Ioanne Blaeu.

AMSTERDAMI,
Apud Iohannem
et Cornelium Blaeu.
ANNO cIɔ Iɔc XXXX.

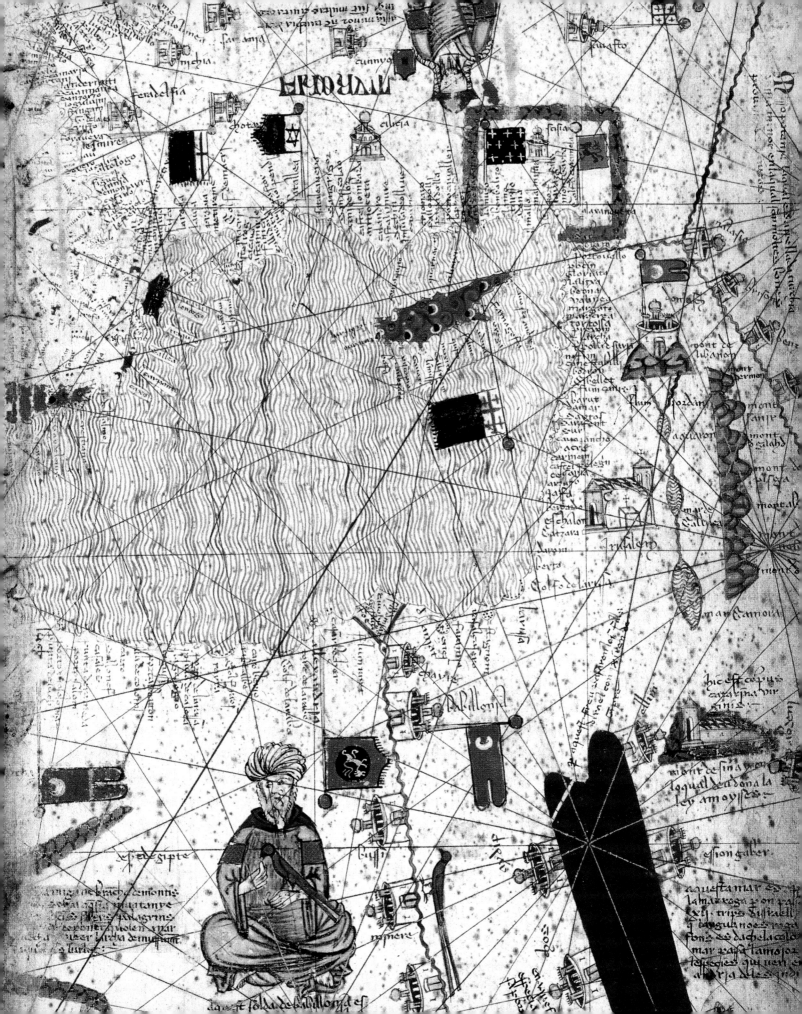

Land, which were historical-biblical, the maps came to include the most up-to-date information on the lands they described, encompassing not only topographic features, but bodies of water, human settlements, roads, and borders as well.

One of the most outstanding for its quality and elegance was the Atlas Novus (1638) prepared by the Dutch cartographer Willem Janszoon Blaeu. This work, containing a magnificent historical map of the Land of Israel (see p. 104), was published in a number of editions throughout the 17th century.

During the 18th century the fashion to embellish and glorify the maps in atlases waned, and the maps of this period grew less decorative and colorful. On the other hand they — especially those representing the countries of Europe — became more precise and more densely filled with the names of towns and villages. There was also an improvement in the quality of the raw data used by the mapmakers, as the techniques for measuring and surveying advanced. France now established itself as the center of mapmaking developments and the most important of the atlases of this period was the Atlas Général (1737) compiled by one of the best of 18th century cartographers and geographers, Jean Baptiste Bourguignon d'Anville.

The 19th century saw many changes in the atlas, leading up to its modern design and character. Early atlases had contained general maps describing topographic features, and as the 19th century gave way to the 20th, atlases not only began to include subject maps (providing data on climate, flora, population, etc.) but also grew in diversity of range — they could now be regional, historical, political, municipal, economic, and so on; in addition special atlases dedicated to the "Lands of the Bible" began to appear. A prominent innovation of the 20th century was the national atlas — presenting an in-depth study of a particular country. One of the largest and most elaborate of these was the 90-page Hebrew Atlas of Israel (first edition 1956–1964), depicting in hundreds of maps the country's physical features, geology, climate, resources, and flora, as well as its history — a comparative mapping of past and present — and economy, as well as relating to the multicultural nature of its population, and its major pursuits and achievements.

The first world atlas in Hebrew, compiled by Ze'ev Jabotinsky and Shlomo Perlman, was published in Germany in 1925. A second Hebrew atlas, edited by Avraham Ya'acov Brawer, was produced in England in 1935. Both were intended primarily for school use. Since then numerous Hebrew atlases have been published in Israel.

M. B.

L. Bagrow, History of Cartography (London, 1964).

W. Bormann, Atlas Kartographie (Gotha, 1957).

M. Brawer, "The Atlas as Source of Knowledge," in Maps and Mapping, ed. N. Kadmon and A. Shmueli (Jerusalem, 1982), pp. 258–63 (in Hebrew).

M. Brawer, The New University Atlas (Tel Aviv, 2001) (in Hebrew).

H. G. Fordham, Maps: Their History, Characteristics and Uses (New York, 1943).

Portolan Atlases: The Medici Atlas

Giovanni Battista Cavallini,
Italian, active in Livorno,
mid-1630s until ca. 1670
Portolan Atlas –
The Eastern Mediterranean
(detail of map no. 3), 1635
Ink, gouache, wash, and gold
paint on vellum, 550x382 mm
Made for Ferdinando II
de Medici
Private Collection

The late 13th century saw the emergence of a new mapping tradition in southern Europe. The Early Renaissance yielded three important developments, which quite suddenly widened the horizons of mariners sailing the open seas. From the East the magnetic compass was introduced. New sailing methods resulted in the highly seaworthy caravel sailing ships, thus dispensing with manpower-intensive rowing vessels; and the conservation of food in the form of salted dry meat and bread enabled long voyages to be made, crossing oceans and not just hugging the coasts as hitherto. On the one hand, sailors demanded better maps; on the other, they provided mapmakers with extensive new data. As a result the so-called portolan charts came into existence. These differed from the Ptolemaic tradition in that they dispensed with the geographical graticule of parallels of latitude and meridians of longitude, or the grid of squares as seen in the map of the Holy Land by Petrus Vesconte (see p. 74), replacing them with so-called rhumb lines (also known as loxodromes) indicating constant compass direction. These lines take the form of numerous "wind roses" covering the entire map sheet. The portolan charts (a sea map is called a chart) are represented here by the Medici Atlas.

This portolan atlas, made 260 years after the well-known Catalan Atlas, represents the mature stage of the genre. It was prepared for Ferdinando II de Medici, grand duke of Tuscany and hereditary grand master of the order of San Stefano, born in 1610. His father, Cosimo II, died in 1621, and it was only after an interim period of regency that Ferdinando succeeded him in 1627. He himself died in 1670. Together with his brother Leopold he was a patron of art and literature and encouraged the growth of science and education, founding the Accademia del Cimento. For centuries, the Medici family were renowned as patrons of cartography, and it is known that several additional portolan atlases were prepared for the family, one at the beginning of the 14th century and two more for Ferdinando's successors.

The present map, the third in the atlas, is signed by the artist-cartographer "Johan B. Cavallini in Livorno Anno M.D.C.XXXV" (for an unknown reason the last numeral of the date is written over an erased number). Other maps by Cavallini appear in a number of collections around the world.

Each of the maps in the atlas is framed by a double ruled border and is drawn in brown ink; the continental coastlines are in a shade of yellow, while island coastlines are reddish, blue, or gold. Many details cover the landmass — including mountains, houses, castles, churches — while the sea is filled with ships, sea monsters, and large, colorful wind roses. In the upper portion are the coats of arms, and the map's scale, together with a type of cartouche and rippling pennants. Flying from the mast of most of the ships is a flag of the order of San Stefano, founded by Cosimo de Medici to commemorate the victory over the French at the Battle of Marciano in 1554. The aims of the order were to defend the Catholic faith and to expel Turkish pirates from the waters of the Mediterranean.

The atlas includes three regional maps with half wind roses at top and bottom and a crisscross of rhumb lines — characteristic features of portolan atlases. These maps delineate the western, central, and eastern Mediterranean — including the coastline of the Land of Israel. Most of the atlas's 13 maps represent various Mediterranean islands, with the rhumb lines fanning outward from the center of the map, which is also the center of the island. The style exemplifies a type of book known as *Isolario*. The final map in the atlas is of the world, and includes north and south America, Japan, and a large part of Australia.

The map of the eastern Mediterranean shown here covers the area from Dalmatia (Yugoslavia) in the northwest to Libya in the southwest, and from Anatolia to the Land of Israel in the east, with most of its coastal cities marked, and the inland filled with illustrations.

N. K. A. T.

Important Atlases and Cosmographies (Sotheby's, London, March 1999), pp. 75–77.

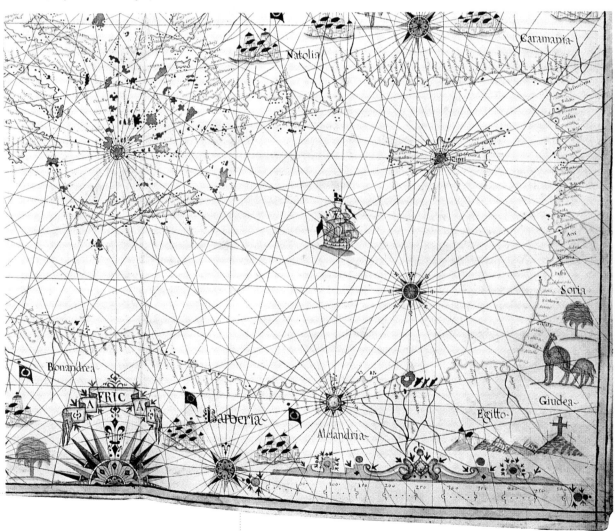

Maps and Globes

The geographical map can be traced back to graphic representations of the immediate environment, which, apart from hills and valleys, has the appearance of a flat disk, bounded by the horizon. Such representations, with agreed marking points, can serve as a means of orientation, and hence of sharing one's knowledge of an area with others.

A globe requires a totally different approach. One needs to be aware that planet Earth is a large sphere on which land and sea are distributed unequally. The small scale of a globe means that a model of the Earth must be limited to representation of vast areas such as continents and oceans.

The leap from the belief that the Earth is flat to the realization that it is spherical should probably be attributed to the philosophers of ancient Greece and of the Hellenistic period. One extant visual example is a mosaic from the latter period discovered in a district of villas at Palermo, Sicily. It depicts an armillary sphere consisting of strips of sheet metal that represent a reconstruction of imaginary lines of the celestial equator, the eclipse or apparent orbit of the sun throughout the year, the tropics and polar circles, as well as lines called "colures" (great circles connecting the celestial poles and the axis linking them). The mosaic clearly reveals a smaller sphere in the center of the armillary sphere, also called the "ring globe," which must be planet Earth.

Representations of globes can also be found on ancient coins. They may either be models of the Earth or else models of the "celestial" or "star" globe. Models of celestial globes seem also to have been produced in earlier periods, and in Greece as early as the 3rd century BCE.

Whereas a very small number of ancient celestial globes are extant, no terrestrial globes of this early period have been found. One must suppose that terrestrial globes were rarely produced in antiquity, since at the time only 15 percent of the Earth's surface was known. This limited knowledge, obtained from travelers and through trade relations, was perhaps also gleaned from myths and stories.

Things were to change with the discoveries of the Portuguese and Spanish in the late Middle Ages and toward the beginning of modern times. There was an increasing interest in the Earth's appearance. Though its spherical shape was common knowledge in educated circles, the distribution of land and sea was only gradually deciphered through the various expeditions of Bartolomeo Diaz, Vasco da Gama, Columbus, Vespucci and, particularly, Magellan's circumnavigation of the globe.

The oldest preserved terrestrial globe was constructed by Martin Behaim and notable artists in 1492. It was hand-colored and did not yet show America. The first globe gores, dating from 1507, were woodcuts printed on paper that could be glued to the globe. They already represented the continent of South America and the route to East Asia though the South Atlantic and Indian oceans. More and more globes were being produced, both individual pieces engraved with hand-colored details and serially produced globes. The oldest known serial globes, still hand-decorated, date from the first two decades of the 16th century. New editions of the prints had to be produced at a rapid pace in order to incorporate the findings of each new exploration on the globe. However, few of these early terrestrial globes have withstood the ravages of time and the elements and survived to the present day.

Whereas on the flat map one can establish one's chosen standpoint as the center — e.g., with regard to Jerusalem in medieval maps — this is not possible on a globe. A globe can, however, indicate whether a certain site is located further to the north or south, or whether it is more remote from the chosen zero meridian. The globe is thus a realistic illustrative model, a necessary and meaningful complement to the detailed map. Moreover, the globe indicates, better than the global map, great-circle distances, and enables size comparison and the determination of time differences. An overall view of the world on a flat plane shows strong distortions toward the margins of the map and thus is no longer a true model of reality.

R. S.

Maps of the Holy Land

"and they shall rise
and go through the land,
and describe it according to
the inheritance of them . . ."

Joshua 18:4

The Madaba Map

The Madaba Map is a mosaic depiction of the Holy Land set in the floor of a Byzantine church in the Jordanian town of Madaba. Although schematic depictions of cities and structures representing settled areas are commonly to be found in mosaics, to date there is no other mosaic that compares with the Madaba Map. Its unique feature lies in its geographic depiction of the Holy Land, which relates to the general topography of Palestine and neighboring countries, and its portrayal of prominent geographic landmarks. Contrary to common practice today, in the Madaba Map the east is at the top, and this is how it is seen by those entering the church and facing the altar. The mosaic's rectangular shape, corresponding to the structural form of the church, forced the artist to introduce a number of distortions, the most prominent being the depiction of the Nile as if flowing from west to east (resulting in the skewed orientation of the Egyptian coast and the Sinai coast as well). On the whole, however, the general layout of the coast, the River Jordan, the highlands, and the location of the major settlements all adhere closely to reality. On the other hand the distances between sites and the relative size of the settlements diverge far from reality. The original measurements of the map are unknown, although it would appear to have been nearly 16 m long (the width of the church) and nearly 6 m wide. Several portions of the map were destroyed, among them the entire northern part of the country as well as regions to the north of it. Isolated remnants that were preserved clearly indicate that the map originally reached beyond Sidon in today's Lebanon.

The map was discovered in 1884 when a new church was being erected by Christian monks over Byzantine ruins. It became known to the scientific world only in 1897, after Kleopas Koikilides, a monk of the Greek patriarchy in Jerusalem, documented the discovery, incorporating an initial drawing of the map in a scientific publication. News of the discovery soon spread throughout the world, and hundreds of essays have been written on it since that time. In 1906 Palmer and Guthe published an accurate colored drawing of the map that served as a basis for all the scientific works produced up to the second half of the 20th century, when the map was photographed in color.

During the years immediately following the discovery, the map was drawn several times in colored ink. Apart from actual documentation, commercial intent also appears to have been involved, the idea being to sell the drawings to tourists and collectors. About a dozen maps of this type are extant in Israel and elsewhere; the largest of them, represented in this exhibition, is in

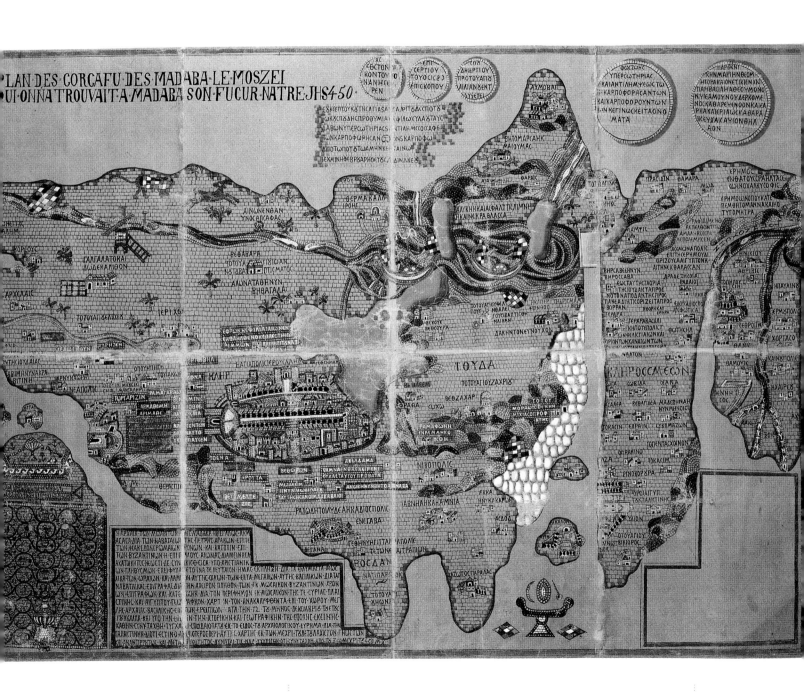

Jerusalem's National and University Library. It is accompanied by copies of the Greek inscriptions from churches in Madaba and text based on Koikilides's publication.

The map depicts the greater Land of Israel from a biblical viewpoint, even denoting the patrimonial lands of the Twelve Tribes. The inscriptions on the map include quotations of verses from the Old and New Testaments. Many of the map's details have been verified over the years by archaeological excavations and surveys, a clear example being the city of Jerusalem with its pillared streets, Damascus Gate and its courtyard, and some of the city's churches.

The map not only presents precise geographical and archaeological facts, as do modern maps; it goes further by embodying "sacred geography" as well as traditions and ideas common to the period in which it was drawn. For example, Jerusalem is enlarged beyond proportion and placed in the middle of the map, with the entrance to the Church of the Holy Sepulchre centrally situated within the city. These were inaccuracies intended to place the Holy City and the Holy Sepulchre — the new Christian temple — firmly at the center of the world.

The exact date of the Madaba Map's execution remains a mystery. However, it undoubtedly illustrates conditions in the Byzantine period, which leads most scholars to date it to the second part of the 6th century, a time when an important mosaic industry was developing around Madaba. Given

that the map includes a drawing of the New Church of Mary (the "Nea") in Jerusalem, which was inaugurated in 543, it is clear that it was created after that date. Another possible factor in dating this map is the depiction of a church at the entrance to Saint Lot's Cave near Zo'ar (es-Safi), southeast of the Dead Sea. A mosaic inscription discovered in that church indicates it was founded in the year 605, suggesting that the Madaba Map was made after that date. However, this is not a reliable determinant, since the artist may have depicted an earlier church built on that site.

The cartographer made use of several sources of information. From the outset scholars pointed to the connection between the map and Christian exegeses describing the Holy City — such as the *Onomastikon* written by Eusebius — as well as pilgrims' guides and their itineraries. It is probable that at least some of these compositions were accompanied by parchment maps depicting the Holy Land with its major towns, pilgrim sites, and routes. Such a map may well have been the primary source used by the Madaba mosaic artist and could have provided him with most of the data: names of settlements and particularly places mentioned in the Old and New Testaments together with relevant verses. At least some of the sites on the map were included because of their location on main roads. They include "the Fourth Mile" and "the Ninth Mile" northwest of Jerusalem and settlements called Aya and Tharais in Moab. Another source of information must have been the personal knowledge of the artist or of those who commissioned the map. The minute detail in which small villages in the Gaza region and in the south of the country were depicted can be attributed to such knowledge — it could not have come from any other source — as can the description of the settlements around Madaba. The drawing of the town of Madaba itself was not preserved, though no doubt the city was placed exactly to the east of Jerusalem, between the map's depiction of the latter and of the church's altar.

Most of the settlements and sites are drawn schematically: a building or group of buildings is usually depicted without any distinctive features. However, in the drawings of large cities such as Gaza, Ashqelon, Neapolis (Nablus) or Pelusion there is clear evidence of the artist's attempt to approach reality. This realism is particularly noticeable in the depiction of Jerusalem. The picture of the city — apparently also based on a cityscape used by pilgrims — conveys to the observer the major outlines of the Roman city that was constructed over the ruins of the Second Temple.

The city is rendered as an oval surrounded by walls, and within the main gate (Damascus Gate) there is a plaza on which stands a monumental pillar. Pillared streets transverse the city. Its southern part, near Mount Zion and Siloam, which was built in Byzantine times, is depicted as an irregular group of buildings. Within the walls are Jerusalem's major churches, among them the Holy Sepulchre, the Church of Zion, the "Nea" and the Probatica Church in the city's northeastern part. Other buildings and churches can be discerned only with difficulty, and most of them may not represent anything in

particular. The Christian ideological approach predominates, particularly in the placement of the Church of the Holy Sepulchre at the center of the city and to no lesser degree in the absence of the Temple Mount compound, which, although deserted, was still a significant architectural component of the urban topography.

Human images as well as most of the animals depicted on the map were vandalized in the course of the Islamic iconoclasm that swept the country around the year 720. (Similar destruction was wrought in many of the churches and synagogues in what are today Israel and Jordan.) Restoration of the damage has revealed that the church continued to be used, and that the mosaic could be viewed by worshipers as late as the 8th century. No information is available as to when the church was abandoned, although it was probably at the end of the 8th century or during the 9th.

Y. T.

M. Avi-Yona, *The Madaba Mosaic Map* (Jerusalem, 1954).

M. Piccirillo and E. Alliata, ed., *The Madaba Map Centenary — 1897–1997* (Jerusalem, 1999).

Ptolemaeus/Servetus: *Tabula Quarta Asiae*

After Claudius Ptolemaeus,
Alexandria, ca. 90–ca. 168
Tabula Quarta Asiae
Woodcut, 1541, 423x573 mm
(sheet); 310x453 mm (image)
From Claudius Ptolemaeus,
Geographia, edited by
Michael Servetus,
Hugo a Porta, Lyons, 1535
Second edition, Vienne, 1541
The Israel Museum, Jerusalem
Gift of Norman and
Frieda Bier, London

It is no exaggeration to say that the work of Klaudios Ptolemaios of Alexandria (Claudius Ptolemaeus in Latin) marks the beginning of the science of cartography, as distinct from the mere drawing of maps. Ptolemy — as he is known in the English-speaking world — collected and collated all information on the compilation and drawing of geographical maps produced by his predecessors and the geographers of his own time in his great work *Geographiki Yphigisis* — a guide to describing (i.e., drawing) the Earth, usually known as Ptolemy's *Geographia*, and later also as the *Cosmographia*. In general terms, the eight books of the *Geographia* can be regarded as consisting of three sections, later published in a single large volume. The first section, consisting of book 1 and parts of book 8, presents Ptolemy's views on mapmaking in general and includes, in particular, precise geometric and partly mathematical instructions for producing maps. These instructions refer in graphic detail — for the first time, to the best of our knowledge — to the necessity of representing the spherical world on a flat surface such as a sheet of vellum or, later, paper. The new approach initiated the important branch of cartography known as map projections, and in his *Geographia* Ptolemy provides detailed guidelines for producing two such projections. In addition, he furnishes the would-be cartographer with instructions for dividing a map of the world into separate, partial maps.

As a second topic, Ptolemy deals with geographical names, not from a linguistic viewpoint but from a geographical-locational one. He produced the very first geographical gazetteer — i.e., a list of place names together with quantitative coordinates of their location. This list, encompassing some 8,100 items, occupies books 2 to 7.

The final part of the *Geographia* consisted of the maps and apparently constituted the first atlas-like product. Without explicitly defining or naming this concept, Ptolemy established the today universally accepted notion of reduction factor and its inverse, map scale (i.e., the ratio between the distance in a map and the corresponding distance in nature or reality). The map of the entire known world, which in most printed versions of the *Geographia* appears at the end, is thus subdivided into several partial maps of larger scale and therefore of greater detail. These include ten maps of Europe, four of Africa, and 12 of Asia. Shown here is the fourth map of Asia — *Tabula Quarta Asiae* which includes Israel, the Holy Land, as well as large parts of the Middle East. It is thus the earliest known map of the area based on actual "geodetic" measurements of latitude and longitude. No original manuscripts of Ptolemy's time have survived, only copies in Greek, Arabic adaptations, and later translations into Latin and then into other European languages. Whereas Ptolemy's written work, including the verbal parts of the *Geographia*, apparently reached the Western world mostly intact, his original maps were lost. It is still unclear whether the maps found — e.g., in Greece (in the Vatopedi Monastery on Mount Athos) — and those produced later in Italy, Germany, and other countries were copies (or copies of copies) of Ptolemy's originals, or whether they were reconstructed on the basis of the ca. 8,100 names with their pairs of coordinates — latitude and longitude — which had survived in the verbal text of books 2 to 7.

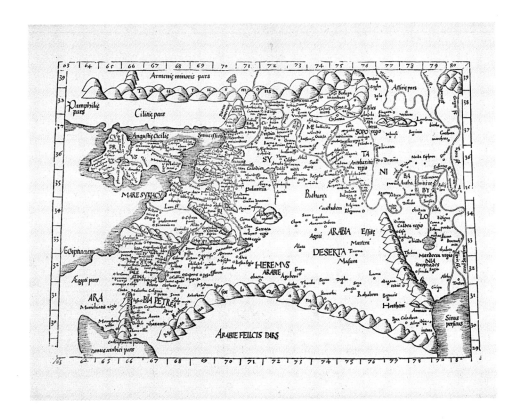

Even the non-professional viewer will note the much-too-flat angle of the Levant coast of the eastern Mediterranean Sea. This error is explained by the fact that whereas in Ptolemy's time latitude was being measured with relatively high accuracy, longitude would have to wait another 1,400 years. Ptolemy relied on the value of the Earth's circumference established by Poseidonius (ca. 135–51 BCE), which resulted in too-short degrees of longitude (with their origin in the Fortunate Isles — the Canaries) and therefore in "flatter" oblique lines. It is significant that the map shown here displays the greatest density of information, in the form of geographical features and names, in the region of the Holy Land.

Ptolemy's *Geographia* appeared in many editions from the late 15th century up to 1730, among others the one edited by the great Flemish cartographer Gerardus Mercator. The copy shown here was edited by Michael Villanovanus, better known as Servetus, printed in Vienne (France) in 1541 by Gasper Trechsel and published by Hugo a Porta. This is the second version of an earlier edition, produced by the same editor and printer, and printed in Lyons in 1535. While the maps in the *Geographia* were unchanged, many derogatory and even heretic remarks on peoples and countries in the text were deleted in the later edition. However, Servetus was burned at the stake in 1553.

N. K.

Michael Servetus Villanovanus, *Claudii Ptolemaei Alexandrini Geographicae Ennarationis Libri Octo* (Lyons, 1541).

H. W. Stevens, *Ptolemy's Geography: A Brief Account of All the Printed Editions Down to 1730* (London, 1908), pp. 48–49.

O. A. Dilke "The Culmination of Greek Cartography in Ptolemy," in *The History of Cartography* vol. 1, ed. J. B. Harley and D. Woodward (Chicago and London, 1987), pp. 177–200.

Eusebius and Hieronymus

Eusebius of Caesarea,
ca. 260–340, and Hieronymus,
ca. 348–420
Map of the Holy Land (detail),
ca. 385, Latin copy, ca. 1150
Manuscript on vellum,
338x225 mm
The British Library, London
Add. Ms. 10049,
fol. 64v

Eusebius, bishop of Caesarea at the end of the 3rd century and beginning of the 4th, was an important Father of the Church. One of his works was the *Onomastikon,* in which he presented in detail the names of the settlements mentioned in the Scriptures, noting each with information relevant to his time. This composition was translated into Latin from the Greek about a hundred years later by Hieronymus (St. Jerome), who added many notations of his own. Hieronymus was himself a Father of the Church and a noted Bible interpreter, whose fame lay in the translation of the Bible from Hebrew into Latin (the Vulgata). The map accompanying the *Onomastikon,* hand-drawn on vellum, is kept alongside it in the library of the British Museum. It is quite possible that Eusebius's original work included a map, but we are not able to reconstruct its form or contents. In any case, the present map is not the original as drawn in the 12th century; in content and in style it is a medieval map.

The map depicts the Orient, from the Ganges and the upper part of the Indus to the Nile delta and Alexandria in the lower right-hand corner and Constantinople in the lower left-hand corner. The Holy Land is at the center of the map, and at its core is Jerusalem. The city is shown as a walled circle with four unequally spaced gates, and next to it is the Citadel (David's Tower). East of the city (seen above it) are marked the Valley of Jehoshaphat, the Mount of Olives, and Bethany, and above them are the Jordan, the Sea of Galilee, and the Dead Sea. The Jordan has two sources — the Yor and the Dan, its two tributaries according to the tradition stemming from Byzantine times and continuing through the Middle Ages. Across the Jordan are Mount Hermon, Mount Lebanon, and Mount Gilead. In the center of the country appear the names of various sites mentioned in the Bible. To the right of Jerusalem are Bethlehem, Hebron, Ein-Gedi, Beersheba, and Rafiah; to the left of it are Bethel, Shiloh, Beth-Shean (Scythopolis), Samaria, Modi'in, and other sites. Shechem is inadvertently mentioned twice, once as "Shechema" and once as "Neapolis." In this part of the map we also find Mount Ephraim, Mount Gilboa, Mount Carmel, and Mount Tabor. The cities of the coastal plain appear as a set of rectangles strung out between Sidon on the left and Gaza on the right. On the southern border of the country we find a river that marks the border between the Land of Israel and Egypt and flows into the Mediterranean near Rinocorura (El Arish). It represents "the River of Egypt," mentioned in the Bible as the southern border of the Land of Israel. The contents of the map, especially the names and some terms, are typical of the cartographic tradition of the 12th century and relate to Crusader traditions. It is interesting to note that another map, depicting all of Asia, was drawn on the reverse side of the same vellum.

R. R.

D. Woodward, "Medieval Mappaemundi," in *History of Cartography*, vol. 1, ed. J. B. Harley and D. Woodward (Chicago, 1987), pp. 286–370.

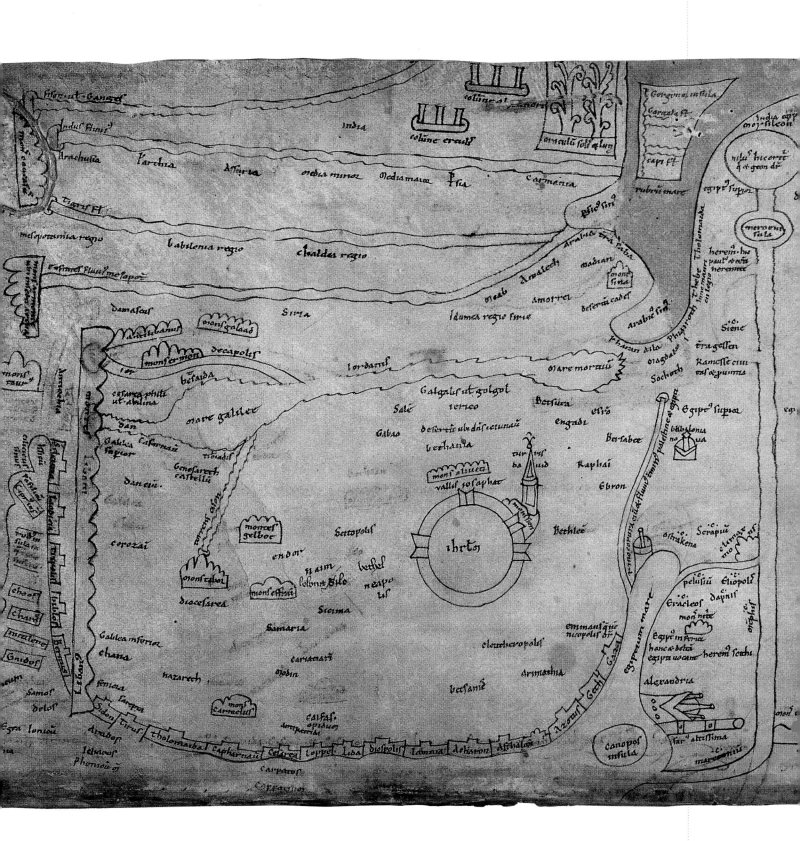

Marino Sanuto and Petrus Vesconte

Marino Sanuto, Italian,
ca. 1260–1338, and
Petrus Vesconte, Italian,
d. ca. 1350
Map of Palestine (detail)
Manuscript on vellum,
350x510 mm
From *Liber Secretorum
Fidelium Crucis . . .*, ca. 1320
The British Library, London
Add. MS. 27376,
ff. 188v–189

Marino Sanuto was a Venetian nobleman well acquainted with the Crusader Kingdom of Jerusalem, having stayed in Acre in 1285–86 and visited the Holy Land again in 1306, a few years after the fall of Acre. That defeat put an end to the Crusader Kingdom; however, some Christians in the West still entertained hopes of reconquering the Holy Land and restoring the golden days of the Kingdom. Among them was Marino Sanuto, whose family had interests in the eastern Mediterranean. With this aim in mind, he presented the pope in 1321 with a copy of his book *Liber Secretorum Fidelium Crucis super Terrae Sanctae Recuperatione et Conservatione* (Book of secrets of the faithful to the Cross on the recovery and protection of the Holy Land), hoping to persuade him to proclaim a new crusade.

Sanuto's book contains several maps, among them a world map, a map of the Holy Land, a map of Jerusalem, and a map of Acre — all drawn by Petrus Vesconte, a renowned Genovese cartographer of the time working in Venice. Vesconte compiled maps of various parts of Europe, Asia, and Africa as well as navigational charts; we are acquainted today with seven atlases drawn by him. He was one of the first to use a compass and work with a grid; the maps in the *Liber Secretorum* therefore differ significantly from earlier ones of the Holy Land and Jerusalem. Here for the first time the aim was to render a map true to reality and precise in both detail and scale. Given the close correspondence between the maps and the text, it is evident that Vesconte drew his maps of the Holy Land according to Sanuto's directions, integrating into them information he derived.

The Sanuto–Vesconte Map of Palestine was unique in its day and for a long time after. Here, for the first time, the cartographer attempted to draw a map on a uniform scale: The map, facing east, is placed on a grid each of whose squares represents a distance of one league (a varying measure that in the present case is about 7 km). It is a pioneering effort to draw a map in the modern sense of the word — i.e., showing the relative directions and distances between the sites. In contrast to earlier (and later) maps, Sanuto and Vesconte's map of Palestine, like their map of Jerusalem, lacks almost any illustrations other than mountains and streams. Not only are drawings of holy places entirely absent, but the inscriptions are all uniform, the size of the letters not varying with the relative importance of the site. The map therefore appears to be an entirely impartial, factual graphic text. This approach, much ahead of its time, is probably attributable to the cartographer's being, in contrast to previous and later cartographers of Palestine, a maker of portolans — navigational charts whose aim is to delineate the topography and note distances as accurately as possible so as to serve as a reliable guide for seafarers. Indeed, the spatial distribution of the sites is relatively accurate, as is the shoreline, richly dotted by the coastal settlements of that time, among them Iscandrone (Scandalion), Sidon, Tyre, Acre, Athlit (Castrum Peregrinorum), Haifa, Caesarea, Arsuf, Ramla, Ashqelon, and Gaza. Among the castles and Crusader sites appearing on the map are Mons Fortis (Montfort), Belvoir, Alba Specula (Blanche Garde, today al-Safi), and Castrum Beroardi (Mint al-Qala'a, south of Ramla). Yet it is clear that Sanuto, having stayed in Acre, knew the

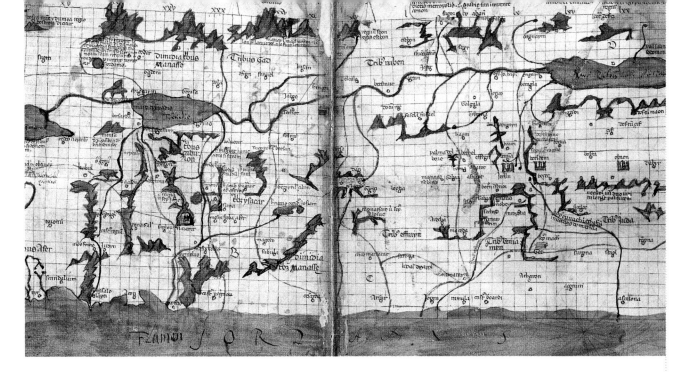

coastline much better than he did the hinterland. For the latter he apparently relied heavily on the traveler Burchard of Mount Sion, who had published a description of the Holy Land in 1283. Sanuto even repeats a gross error made by Burchard, who described the Kishon River as emenating from the Sea of Galilee. Because the Sanuto—Vesconte map was published quite early and was widely used, it served as a model for the "modern" maps appended to all the editions of the "revived" Ptolemy. It was thus very influential, and its inaccuracies were repeated in maps up to the 19th century.

Despite its largely "practical" orientation, this map of Palestine is neither "dry" nor impartial. Its aim was to offer a reliable tool for the planning of a crusade to recapture the Holy Land. Emphasizing the division of the country among the Twelve Tribes (their respective names are the only legends written in larger letters and colored red), it is also rich in Christian holy sites. Aside from Capernaum, Magdala, Bethsaida, the Church of Baptism on the Jordan River, Nazareth, and Bethlehem, we see, on the eastern bank of the Jordan, Baal Gad, Penuel, Succoth, Mount Nebo, Jabesir, Mount Seir (where Lot's wife turned into a

pillar of salt), and Job's grave. Near Hebron are depicted Dvir and Ziph, and south of them the house of Nabal the Carmelite; west of Jerusalem, ear Emmaus, are Shiloh, Givah, and Socho; and west of Emmaus is marked even the site of the Maccabees' graves.

In the Valley of Jezreel various traditions are marked in great detail, among them the battle sites of Barak against Sisera and of Gideon against the Midianites, as well as the defeats of Ahab and Josiah.

M. L.-R.

P. D. A. Harvey, "Local and Regional Cartography in Medieval Europe," in *The History of Cartography*, ed. D. Harley and D. Woodward (1987), pp. 496—97.

M. Levy, "Medieval Maps of Jerusalem," in *The History of Jerusalem: The Crusaders and the Ayyubids (1099—1250)*, ed. J. Prawer and H. Ben-Shammai (Jerusalem, 1991), pp. 418—507 (in Hebrew).

K. Nebenzahl, *Maps of the Holy Land* (New York and Tel Aviv, 1986), pp. 42—45.

J. Prawer, "Foreword," in reprinted edition of Marinus Sanudus Torsellus, *Liber Secretorum Fidelium Crucis super Terrae Sanctae Recoperatione et Conservatione* (Hanover, 1611; repr. Jerusalem, 1972), pp. v—xix, incl. bibliography.

William Wey

William Wey, English,
1407–1476
*Map of the Holy Land
from the Spring Voyage
of 1458* (detail),
Eton, ca. 1462
Lithographic facsimile,
London, 1867, 420x2200 mm
The Jewish National and
University Library, Jerusalem
The Eran Laor
Cartographic Collection

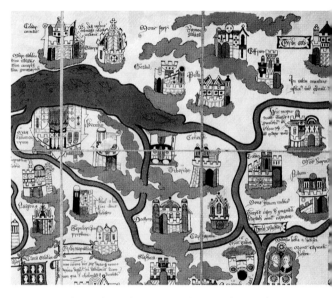

William Wey was a fellow of the "King's College of Our Lady of Eton beside Windsor" situated in the town of Eton on the banks of the Thames. Founded by King Henry VI ca. 1440, this was the largest of the private schools in 15th-century England. After making a pilgrimage to Santiago de Compostela in northwestern Spain, Wey obtained a leave of absence from the college to go to the Holy Land in the framework of the annual "Spring Voyage."

Pilgrimage — to Rome, Spain, and the Holy Land — became increasingly common after the Crusades, spurred by the belief that it would gain the pilgrim full redemption (*indulgentsia*) for his sins after death. In this spirit, Wey boarded a ship sailing from Venice to Jaffa in May 1458. Among the 197 pilgrims were the cousins Gabriel and Antonio Capodilista, who were later to become famous as the creators of a map of the Holy Land, and Lord Caiazzo, who wrote a detailed account of their journey. After remaining in Jaffa for a full month, they visited the Church of the Holy Sepulchre and the Via Dolorosa in Jerusalem, as well as Bethlehem and the banks of the Jordan, setting sail on their return journey in early July. Four years later Wey made a second, week-long visit to the Holy Land, following which he wrote a travelogue describing his experiences in detail, including information about the political situation in different areas. He added to this various suggestions for pilgrims, including a short dictionary of terms in Greek, Hebrew, and English, and a list of distances.

Wey recorded the itinerary of his two journeys in a legible hand on parchment, adding a map of the Holy Land. Of interest is the list of equipment he recommended taking from Jerusalem to the Jordan Valley: "Also whan ye schal ryde to flvm Jordan take wyth yow out of Jerusalem bred, wyne, water, hard chese, and hard eggys, and such vytellys as ye may haue for too dayes . . ."

Moreover, he was one of the first to describe the "14 Stations of the Cross," the accepted number of stations to this day. In fact, the Via Dolorosa tradition and the enumeration of the stations along the route date back to the 4th century, though they underwent many changes in the course of the intervening centuries.

Wey's map shows the Holy Land and its traditional borders with an easterly orientation. The coastline reaches from Sidon in the north to Gaza in the south, and the eastern border runs from Damascus in the north to Beersheba and Hebron in the south. A detailed table of distances appears in the right-hand margin. Jerusalem and Damascus are greatly enlarged, with the southern section contrastingly

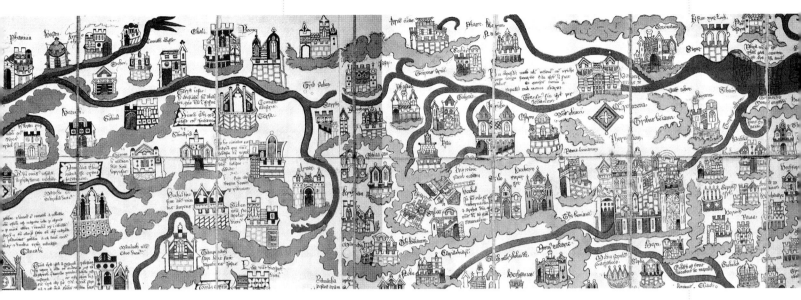

compressed. Placard-like markers denote the Twelve Tribes on both banks of the Jordan.

Even though Wey had firsthand experience of the area, he embellished his map in the spirit of the time, with a rich assortment of architectonic illustrations suggestive rather of the English urban landscape. The map is overflowing with medieval castles, each with its Gothic pennants, gateways, turrets, and arches; the paucity of both crosses and crescents on the roofs of the buildings is striking.

The map is drawn from a horizontal bird's-eye view, but the buildings are shown from a front elevation. The rivers, flora, and mountain ridges are colorful and stylized, somewhat reminiscent of early Muslim maps.

Yet it is impossible not to notice the direct influence of the Sanuto—Vesconte Map (see p. 74) on the general layout, and of Burchard of Mount Sion's book, presumably the source of some of this map's inaccuracies. Figures and captions — mainly the latter — indicate important biblical events close to the historical sites with which they are associated: for example, at Beit-El (the only structure on the map shown upside down) a ladder symbolizes Jacob's dream; and six water jugs mark Christ's miracle at Canna.

Wey's illustrated map exemplifies mapmaking in the period toward the end of the Middle Ages and beginning of the Renaissance, shortly before the printing press and new geographical discoveries brought about revolutionary changes in science and cartography.

A. T.

Itinerary of William Wey, Fellow of Eton, to The Holy Land, A.D. 1458 and 1462, from the original manuscript in the Bodleian Library (London, 1857).

A. Liron, *Christianity Arose in the Holy Land* (Tel Aviv, 1997) (in Hebrew).

K. Nebenzahl, *Maps of the Holy Land* (New York and Tel Aviv, 1986), pp. 49—57.

Pierre le Rouge, after Lucas Brandis de Schass

Pierre le Rouge, French,
15th century
After Lucas Brandis de Schass,
15th century
Map of the Holy Land
Woodcut on 2 blocks, 1488,
387x552 mm
From *La mer des hystoires*,
Pierre le Rouge for
Vincent Commin,
Paris, 1488
The Israel Museum, Jerusalem
Gift of Norman and
Frieda Bier, London

This rare woodcut comes from the French edition of a book by Lucas Brandis de Schass, *Rudimentum Novitorum*, a history of the world according to the medieval Christian theological view. It is replete with illustrations, among them two maps: a world map, and the present one of the Holy Land, which are among the earliest printed maps. Oriented to the east and drawn from a diagonal bird's-eye view, the map has Jerusalem at center, depicted in the medieval pattern of a city surrounded by a circular wall. Here two additional circular walls have been added, in accordance with Josephus Flavius. Since the almost perfect circles do not correspond to the diagonal view, Jerusalem in fact incorporates two different points of view. The map extends from Damascus and Sidon in the north to the Red Sea in the south, with Acre represented as the second most important city after Jerusalem, in commemoration of the Crusader period. The abundant illustrations depict major scenes from the Old and New Testaments: Pharaoh and his armies drowning in the Red Sea at lower right; Moses receiving the Tablets of the Law on Mount Sinai at upper right; John baptizing Jesus at top center; the crucifixion at Golgotha, outside the walls of Jerusalem. While major figures such as Moses and Jesus are depicted clearly and in relative detail, the surface is dotted with small black silhouette-like figures drawn freehand.

The names of the sites appear on banderoles on the mountaintops, which cover most of the land area. The caption, "Cedar et ses Tabernacles," is framed by another such banderole, with the silhouette of a dragon alongside it. The map is encompassed by eight personifications of the celestial directions in the form of human heads. The French edition has some additional figures and illustrations.

A notable characteristic of this map (as well as of the original from which it was copied) is the lack of a true conjunction of the two sheets; they do not fit at the centerline joining the two halves, a defect that may have been caused by an unequal preparation of the two woodblocks.

The book by Brandis de Schass, published in 1475 — some years before the first printed editions of Ptolemy — includes one of the most detailed geographic descriptions of the Holy Land: the *Prologus* by Burchard of Mount Sion, a 13th-century Dominican monk from Magdeburg who lived in the Holy Land for about ten years. In 1283 he drew a unique map, which was later lost. Burchard was the first to divide a map of the Holy Land by both distance and direction. The present map is a highly imprecise interpretation by Brandis de Schass of Burchard's text.

By virtue of the fact that the map bears no resemblance to earlier Holy Land maps, it has remained a singular document, an extraordinary relic in the history of maps of the Holy Land.

A. T.

T. Campbell, *The Earliest Printed Maps: 1472–1500* (Berkeley and Los Angeles, 1987), pp. 144–51.

E. Laor and S. Klein, *Maps of the Holy Land: Cartobibliography of Printed Maps, 1475–1900* (New York and Amsterdam, 1986), pp. 54, 56, no. 440; p. 180.

K. Nebenzahl, *Maps of the Holy Land* (New York and Tel Aviv, 1986), pp. 59–61.

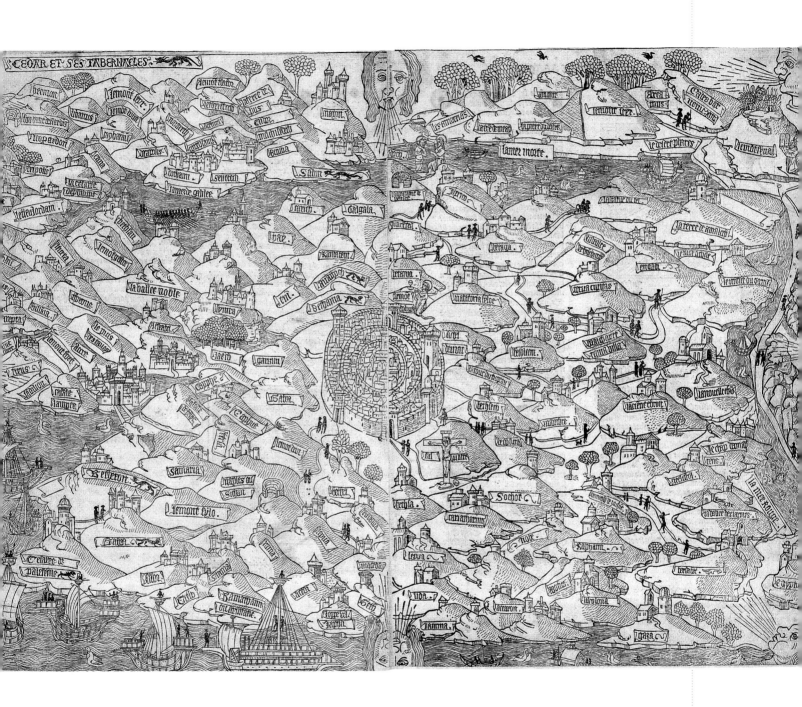

Bernhard von Breydenbach

Bernhard von Breydenbach,
German, ca. 1440–1497
Map of The Holy Land
Woodcut, 275x1270 mm
(mid-section: 275x412 mm)
After Erhard Reuwich, Dutch,
active ca. 1460–1490
Originally Mainz, 1486
In Bernhard von Breydenbach,
*Sanctarum Peregrinationum in
Montem Syon*, Peter Drach,
Speyer, 1505(?)
The Wajntraub Family
Collection, Jerusalem

Bernhard von Breydenbach was a nobleman and cleric who served as a canon in Mainz, Germany. Accompanied by a group of German noblemen, in 1483 he set out on a long pilgrimage to the Holy Land, after which he wrote a thick book about his journey, dedicating it to the archbishop of Mainz. First published in Latin in 1486, and in later editions in several languages, this book is apparently the first of many travel books on the Holy Land. It was printed with illustrations of the journey and the sites, and was considered at the time a valuable source. Among Breydenbach's companions were other writers of travel books — Felix Fabri, Paul Walther, and Georg von Gumppenberg, the first of whom became known for his unique account.

Erhard Reuwich of Utrecht, a professional artist, also accompanied Breydenbach and prepared many illustrations that were later made into woodcuts and incorporated in the latter's book. Among them were images of cities, sites, and buildings visited by the pilgrims, as well as of people and animals encountered during the trip. A map depicting the Holy Land occupied a central place in the book.

The map, originally printed on a long, narrow sheet, is oriented to the east and presents the Holy Land opening up before the pilgrim coming from the Mediterranean. In the right-hand (southwest) border we see Alexandria, the Nile Delta, Cairo, and the pyramids, and behind them the Red Sea, Mount Sinai, and Mecca. On the left-hand (northern) side we see Tripoli in Lebanon and Damascus in Syria. Sites throughout the country are often accompanied by Latin captions, most relating to historic names from the Holy Scriptures as well as later sources. Many of the place names are accompanied by a short sentence, such as, "Here Esau met Jacob when he returned from Mesopotamia." Occasionally confusion arises in the identification of the sites; thus Caesarea on the coast is called "Caesarea Philippi," the former name of the inland Banyas springs. Captions are dispersed throughout the map identifying the heritages of the different tribes, but there is no clear division of the country among the tribes. This map also follows the tradition showing the Kishon River as connecting the Sea of Galilee with Haifa Bay.

In the center of the map's foreground, near semi-destroyed Jaffa, we see a moored ship from which pilgrims would disembark and ascend to Jerusalem. The latter city occupies a prominent space at the center of the map, presented in a size befitting its importance rather than realistically. Preferring to show a view of Jerusalem from the east — from the top of the Mount of Olives westward — the artist has rotated the city by 180^0 in relation to the rest of the map, which faces east.

Nearest the viewer is the eastern wall of the city; the Golden Gate is closed, its upper section partially destroyed. Although Lions Gate is not clearly visible, its place is marked by a caption: "Here Stephanos was stoned." The whole northern part of the wall is also not clear. The Temple Mount area is accorded its full size, the Dome of the Rock being the largest structure in the city. To its right is the Holy Sepulchre, also rotated in the sketch so that its front

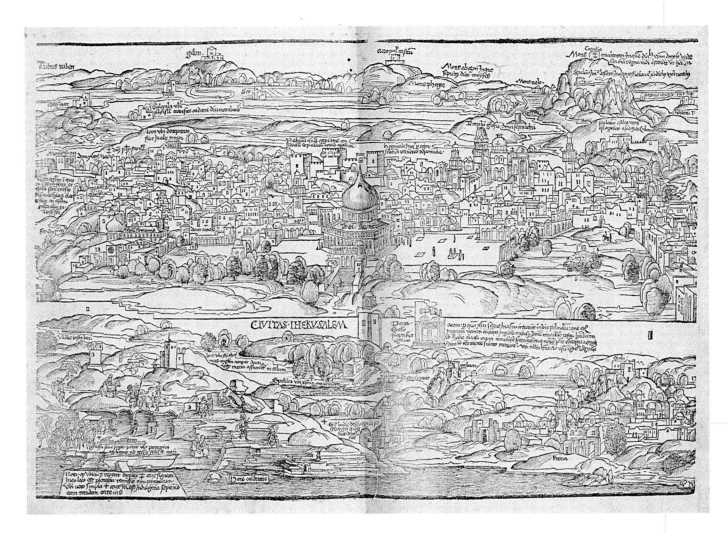

faces eastward, whereas it actually faces southward. Behind the Dome of the Rock and to its left are the turrets of the Citadel of Jerusalem, depicted with almost precise realism.

In the background, behind Jerusalem, are the Jordan Valley, Jericho, and the Jordan River, with the hills of Moab behind them. The Quarantena Mountain, where according to tradition Jesus fasted for forty days, is the most prominent feature of this part of the map. On its left and across the Jordan is "the Mount of the Hebrews, where Moses is said to be buried."

Bernhard von Breydenbach's map, especially its depiction of Jerusalem at center, was the basis for multiple copies and imitations. It is obvious that many of the copiers were unaware that the view of Jerusalem is rotated, in opposition to the general direction of the map.

R. R.

Bernhard von Breydenbach, *Sanctarum Peregrinationum in Montem Syon* (Mainz, 1486).

Bernhard von Breydenbach and His Journey to the Holy Land 1483–84: A Bibliography, compiled by H. W. Davies (Utrecht, 1968, repr.).

Lucas Cranach the Elder

Lucas Cranach the Elder,
German, ca. 1472–1553
Map of the Holy Land
Woodcut on 6 blocks,
1522 (?), 540 x 605 mm
The Jewish National and
University Library, Jerusalem
The Eran Laor
Cartographic Collection

In the early part of his artistic career, ca. 1501–3, the German artist Lucas Cranach the Elder lived in Vienna and was associated with the humanistic circles there. He moved to Wittenberg, where he was appointed court painter to the Saxon elector Frederic III, known as "the Wise," and founded a large workshop with his two sons. His oeuvre, most of it in a late Gothic style, includes paintings and woodcuts of religious scenes and portraits, as well as of classical mythological themes. A friend of Martin Luther, Cranach was among the first supporters of the Reformation; he also painted one of the best-known portraits of Luther and illustrated the latter's translation of the New Testament from the Greek into German.

Cranach's prolific oeuvre included one of the most unique and interesting maps of the Holy Land. This map, oriented to the north-northwest, combines a vertical with a diagonal bird's-eye perspective. It encompasses all of the country and shows the division of the tribal lands on either side of the Jordan, from Damascus in the north to the Red Sea in the south, with the coastline reaching from north of Sidon to the Nile Delta. A central motif is the marking of the Israelites' route of wandering in the desert. Many of these scenes are in miniature, with the major encampments named. Among the subjects illustrated are the Red Sea crossing, the collecting of manna, the lost peoples of Korach, Moses receiving the Ten Commandments on Mount Sinai, and the incident of the Golden Calf. Oddly, the names of the Twelve Tribes and the scene descriptions are written in many directions and even

upside down, as are the compass markings in the margins of the map. A narrow strip is missing from its lower part.

Parts of the map have been wrought with amazing detail and exactitude — among them Mount Sinai and Edom in the south (lower edge of the map), the Hermon range in the north, and the sea with its elaborate waves and elegant ships. Large areas, however, entirely lack in such features as mountain ranges and rivers, showing only major settlements, among them Hebron, Jaffa, and Tiberias. This contrasting treatment creates the sense of an unfinished work. And the fact that this is the sole known complete copy allows for the assumption that only a number of test prints of this map were ever produced. It has also been conjectured that Cranach's responsibility was limited to the artistic design, and that the cartographic information was the responsibility of the geographer and scholar Barthel Stein.

Heinrich Röttinger published two fragments of the map in 1921 and was the first to attribute the work to Cranach. In 1981 Eran Laor bought the complete map from Teddy Kollek — then mayor of Jerusalem — and after a worldwide investigation received confirmation from the Swiss cartographic historian Arthur Dürst that this was indeed the Cranach map, until then presumed lost. It was popularly believed at the beginning of the 18th century that Cranach had accompanied Frederic the Wise on his 1493 journey to the Holy Land, and Dürst hypothesized that the map was made to commemorate this pilgrimage. At any rate the Saxon coat of arms, with its crossed swords, can be seen hoisted from a sail of the uppermost ship. While this insignia, with variations, is to be found in most of Cranach's prints, the ornate version see here probably appeared for the first time in 1515.

There are two known copies after this map. The first, turned around (left becoming right) in the printing, appears in the Zurich Bible published by Froschauer in 1524 and is thought to be the first map of the Holy Land to be included in a Bible. The second, copied from this book, but with the error corrected, was printed in the Dutch Bible by Jan Liesvfeldt in Antwerp in 1526. The fragments having been discovered, it is possible with the help of the copies to reconstruct the strip that, as mentioned, is missing from the lower part of the map under discussion here.

With regard to its cartographic origins, there is no doubt that the main source of reference for Cranach's map is Ptolemy's *Quarta Asiae Tabula* or *Asia Part IV* (see p. 70). In the opinion of Armin Kunz, most of the additional cartographic information in the map and the softening of the coastline derived from Sanuto–Vesconte's *Modern Map of Palestine*, which was appended to new editions of Ptolemy's *Geographia* (see p. 74). It is interesting to note a certain correspondence, in subject matter and design, between this map and the first printed Hebrew map from Zurich (see p. 120) — particularly in the prominence given to Mount Sinai and Mount Seir in both. The division of the land among the Twelve Tribes, with their names inscribed in Latin, follows the Ptolemy maps. But unlike those maps, which pay little heed to the Israelites' wanderings, here the topic receives particular attention. Considering the date of the map, the detailing of the stops along the way according to the biblical text can be compared only to that in Hebrew maps. Indeed, the very fact that Cranach included such a systematic account in this type of map reveals him to be one of the pioneers of European Christian mapmaking.

The map's date attribution ranges from 1508 to 1515. Kunz draws attention to the word *Blachfeld* — (meaning "dry land" or "plain") ("And they possessed his land. . . . And all the plain on this side Jordan eastward, even unto the sea of the plain, under the springs of Pisgah" (Deut. 4:47–49) — appearing near the end of the route, northeast of the Dead Sea. The first use of this word in written German can be traced to Luther's translation of the Bible, published in 1522. It therefore seems plausible that the map was first used to illustrate this translation.

From a stylistic point of view, it is worth noting the firm lines and original rendering of the mountains and waves. Similar features appear also in Cranach's woodcuts of the Passion, dated 1509, and his scene of prayer at Gethsemane. They can also be found in the waves and clouds in Cranach's 1519 woodcut of the Apocalypse. Intriguing too, is the possible influence here of Jacopo de Barbari's portrayal of the city of Venice, ca. 1500, de Barbari having been Cranach's predecessor as Saxon court painter.

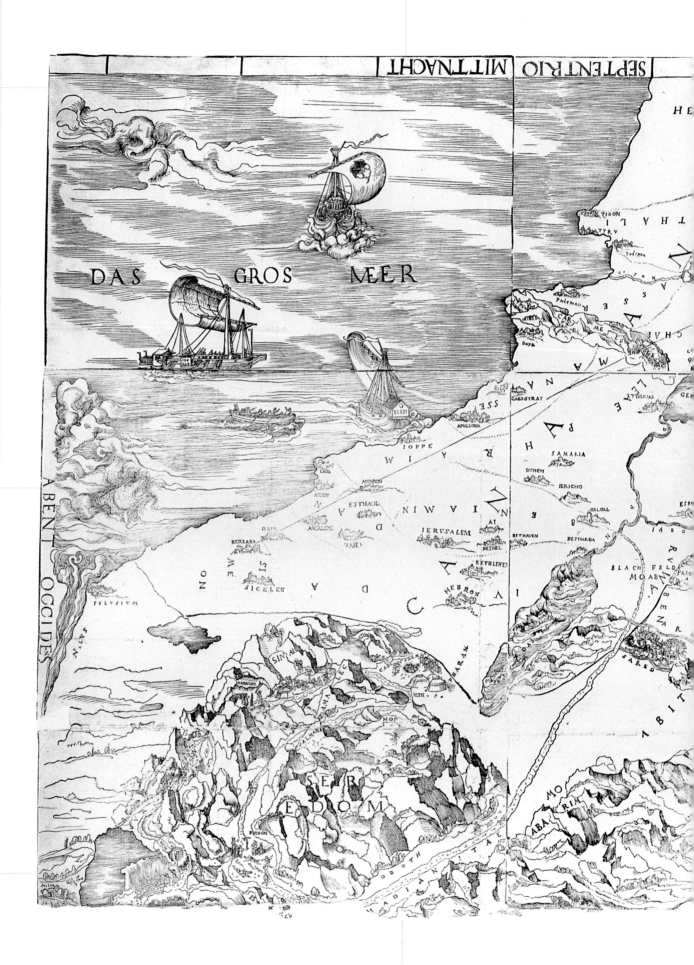

DAS GROS MEER

ABENT OCCIDES

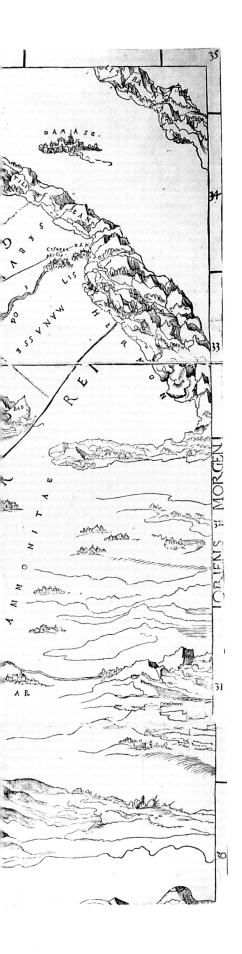

Michael Liebmann has noted affinities between the two works, especially in the depiction of nature in a rich style entirely devoid of schematization.

Various scholars have discussed at length the purpose of this map and its historical and theological import. It appears that Joachim von Watt (1484–1551) (known in Latin as Vadianus), humanist poet, historian, and reformer, who served as rector of the University of Vienna, sponsored the copy of the Cranach map that appears in the Zurich Bible. Being in addition a geographer, he emphasized the need to comprehend the Bible geographically. The purpose of this map, then, may have been to serve as a "teaching aid" at the University of Wittenberg, perhaps explaining why only one copy has come down to us.

It seems that even after the extensive research carried out by such scholars as Dürst, Liebmann, and especially Kunz, on which much of the above information is based, a number of puzzles relating to this map remain unsolved.

A. T.

A. Dürst, "Zur Wiederauffindung der Heiligland-Karte von ca. 1515 von Lucas Cranach dem Ältern, in Memoriam Eran Laor (1900–1990)," in *Cartographica Helvetica* 3 (January 1991), pp. 22–27.

M. Liebmann, "Die Heiligland-Karte von ca. 1515 von Lucas Cranach dem Ältern: Ein Kunstgeschichtlicher Bericht," *Wiener Jahrbuch für Kunstgeschichte* 45 (1992), pp. 195–99.

A. Kunz, "Cranach as Cartographer: The Rediscovered Map of the Holy Land," *Print Quarterly* 12, no. 2 (June 1995), pp. 123–44.

Jacob Ziegler

Jacob Ziegler, German,
ca. 1470–1549
*Quinta tabula universalis
Palestinae*
(The fifth map of all of
Palestine)
Woodcut, 232x343 mm
From Jacob Ziegler,
Terrae Sanctae. Descriptio,
Petrus Opilius,
Strasbourg, 1532
The Wajntraub Family
Collection, Jerusalem

Jacob Ziegler, theologian, historian, and mathematician, was also a geographer and in 1504 published a book on the mathematical basis of cartography. From 1529 he was a professor at the University of Vienna and at the same time maintained close contact with centers of learning in Italy, Germany, and Scandinavia. His book on the Holy Land, which appeared in 1532, with a second edition in 1536, included seven maps illustrating the Bible and, somewhat surprisingly, a map of Scandinavia. In a letter to the renowned Nuremberg humanist Willibald Pirkheimer, he spoke of his desire to map various regions in accordance with the new scientific principles of the Renaissance. However, his hopes that the mathematical data of the maps would be drawn from astronomical measurements, to be made by special emissaries in various places in the world, were not realized.

This map, oriented to the northwest, is a detailed depiction of the Land of Israel on either side of the Jordan, with a coastline extending from Sidon in the north to Rhinocorura (El Arish) near Rafiah in the south. It also encompasses a large section of the Arabian Desert (not shown in detail) as well as Damascus in the north. The inheritances of the Twelve Tribes are indicated by straight schematic lines, and their names, written in large, well-spaced letters, are mostly derived from Greek and Roman sources. Thus Jerusalem is called "Aelia."

The map influenced a number of major cartographers, among them Gerardus Mercator (in his first map of the Holy Land in 1537), Sebastian Münster, and Tilemannus Stella in 1559. This influence is evinced in their adoption of Ziegler's crescent-shaped Dead Sea, which partly runs parallel to the Mediterranean coastline, and of his tracing of the Kishon River along a course that does not directly link the Sea of Galilee to the Mediterranean — as incorrectly shown on many maps — but originates in the Gilboa range and divides into two, right-angled branches.

The book containing this map has been regarded by some as the first "atlas" of the Holy Land. Ziegler has indicated his sources; he quotes at length from the writings of Josephus Flavius, Eusebius's *Onomastikon*, Hieronymus, Strabo, Pliny, and the account of Antonius's journey, and also refers to the descriptions of Burchard of Mount Sion and Bernhard von Breydenbach. But his map was indisputably based mainly on Ptolemy's *Asia Part IV* (see p. 70) and illustrates the enormous influence of the "Ptolemaic revival." Although new astronomical measurements were unavailable, he tried to base his data on at least two different parallel sources and to remove or revise geographical information he thought to be incorrect. Thus in a sense this may be considered the first "scientific" map of the Holy Land. Yet it contains many inaccuracies. For example, apart from the distortions in the shape of the Dead Sea and of the Mediterranean coastline, he placed Ein Gedi to the south of Masada.

It should be borne in mind that the innovative map of Lucas Cranach the Elder (see p. 82) preceded Ziegler's by a decade. Nevertheless, two new cartographic elements in the map should be noted:

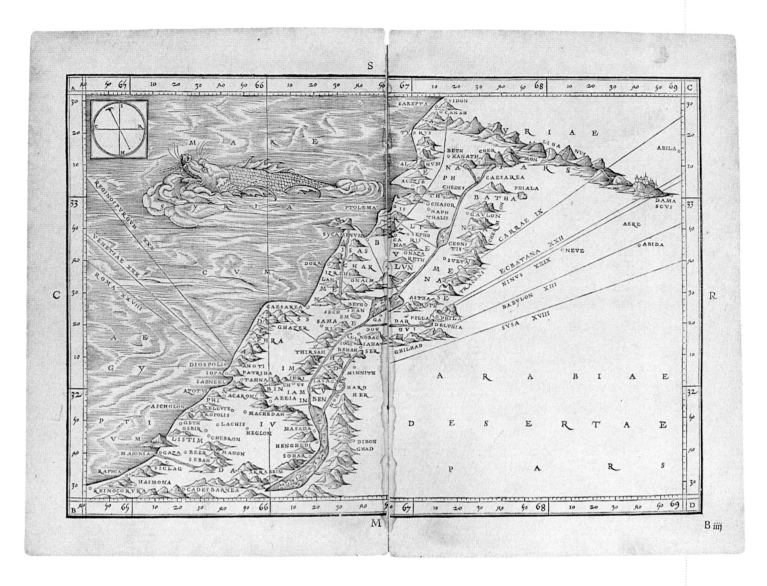

first, the listing of distances from Jerusalem of eight different places to the east and west of the city, and second, the indication of the magnetic deviation in the compass rose at top right. The magnetic deviation had been noticed long before and had troubled Columbus, but it was first pointed out in a map in Apianus's *Cosmographia*, published in Ingoldstadt in 1529, only three years before Ziegler's map.

A. T.

E. Laor and S. Klein, *Maps of the Holy Land: Cartobibliography of Printed Maps, 1470–1900* (New York and Amsterdam, 1986), pp. 117–18, nos. 866–860.

K. Nebenzahl, *Maps of the Holy Land* (New York and Tel Aviv, 1986), pp. 70–71.

Petrus Laicstain and Christian Schrott

Petrus Laicstain, Dutch, active
ca. 1556–1570, and
Christian Schrott, Dutch,
ca. 1532–1608
*Nova descriptio amplissimae
Sanctae Terrae*
(New description of the entire
Holy Land)
Engraving on 9 plates by J. and
L. Doetechum, Antwerp, 1570,
second state 1676,
1110x1170 mm
The Moldovan Family
Collection, New York

This is a rare, impressive, and most important 16th-century map of the Land of Israel. Petrus Laicstain, a Dutch cartographer and astronomer, returning from a visit to the Holy Land in 1556 with the draft of a map, gave it to the cartographer Christian Schrott, who published it in 1570. This information is provided on a scroll centered at the top of the map. The printer was Hieronymous Cocq. A few copies are known to us, two of them in the British Library, London. Laicstain is also known to have made two maps of Jerusalem — one of the "modern," the other of the historic city — which were sold in two sheets in copies made by Gerard de Jode, and later in a single sheet in a copy made by Braun and Hogenberg.

Schrott was cartographer to the court of Philip II of Spain, and one of his commissions was to produce an atlas of Europe for the duke of Alba. In the cartouche beneath the medallion is a dedication to Bishop Gerard of Groesbeck, and in a frame lower down a geographic-historical description of the Holy Land.

Here we in fact have two maps: a large one and to the left of it a smaller one in a separate frame. The former, oriented to the north, shows the Land of Israel on either side of the Jordan and the inheritances of the Twelve Tribes. Judea, Samaria, and the Galilee are marked in large, spaced letters. The curves and indentations of the coastline, which extends from Beirut in the north to Gaza in the south, are delineated with exceptional skill, and the bends in the Jordan are emphasized. The map is rich in topographical detail and demarcated settlements, especially biblical sites. The southern portion of the Dead Sea is cropped by the decorative frame. Both the engraving of the map itself and the execution of the frames and medallions evince outstanding artistry.

The other map, though smaller, encompasses a wider area. Devoted to the biblical Exodus, it includes the Sinai Desert and the Nile Delta. It has the southern part of the Dead Sea turning eastward, almost at a right angle, but it does not have the Kishon linking the Sea of Galilee to the Mediterranean — as do many other maps of this time. The route of the Israelites' wanderings in the desert, delicately marked but devoid of figural images, includes the crossing of the Red Sea. The southern shoreline of the Sinai Peninsula is flattened and distorted; Mount Sinai is given prominence, with the name of the Saint Catherine Monastery appearing next to it.

Apart from his visit to the to the Holy Land and the Bible itself, Schrott's sources for this groundbreaking map are a mystery. Its influence, on the other hand, can be easily traced, as the two maps were copied by the greatest Dutch and Flemish cartographers. In 1584 Ortelius copied the larger map, noting its derivation but changing its orientation. Mercator also copied Schrott's map, with minor changes (see p. 92), presenting it in 1570 as a different version of Ortelius's map, after Tilemannus Stella. The Fleming Jodocus Hondius (1563–1611) copied the smaller map for a table acquired by Blaeu on Hondius's death, and Blaeu published it, giving it a western orientation.

Two differences between the present map and the earlier state in the British Library are worthy of note.

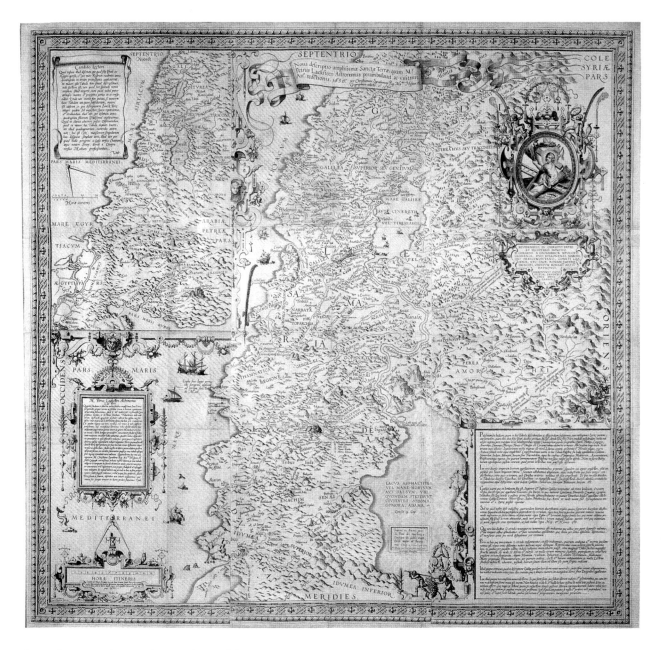

First, whereas in the British copy the medallion at top right is empty, in this version it contains a figure of a child. The attributes of the cross, the letters INRI, and the crown of thorns imply that the figure is Jesus. Second, in the frame giving the origin of the map and the names of its authors, an unknown hand changed the date, and the year 1556 became in the present copy 1676, probably indicating that this is a second state.

A. T.

Johannes Keuning, "XVIth Century Cartography in the Netherlands," *Imago Mundi* (1952).

E. Laor and S. Klein, *Maps of the Holy Land: Cartobibliography of Printed Maps, 1470–1900* (New York and Amsterdam, 1986), p. 180.

K. Nebenzahl, *Maps of the Holy Land* (New York and Tel Aviv, 1986), pp. 82–83.

Gerard de Jode

Gerard de Jode, Flemish,
1509–1591
After Tilemannus Stella,
German, 1525–1589
*Terrae Sanctae, quae
Promissionis terra . . .*
(Description of the Holy Land,
or the Promised Land . . .)
Hand-colored etching by
Johannes and Lucas
Doetechum, 1578,
307x513mm
From Gerard de Jode, *Speculum
orbis terrae,* edited by the
author's son,
Cornelis de Jode,
Antwerp, 1593
The Israel Museum, Jerusalem
Gift of Norman and
Frieda Bier, London

Gerard de Jode (whose name indicates his Jewish origins) was a researcher, engraver, and publisher living in Antwerp. He published single maps in various formats, including two views of Jerusalem at different periods, after Petrus Laicstain.

This map belongs to a familiar genre, in which a view or a map of Jerusalem is appended to a map of the Holy Land. The view of the "modern" Jerusalem (i.e., as it was in the cartographer's time) at lower right — incorporating illustrations of Bethlehem's Church of the Nativity on the left and of the monument marking the site of Jesus' tomb in Jerusalem's Holy Sepulchre on the right — belongs to a series of five maps apparently copied from each other in the 16th century in Italy (see p. 144). The prototype of this series was probably the map of Hermanus Borculus, dated 1538.

The map is oriented toward the northwest, and shows the patrimonial lands of the Twelve Tribes. The coastline, extending from Tyre to Beersheba (!), with many bays and inlets, is inaccurate, and the Dead Sea is, perculiarly, crescent-shaped. In the east, the map depicts Transjordan as far as Philadelphia (Amman) and the Arab Desert. As indicated in the cartouche at bottom left, de Jode based this map on Tilemannus Stella's map of the Holy Land, which served as an influential source for many cartographers. But it also owes much to an earlier map by Jacob Ziegler (see p. 86), especially in its drawing of the coastline and the shape given to the Dead Sea. Ziegler himself drew upon Ptolemy's *Asia Part IV.*

De Jode's map is outstanding in its exquisite artistic design and coloring, and illustrates well the complex combination of several prototypes exerting their influence on the design of ancient maps of the Holy Land.

K. Nebenzahl, *Maps of the Holy Land* (New York and Tel Aviv, 1986), pp. 76–77.

R. Rubin, *Image and Reality: Jerusalem in Maps and Views,* (Jerusalem, 1999), pp. 76–87.

A. T.

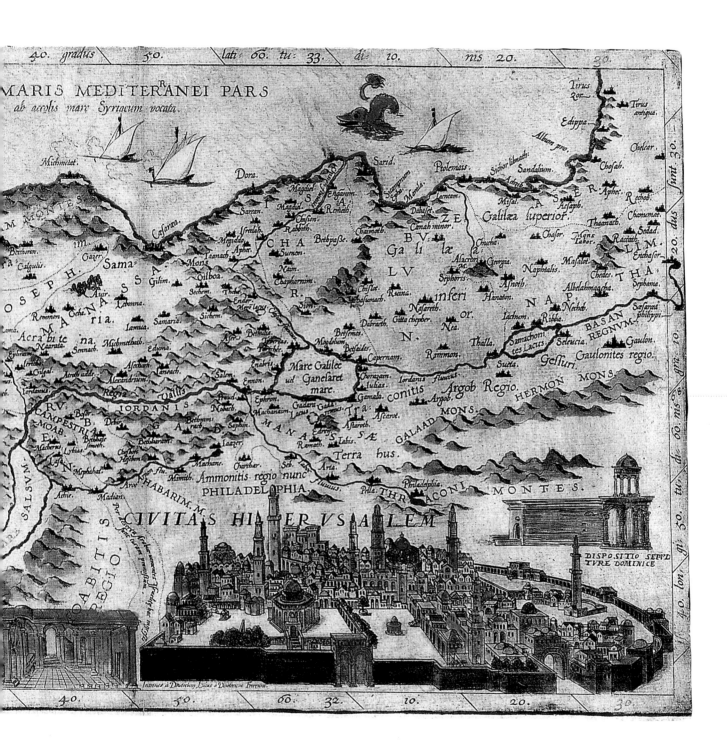

Gerardus Mercator

Gerardus Mercator, Flemish,
1512–1594
After Abraham Ortelius,
Flemish, 1527–1598
After Laicstain–Schrott,
*Map of the Holy Land – the
Promised Land*
Hand-colored engraving,
ca. 1585, 360x502 mm
From Gerardus Mercator,
*Atlas sive Cosmographicae
Meditationes*,
Henricus Hondius, Amsterdam,
ca. 1623
The Israel Museum, Jerusalem

This map underwent many developments. In 1556 the Dutch astronomer Peter Laicstain visited the Holy Land and recorded his impressions. The Dutch cartographer Christian Schrott then designed a map accordingly (see p. 88). Abraham Ortelius copied the present map from the former, introducing some changes of his own. He altered the orientation from north to east, omitted the inset map in the Laicstain–Schrott version, and added a pictorial depiction of the story of Jonah and "the great fish," as well as individual cartouches. The coastline, the Sea of Galilee, the Dead Sea, and the various rivers were copied nearly exactly, whereas the representation of the mountains was schematized. Ortelius was the follower and heir of Gerardus Mercator (Gerhard Kramer), considered the greatest cartographer of the 16th century (see p. 94). Yet in the case of the present map, Mercator was the copier, with slight changes, of Ortelius's map.

Oriented to the east, the map shows the Holy Land on both sides of the Jordan, with a coastline extending from Beirut to Gaza. The craggy and indented coastline and the twists and turns of the Jordan are more fanciful than realistic.

The map cites a long list of places by both their biblical and modern names, using different-styled scripts. Sodom and Gomorrah, Admah and Zeboim, the cities destroyed by God according to Genesis 19, are shown near the Dead Sea. The geographical symbols used in this map are also a combination of old and new. This is especially apparent in the delineation of the cities, their magnitude indicated by the number and bulk of the fortifying towers, as was customary in ancient maps, along with circles of varying size with a dot at the center, according to the method used in modern maps. With these features epitomizing the change from a pictorial to a graphic-scientific depiction, the map reflects a significant shift of *Weltanschauung*.

A. T.

H. M. Z. Meyer, *Palestine in Ancient Maps* (Jerusalem, 1986) (in Hebrew).

K. Nebenzahl, *Maps of the Holy Land* (New York and Tel Aviv, 1986), pp. 72–73.

Abraham Ortelius

Abraham Ortelius, Flemish,
1527–1598
*Abrahami Patriarchae
peregrination et vita*
(The wanderings and life of
Abraham the patriarch),
First edition, Antwerp, 1590
Hand-colored engraving by
Frans Hogenberg, ca. 1603,
360x470 mm (plate)
From Abraham Ortelius,
Theatrum Orbis Terrarum,
Johannes Baptista Vrients,
Antwerp, 1603
The Israel Museum, Jerusalem
Gift of Norman and
Frieda Bier, London

Abraham Ortelius was the first cartographer to gather maps of a uniform size, with explanatory texts on the reverse side, into a kind of atlas. He started out studying Greek, Latin, and mathematics, but later devoted himself to the pursuit of geography. Having begun his professional life as a dealer in maps, which he enriched by hand-coloring, he became the follower and partner of the greatest geographer of his time, Gerardus Mercator. Ortelius was the first publisher to mention the sources of his maps. Thus, apart from the obvious similarity, we know that the source of his map of the Holy Land was Tilemannus Stella of Siegen, Germany (1525–1589) (see p. 90). His book *Theatrum Orbis Terrarum*, published in 41 editions in several languages, included 219 maps, six of them biblical.

The present map depicts the Land of Canaan and part of Egypt, from the Dan River to the Nile Delta. The coastline is emphasized by the customary technique of dense hachuring; the mountains, cone-shaped and round-peaked, are grouped together. The territorial division of the map among the Canaanite peoples — Philistines, Amalekites, and Jebusites, among others — follows the story of Abraham in Genesis. The map is decorated with 22 medallions, after the Dutch artist Maarten de Vos, picturing scenes from the life of Abraham. Starting to the right of the title cartouche and continuing clockwise, they depict, *inter alia*, Abraham's departure from Ur of Chaldaea (in Mesopotamia), his receiving the divine promise of the Land of Israel, the birth of Isaac, the expulsion of Hagar and Ishmael into the wilderness, the binding of Isaac, and the burial of Abraham and Sarah. The source of the right-hand cartouche's decorated frame, with

three different yardsticks appearing below it, is probably Hans Vredman de Vries. At upper left is an additional inset map of the Middle East on which are marked the wanderings of Abraham from Ur to Shechem. The text above and below the map is a quotation from Genesis 12:1: "Get thee out of thy country, and from thy kindred, and from thy father's house, unto a land that I will shew thee."

As in many other maps of Canaan, the Dead Sea does not yet exist in this map. Instead, there is a valley in which we see Sodom, Gomorrah, Admah, and Zeboim, before their destruction.

Ortelius's map represents the growing interest in the 16th century in historical geography, mainly linked to biblical topics. The delicate portrayal of Abraham's wanderings also bears witness to the cartographer's expertise as an engraver.

In its cartographic design this map is almost identical to Ortelius's map of the Promised Land, which includes great parts of Syria, Transjordan, the Sinai Peninsula, and northern Egypt, and depicts the Israelites' wanderings after leaving the land of Egypt and the division of the country among the Twelve Tribes.

Of particular interest is the design of the inner frame of the map: it appears as if stretched on fabric and hanging on a wall, like a rich Flemish tapestry. Indeed, this was a common method of displaying maps in the Netherlands, even in private houses. It is possible that beyond indicating an appreciation of the map's artistic value, it was a status symbol representing the affluence and education of the family.

A. T.

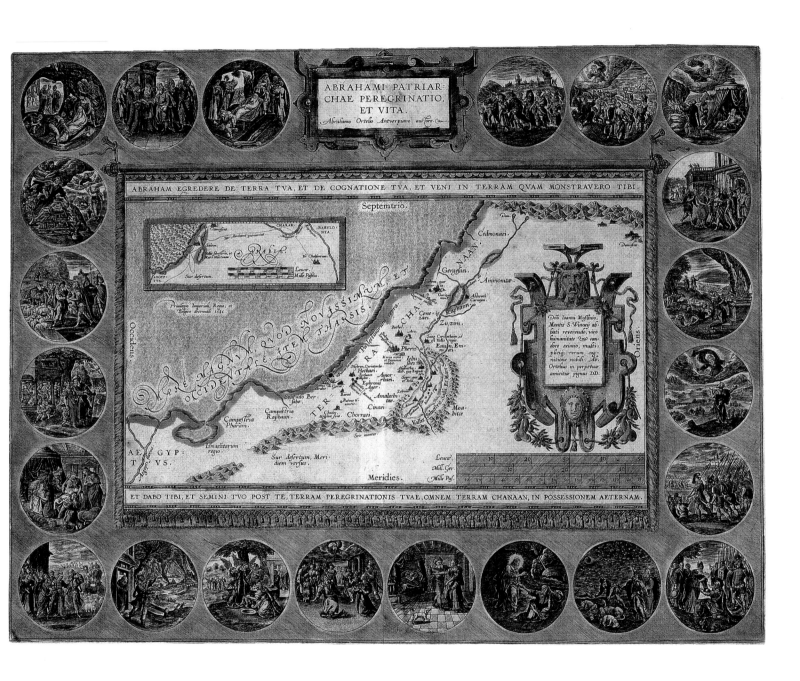

K. Nebenzahl, *Maps of the Holy Land* (New York and Tel Aviv, 1986), pp. 84–85, 92.

J. A. Welu, "The Sources and the Development of Cartographic Ornamentation in the Netherlands," in *Art and Cartography*, ed. David Woodward (Chicago, 1987), pp. 147–73.

Chistian van Adrichom

Christian van Adrichom, Dutch,
1533–1585
*Situs Terrae Promissionis
SS Bibliorum intelligentiam
exacte aperiens*
(The disposition of the
Promised Land precisely clarifies
biblical writings)
Hand-colored engraving,
ca. 1585, 354x1010 mm
From Christian van Adrichom,
*Theatrum Terrae Sanctae et
Biblicarum Historiarum*,
Cologne, Officina Birckmanica,
1590
The Israel Museum, Jerusalem
Gift of Adam Mekler in honor
of Ariel Gabriella Mekler

Christian van Adrichom created this map for his comprehensive work Theatrum Terrae Sanctae, in which he surveys the Holy Land. The book is divided into seventeen chapters; fourteen detail the patrimonial lands of the Twelve Tribes, with ten accompanying maps depicting the settlements, the lie of the land, and some of the events that took place in the region. Another chapter with its detailed map portrays the Paran desert and includes a description of the encampments of the Children of Israel on their travels from Egypt to the Land of Israel. Yet another chapter, with accompanying map, is devoted to Jerusalem, and a "chronicon" — a detailed historical record. Adrichom marked every site and event with a number and gave a brief account of each in his book.

At the end of his life, Adrichom appears to have entrusted his manuscript and the maps to Georg Braun, who indeed published the book in Cologne several years later, in 1590, adding an introduction signed by himself.

Beneath the central inscription is a drawing of a shield emblazoned with a snake and the name Adrichom under it — an emblem that appears on a number of maps drawn by him. In the lower left-hand corner is the scale of map and a compass. The map faces east.

In the east (the top part), the map is delimited by a line running between the cities of Amalek and Petra in the southeast, past the desert of Moab, the Arnon Ravine, and the Gilead Mountains in the east, up to Mount Hermon and the cities of Tzuba and Aroer in the northeast. In the west (the lowermost part of the map) is "the Great Sea" — i.e., the Mediterranean, a number of sailboats and legendary sea monsters lurking in the water. In the center we see the prophet Jonah being thrown to the whale. On the northeastern coast are the Phoenician cities, Mount Carmel, and Strato's tower. "The Land of the Philistines" lies to the west of the coast, and the Nile Delta and the city of Alexandria are in the southwest.

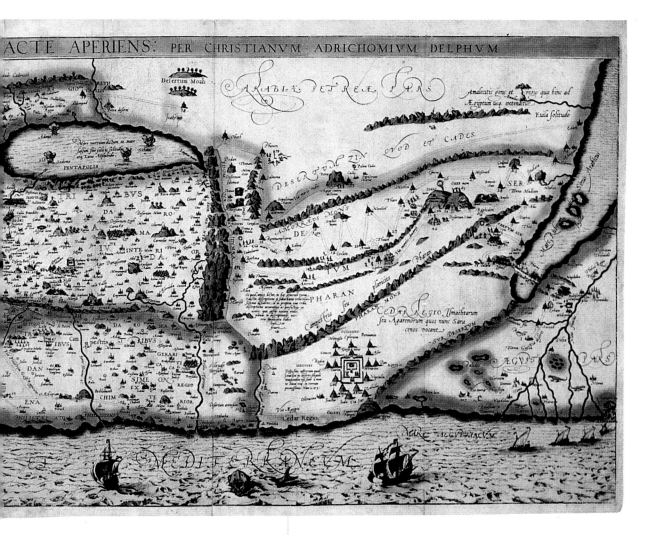

In the north (on the left) the map is delimited by an imaginary line running through the city of Palmyra (Tadmor), the rivers Amana and Parpar in the northwest, and the Lebanon mountains in the north, up to the Forest of Lebanon and the city of Sidon, on the northwest coast. In the south the frontier runs between Alexandria in the southwest, the pyramids, and the city of Memphis, up to the Red Sea and the town of Elath in the northeast.

The most prominent feature of the "Promised Land" map is its partition into patrimonial lands. Marino Sanuto was probably the first cartographer to make this division (see p. 74). Despite the general similarities between Sanuto's map and Adrichom's, we cannot be sure that Adrichom based his map on that of Sanuto. Adrichom revealed his sources in his book, mentioning Jacob Ziegler and Tilemannus Stella, who also made maps of the Land of Israel, though neither of their maps is identical to Adrichom's. Marino Sanuto's map is not even listed among Adrichom's sources.

On Adrichom's map, hatching is used to denote the borders between the tribal patrimonial lands, with emphasis added by coloring in shades of yellow, green, pink, and brown. Adrichom also denoted the different regions by name: (Trachon, Galila, Phoenicia, Samaria, Daroma, the deserts of Tzin and Shor, etc.) as well as the "Kingdom of Edom," the "Land of the Philistines," the "Kingdom of Kedar," etc.

Over 800 sites and events are scattered across the map. In an introduction to his book Adrichom added a sort of key: a cluster of buildings denotes a settlement, a tower topped by a flag a fortress; a triangle enclosing a circle a place that can be accurately identified; a circle within a circle a site Adrichom was not able to identify with any certainty; L the cities of the Levites, and X the Roman cities of Decapolis.

A relief depiction of the area includes mountain ranges (Mount Seir, the mountains of Gilead, the mountains of Emori, etc.), single mountains (Carmel, Sinai, Horev, etc.), rivers (Jordan, Arnon, Kishon, etc.), and lakes (Lake Hula, the Dead Sea, etc.).

Events portrayed on the map span the period from the creation of the world — Cain slaying Abel (91; Judah), followed by the four cities of the plain (228; Judah), and Jacob going down to Egypt (110; Paran) — up to the 6th century CE: the Monastery of Saint Sabas (208; Judah).

This is a richly illustrated map showing famous biblical scenes: the destruction of Sodom and Gomorrah (228; Judah); Malkizedek offering Abraham bread and wine (28; Issachar), Lemech killing Cain in error (16; Issachar), Joseph meeting his brothers in Dotan and being sold to the Ishmaelites (36; Zevulun), Jacob going down into Egypt (110; Paran), Samson striking down the Philistines with the jawbone of a donkey (43; Dan); Elijah and the prophets of Ba'al making sacrifices on

Mount Carmel and Elijah slaying the prophets of Ba'al who remained on the Kishon (19; Zevulun).

Needless to say, traditions from the New Testament and its extrinsic literature are by no means absent from the map, among them Miriam going down into Egypt (107; Simon), Jesus healing a madman (97; Zevulun), Jesus walking on the water (50; Zevulun), and Saint George killing the dragon (91; Asher).

The map of the Paran desert contains artistic depictions of the departure from Egypt; Moses stretching out his hand over the sea and the Children of Israel crossing the dry sea bed (86); Moses striking the rock and drawing water from it for his people (59). The bottom of the map shows the Children of Israel in their encampment around the Tent of Congregation, when they stopped north of the Paran desert; and near the boundary of Simon's patrimonial lands one can see the scouts bearing their clusters of grapes.

The tiny figures featured in depictions of the various events were carefully drawn by the hand of an artist, and they embellish the map with a fascinating touch of the legendary.

S. C.

C. Adrichom, *Theatrum Terrae Sanctae et Biblicarum Historiarum*, Officina Birckmannica (Cologne, 1590).

E. Laor and S. Klein, *Maps of the Holy Land — Cartobibliography of Printed Maps, 1475—1900* (New York and Amsterdam, 1986), pp. 1—5.

John Speed

John Speed, English,
1552–1629
*Canaan as It was Possessed both
in Abraham and Israels Dayes
with the Stations and
Bordering Nations*
Engraving on 4 sheets, 1595,
745x957 mm
The Jewish National and
University Library, Jerusalem
The Eran Laor
Cartographic Collection

When John Speed, an English historian and cartographer, became a member of the Antiquarian Society, he met Sir Robert Cotton and William Camden, who encouraged him to realize his cartographic talents by mapping the British Isles. In addition to single maps and historical works, he also published in 1611 an atlas of Britain, which included 54 maps; and in 1627 he published an atlas of the world. The large wall map of the Land of Israel under discussion here was apparently Speed's first map; it is also the only known extant copy.

On the left, above an illustration of Jonah and the whale enclosed in a small cartouche embellished with a heraldic eagle, is a dedication to the above-mentioned Sir Robert. The source of the map, as stated by its creator in small letters under the title, is one by Benedictus Arias Montanus (1527–98), a Spanish scholar specializing in the history of the lands of the Bible and research of the Hebrew language. In 1572 Montanus published a multilingual edition of the Bible, including a map based on the Sanuto–Vesconte Map (see p. 74), but with an altered orientation. Speed enlarged the illustrated areas, so that his map also includes Mesopotamia, the Arabian Desert, the southeastern coast of Turkey, Cyprus, and almost all of the Nile Delta. In addition, he included the borders separating the tribal lands, drawn in a light dotted line, and marked the route of the Israelites' exodus from Egypt as a narrow path with miniature figures. Borrowing Montanus's covention, Speed sketched three single pillars to mark the borders of the Land of Israel.

Along the lower left and right margins is a long list of places appearing in the map, along with their coordinates. However, the uniqueness of Speed's work lies in its pictorial cartouches at top right and left. On the right, below two cherubs and the name "Elohim" (God in Hebrew), are the figures of Adam and Eve. They duplicate the pair as they appear in the well-known 1504 etching by Albrecht Dürer (1471–1528), with some modifications.

The quoting of Dürer's figures is especially interesting as an illustration of the development of iconography — symbols and formal motifs — in the history of art. Similar developments exist in cartography, in the layout of maps, and in their incorporation of artistic sources. Dürer himself had based the figure of Adam on the well-known Hellenistic statue Apollo Belvedere, and Eve on the type of statue known as "Venus Pudica." The iconography in Dürer's etching is characteristically rich: animals represent the four humors, and the branch in Adam's hand apparently stands for the Tree of Life.

Speed's addition of the title "Elohim" in Hebrew letters is not coincidental — it relates to Genesis 1, describing the creation of the world and man, even though the name of God (in the original Hebrew) is not specifically given there, as opposed to Genesis 2. Nevertheless, above the second cartouche, where Moses and Aaron are shown holding the tablets of the Ten Commandments, the Tetragrammaton (YHVH in Hebrew letters, that is, Yahweh or Jehovah) appears. It could be that Speed is

referring to Exodus 3:13—14, where God answers Moses' question: "... and they shall say to me What is his name? What shall I say unto them? And God said unto Moses, "I AM THAT I AM." Aaron is dressed in the fineries of the high priest, while Moses has the aspect of a vagabond. Around the figures are depictions of the altar, the table of the shewbread, the Menorah, and the Ark of the Covenant; there is even a miniature Tower of Babel.

The placing of Adam and Eve, Moses and Aaron, in two parallel cartouches was a recurring motif in maps of the Holy Land. The figures appear as heraldic symbols rather than as figures with narrative iconographical meaning.

A. T.

E. Laor and S. Klein, *Maps of the Holy Land: Cartobibliography of Printed Maps, 1475—1900* (New York and Amsterdam, 1986), pp. 102—3, no. 736.

K. Nebenzahl, *Maps of the Holy Land* (New York and Tel Aviv, 1986), pp. 106—7.

Thomas Fuller

Thomas Fuller, English,
1608–1661
Zabulon [sic]
Hand-colored engraving by
Robert Vaughan, 1650,
283x360 mm
From Thomas Fuller, *A Pisgah
Sight of Palestine*,
John Williams, London, 1650
The Israel Museum, Jerusalem
Gift of Norman and
Frieda Bier, London

Thomas Fuller was a scholarly English clergyman and the author of books on history and theology. The present map is part of his biblical study *A Pisgah Sight of Palestine*, containing a full map of the Holy Land and detailed double-page maps of the patrimonial lands of the Twelve Tribes. Beyond general interest in the history of the land of the Bible, the tribes of Israel exerted a special fascination and became a sub-genre in Christian theology ("And I appoint unto you a kingdom, as my Father hath appointed unto me; That ye may eat and drink at my table in my kingdom, and sit on thrones judging the twelve tribes of Israel" [Luke 22:29–30]).

Fuller relied mainly on the maps of Adrichom (1533–1585) (see p. 96), adding an abundance of illustrations and decorative features, which rendered his maps very picturesque. The production of the book with its many maps was made possible by an array of benefactors; their coats of arms accompanied by dedicatory inscriptions adorn the maps, along with the symbols of the tribes. Fuller's moderate and tolerant religious outlook was attacked by the Puritans, as is recounted in the text of the book.

The map represents the land allotted to the tribe of Zebulun: the lower Galilee (*Galilaea inferior*) between the Carmel and the Sea of Galilee (Josh. 19:10–16). At upper right is the tribal symbol: a ship with a mast. Included are numerous illustrations of events from the Old and New Testaments: on Mount Carmel, by the Kishon River,

Elijah killing the prophets of Baal (1 Kings, 18); on the shores of the Sea of Galilee the miracle of the loaves and the fishes, when Jesus fed 4,000 people and "seven baskets full" were left over (Matt. 15:32–38); and on Mount Tabor the Transfiguration, where Christ's "face did shine like the sun, and his raiment was white as the light," and Moses and Elias appeared before the three disciples (Matt. 17:1–3).

Fuller placed particular emphasis on geographical data such as mountains, rivers, and flora. He also devised special categorized symbols for settlements: crowns for the seats of kings, a double circle surrounding the four Levite cities (Josh. 21:34–35), etc.

A. T.

E. Laor and S. Klein, *Maps of the Holy Land: Cartobibliography of Printed Maps, 1475–1900* (New York and Amstedam,1986), p. 37, no. 285.

K. Nebenzahl, *Maps of the Holy Land* (New York and Tel Aviv, 1986), pp. 128–31.

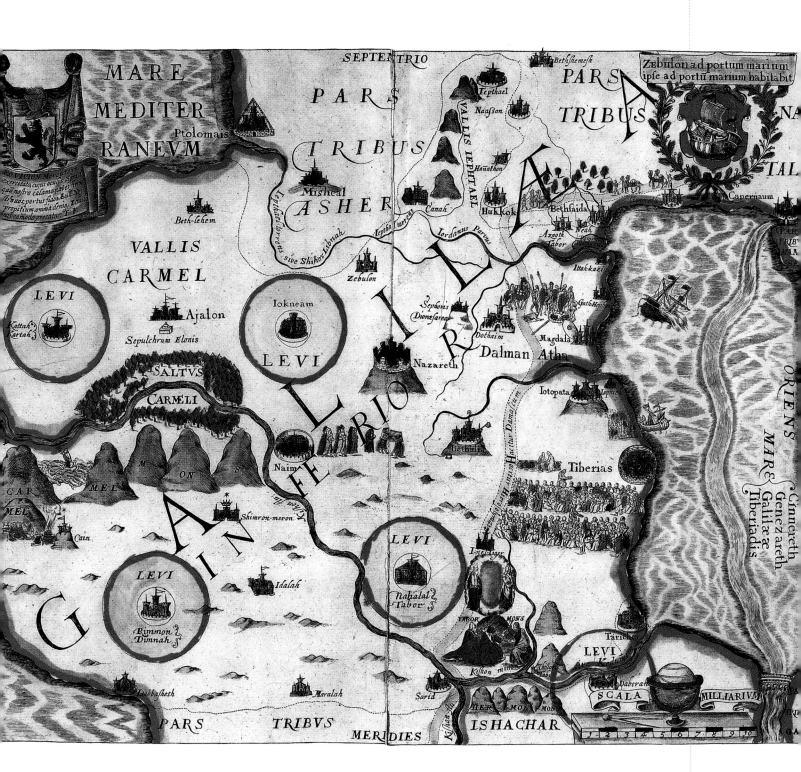

MARE
MEDITER
RANEUM
Ptolomais

SEPTENTRIO

PARS
TRIBUS
ASHER

PARS
TRIBUS

Zebulon ad portum marium
ipse ad portū marium habitabit

Bethshemesh

Iepthael

Naaßon

VALLIS IEPHTAEL

Hanathon

Misheal

Canah

Hukkok

Bethsaida

Capernaum

VALLIS
CARMEL

Beth-lehem

Iepthael torrens
sive Shihorlibnah

Iepthac torrens

Iordanus Parvus

Aznoth
Tabor

Neah

LEVI
Kattah
Kartah

Ajalon

Ioknean

Zebulon

Iottah-kazin

Gath-Hepher

Sepulchrum Elonis

LEVI

Sephons
Dionæsarea

Dothaim

SALTVS
CARMELI

Nazareth

Magdala
Dalman Atha

ORIENS

MARE

Cinnereth
Genezareth
Galilæa
Tiberiadis

MONS
MEL

CAP
MEL
Cain

Shimron-meron

Kishon flu.

Naim

Iotopata

Iaphie

Bethulia

Hattin Damalium

Tiberias

LEVI

Idalah

LEVI
Nahalal
Tabor

Ingela

TABOR MONS

Tariche

LEVI
Kedes

Dabbasheth

Maralah

Sarid

Kishon minor

Chislot
Tabor

Kishon flu.

Rimmon
Dimnah

Kison flu.

HERMON
MONS

Daberah

SCALA

MILLIARIVM

PARS
TRIBVS
MERIDIES

ISHACHAR

Willem Janszoon Blaeu

Willem Janszoon Blaeu, Dutch,
1571–1638
After Jodocus Hondius Jr.,
Dutch, after Laicstain–Schrott,
*Terra Sancta quae in Sacris
Terra Promissionis
olim Palestina*
(The Holy Land, known in the
Scriptures as the Promised Land,
formerly Palestine)
Hand-colored engraving, 1629,
386x503 mm
From *Le théâtre du monde ou
nouvel atlas*, Amsterdam, 1640
The Israel Museum, Jerusalem
Gift of Karl and
Li Handler, Vienna

Willem Janszoon Blaeu was a pupil of the astronomer Tycho Brahe (1546–1601). Around 1640 he founded in Amsterdam a cartographic institute where he engraved and published, with his sons Johann and Cornelius, terrestrial and celestial globes, maps, and atlases.

This map, oriented to the west (as Moses saw the land from Mount Nebo), represents the Holy Land on both sides of the Jordan, the coastline extending from Tripoli to the Nile Delta. It includes a depiction of the Red Sea crossing and the drowning of Pharaoh and his armies, while broken lines indicate the wanderings of the Israelites in the desert. The outlines of the Jordan Valley and of the Dead Sea are not true to fact, the latter making a 90° angle to the east at its southern edge. Accurate mapping of the Dead Sea occurred relatively late, as evidenced by its widely varying depictions in ancient maps. Another common error is to have the Kishon River connecting the Sea of Galilee to the Mediterranean Sea, as is the case here. At bottom right, on either side of the cartouche, Moses and Aaron stand proudly. The cartouche is decorated in Italian Renaissance style, with a *trompe l'oeil* stone plate decorated with fruits and flowers and topped by a globe. The sea section features the story of Jonah and "the great fish" (interpreted as a whale), as well as fanciful aquatic monsters and the compass rose.

The history of this map is especially complicated. Originating as an inset in the Laicstain–Schrott map (see p. 88), it was adopted by Jodocus Hondius, Jr. in 1629 as a new addition to the Mercator–Hondius Atlas. But when Hondius died in that year (aged 34) before having a chance to print it, Blaeu seized the opportunity to buy 37 copper plates of his maps. Blaeu's only addition to the present map was to insert his name in place of Hondius's, without even changing the date at bottom right of the cartouche.

This was one of 45 maps published as a new atlas in 1629. Over the next 34 years the atlas was expanded and issued in many editions, forming a series of 12 volumes with over 600 maps, which thus became the most important geographical publication of the 17th century.

A. T.

E. Laor and S. Klein, *Maps of the Holy Land: Cartobibliography of Printed Maps, 1475–1900* (New York and Amsterdam, 1986), p. 15, no. 106.

K. Nebenzahl, *Maps of the Holy Land* (New York and Tel Aviv, 1986), pp. 116–17.

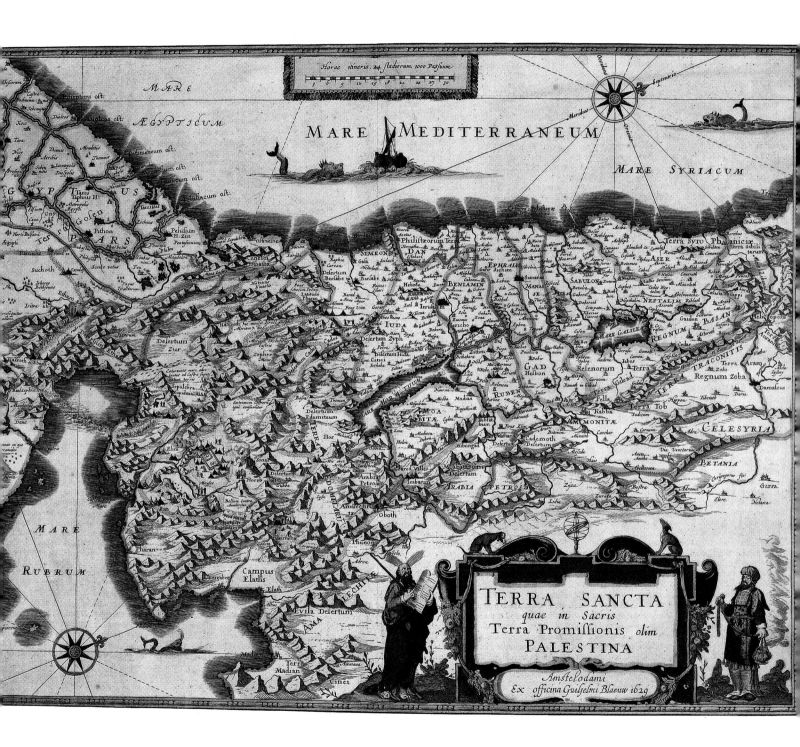

Samuel Heinrich Kiepert and Edward Robinson

Edward Robinson, American,
794–1863
*Map of Palestine, Chiefly from
the Itineraries and
Measurements of E. Robinson
and E. Smith*
Constructed and drawn
by H. Kiepert
Lithograph, 1840,
487x453 mm (sheet);
427X386 mm (image)
The Jewish National and
University Library, Jerusalem
The Eran Laor
Cartographic Collection

Samuel Heinrich Kiepert was one of the foremost German cartographers of the 19th century. In the six decades of his activity he produced over 600 maps, atlases, and globes. Born in Berlin, he studied classical philology but soon found his way to the lectures of Carl Ritter, who together with Alexander von Humboldt is considered the father of modern geography. Ritter, the leading geographer at the University of Berlin, imparted to Kiepert his geographic-historical approach and fostered his interest in cartography.

Kiepert's first maps were published in 1839. He embarked on his research of Palestine one year later, when he began working with the American cleric-scientist Edward Robinson on the preparation of the map attached to the latter's pioneer work, *Biblical Researches in Palestine, Mount Sinai and Arabia Petraea* in 1838 (published 1841). In that same year, 1840, Kiepert's *Map of Palestine, Mainly According to the Descriptions and Surveys of Robinson and Smith* appeared in English and German. The map, on a scale of 1:400,000 and was edited and published by Ritter. Robinson's book was published simultaneously in London, Boston, and Berlin, along with an atlas of five sheets of maps of Jerusalem, Palestine, and Sinai, with an explanatory "memoir" by Kiepert. The direct cooperation between Kiepert and Robinson was renewed in 1852, at the end of the latter's journey to Palestine. It was reflected in *Later Biblical Researches*, which was accompanied by a new map of "Palestine and Phoenicia." Furthermore, an atlas was again attached, this time comprising four maps.

From the beginning of his work with Robinson Kiepert understood the main difficulty dogging all research and writing on the Holy Land: that map preparation was necessarily based on incidental impressions, narrow historical sources, subjective descriptions by travelers and pilgrims, and haphazard and dispersed surveys of doubtful reliability. To overcome this problem he adopted a strict critical approach, consulting as many sources as possible and examining and analyzing them in great detail. He studied continuously, refining his knowledge of historical and current sources and keeping up with every new geographic study.

In 1852, after Kiepert had been head of the Geographic Institute of Weimar for seven years, Ritter initiated his return to Berlin. Ritter's work on his *Comparative Geography* was at its height and, publishing a volume each year, he urgently needed a familiar and reliable cartographer. Kiepert now came to full bloom. It is hard to imagine how one man could have published so many maps, of so many different parts of the world, and yet managed to maintain such a high standard of accuracy. Ritter died in 1859, and Kiepert, the only professor at Berlin University working in this area, replaced him. To fill at least a part of the void left by Ritter, he extended the scope of his interest and lectures to include general and historical geography, the history of geography, and the discoveries and topography of ancient times in the countries of his specialization.

Kiepert's involvement in the mapping of Palestine increased in the course of the 1840s and 50s. He consolidated his leading position by authoring historical and current maps of the area. His maps accompanied the publications of many scholars researching the Holy Land, Syria, Sinai, and Transjordan. Conscious of the importance of maps in the teaching of geography, Kiepert also prepared wall maps of Palestine.

In the spring of 1870 he set off to explore the East in person, directing his attention primarily toward Palestine and Asia Minor, the two areas that were the focus of his scientific work. On his first and only visit to Palestine he made sure to tour mainly the less-frequented areas on both sides of the Jordan Rift. The wealth of material he gathered served him in preparing new editions of his various maps — both historical and current — and in 1891 he published *A Pocket Map of Palestine*, on a scale of 1:800,000.

In Kiepert's 1840 map, the itinerary of the scholars is marked in red. The only historical element emphasized is the borders separating the patrimonial lands of the Twelve Tribes, one of the topics of Robinson's biblical-geographic research. To this end, Kiepert took great pains in finely hachuring and shading the map. Other geographic elements depicted are settlements and ruins, streams and roads. In a note accompanying the map Kiepert emphasized the difficulty in establishing the correct Latin spelling of Arabic names.

H. G.

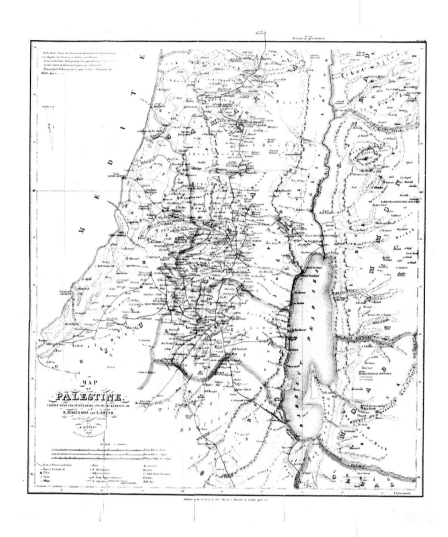

H. Kiepert, "Memoir on the Maps Accompanying This Work," in E. Robinson and E. *Smith, Biblical Researches in Palestine, Mount Sinai and Arabia Petraea*, vol. 3 (London, 1841), first Appendix, pp. 29—55.

H. Goren, "Carl Ritter's Contribution to Holy Land Research," in *Text and Image: Social Construction of Regional Images (Beiträge zur Regionalen Geographie)*, ed. A. Buttimer, S. D. Brunn, and U. Wardenga (Leipzig, 1998), pp. 28—37.

H. Goren, "Heinrich Kiepert in the Holy Land, Spring 1970: Sketches from an Exploration-Tour of an Historical Cartographer," in *Antike Welten Neue Regionen: Heinrich Kiepert 1818—1899*, ed. L. Zögner (Berlin, 1999), pp. 45—61.

Two Hundred Years of Topographic Mapping, 1799–2000

Dov Gavish

"A good topographical map should be looked upon as a national monument," stated Colonel F. J. Salmon, director of the Palestine Survey Department, 1933–1938.[1] Indeed, it should be a cartographic image of the land surface, showing the relief, the land cover, and the distribution pattern of all details of the landscape in a way that emphasizes the uniqueness of the scenery. The method of depiction, the technical format, the information, and the level of specification aspired to in a topographic map — all depend on two factors: the complexity of the landscape and the scale of the map.

A topographic map describes the land surface in symbolic outlines and conventional signs. In the past, it was based on surveys and mathematical calculations; with the development of mapping by means of aerial photography, the main work of mapping was transferred from the field to the office.

The topographic mapping of Palestine-Israel reflects four periods of development:

a. Maps of the 19th century
b. Maps of World War I, 1914–1918
c. British Mandatory maps, 1920–1948
d. Maps of the State of Israel

Maps of the 19th Century

"Napoleon's Map," 1:100,000, 1799[2]

Topographic mapping methods began evolving in Europe in the 17th century, and Napoleon's expedition to Egypt in 1798–99 brought these to the shores of Palestine.

In July 1798 Napoleon conquered Egypt with a view to cutting off England's transportation routes to India. He greatly valued Egypt's cultural heritage, and as a military man with a feeling for science and culture appreciated the geographical importance of a map. He thus added to his expedition scientists who were to carry out a comprehensive survey of the ancient cultural assets of Egypt, among them surveyors proficient in topographic mapping.

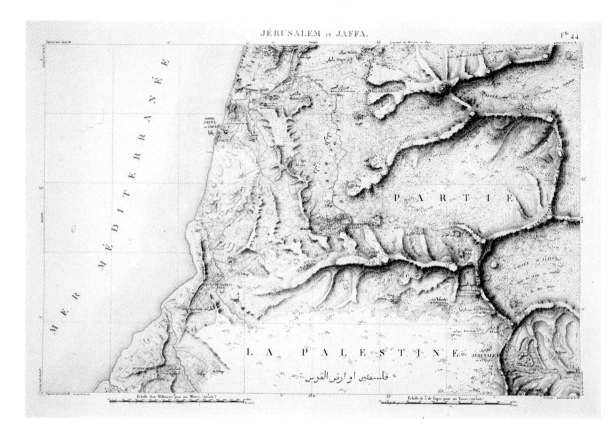

Pierre Jacotin,
Jerusalem and
Jaffa, sheet from
"Napoleon's Map,"
1:100,000,
1799, etching
The Israel Museum,
Jerusalem
Gift of the French
Ambassador,
Alain Pierret

Apprised of an Ottoman force being sent from Syria to Egypt, Napoleon set out in January 1799 to defeat it in Palestine. In February he conquered Gaza; in March Ramla, Jaffa, and Haifa, stopping at the walls of Acre. His reconnaissance troops reached Quneitra on the Golan Heights and Tyre in the north, and the battery of topographic surveyors followed them.

The French military march in Palestine lasted three months, under trying conditions. Its minor successes were offset by recurrent losses, illness in the ranks, and a final failure to storm the walls of Acre. Despite these setbacks the surveyors, until their retreat to Egypt at the end of May 1799, did their best in gathering the

data needed to prepare a topographic map of part of Palestine. The character of the map was determined by the pace and course of the army's advance, and the result was therefore incomplete, being based on non-surveyed and unchecked information, or data copied from other maps during subsequent cartographic editing in Paris. Nevertheless, this was the first topographic map of Palestine.

Napoleon's maps of Egypt and Palestine were edited by Colonel Pierre Jacotin, a cartographer who was appointed chief of the Geographic Engineers' Unit in June 1799, following the retreat. Upon his return to France, Jacotin arranged the maps in 47

Map of the French
General Staff
*(detail), 1:100,000,
1870, Bibliothèque
nationale de France,
Paris*

sheets, six of which were devoted to Palestine. The scale of these maps is 1:100,000. The description of the relief is by means of hachuring, providing no information about exact topographic heights but endowing the map with a topographic appearance that emphasizes the drainage features and the watershed lines. They indicate the settlements and roads in the country, and make profuse use of conventional signs in describing the land surface.

Map of the French General Staff, 1:100,000, 1870[3]

With the occupation of Syria and Lebanon by France in 1860, a French scientific surveying expedition set out to study and map the cultural past of Phoenicia. Ten years later, in 1870, the French General Staff sent surveyors to map Palestine as well, as an extension of the earlier mapping of Syria and Lebanon. The expedition, headed by the officers Mieulet and Derrien, began its work in May of that year in the north, around Acre. A baseline was measured near that city, as were numerous triangulation points and spot heights, enabling the surveyors to draw a map with form lines similar in their significance to contour lines, which gave the map an updated look. Care was taken in marking roads, settlements, streams, and landscape details, with special attention paid to place names and their historical sources. The map encompasses the northern Galilee from the sea in the west to a line in the east connecting Safed with Mount Tabor, Nazareth, and Tiberias — an area of some 2,000 km^2.

The French surveyors were not able to complete their task, being ordered back to France after three months, when France became entangled in war with Prussia in July 1870. The map was published in its incomplete form on a scale of 1:100,000 about three years after the field work.

Map of the British Palestine Exploration Fund, 1:63,360, 1872—1878[4]

The Palestine Exploration Fund (PEF) was established in England in 1865, following the surveys and maps of Captain Charles Wilson, who mapped Jerusalem as early as 1864–65. The fund's emissaries in Jerusalem, mainly Charles Warren, undertook archaeological explorations, surveyed and mapped sites, and came to the conclusion that the explorers needed a comprehensive map of the entire country that would serve as a common basis for all the individual surveys carried out there. In light of this recommendation it was decided to send an expedition to survey the country and map it systematically.

The expedition set out for Palestine in 1871 and began its work on the basis of measured baselines and a network of triangulation points. Directed mainly by Lieutenant C. R. Conder, who commanded the survey in 1872–76, and Lieutenant H. H. Kitchener, who joined it in 1874, the survey was completed in September 1877, and in 1880 a map was published along with three volumes describing the sites and landscapes of the country. This map, printed in 26 sheets, on a scale of an inch to one mile (decimally 1:63,360), was referred to as a "great map" — a title given at that time to large-scale maps covering a broad area. It stretched from a line connecting Tyre and the Banyas springs in the north to a line in the south connecting Rafiah, Beersheba and the southern Dead Sea. To safeguard the PEF's rights and for fear that others would copy the map and publish it in a more compact format, it was printed on a smaller scale.

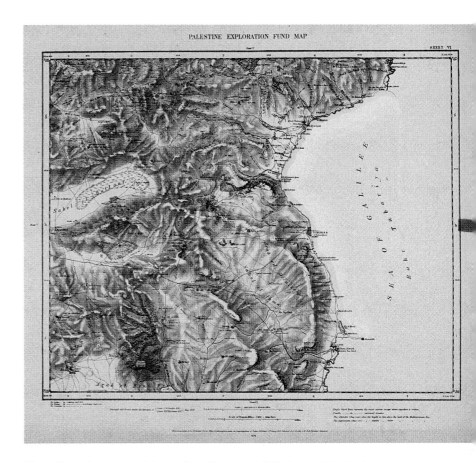

The editors focused mainly on describing the biblical heritage and cultural values of the country, on sites and roads, and on the influence of man on the natural landscape. The relief was depicted by shading, and surveyed measured spot heights.

From a local point of view, this was the first topographic map to cover the country "from Dan to Beersheba"; from an imperial point of view, when World War I broke out, the British had a ready-made map. Although it had to be updated and adjusted to military requirements, it gave them a valuable cartographic advantage.

C. R. Conder and H. H. Kitchener, Tiberias and Surroundings, Palestine Exploration Fund, photo-zincograph, 1878, 690x585 mm

World War I Maps, 1914—1918

World War I saw the confrontation of the British and the Ottoman armies, the latter supported by the Germans. Each of these forces set itself up cartographically to the best of its means.

British Military Map, 1:40,000, 1917—1918[5]

In October 1915, after the British defeat at Gallipoli, which was partly blamed on the lack of proper maps, a topographic unit was set up at the headquarters of the British Expeditionary Force in Egypt. Despite the availability of the Newcombe maps for the southern part of the country and the PEF's maps for the north, the quality of the resulting maps, their scale and actuality, did not satisfy the operational needs of the army command. The unit made great efforts to change the concept and methods of cartography in order to bring existing maps up to date and map the future battleground — the area then in the hands of the enemy — by means of aerial photography, in time. After the failure of the second Turkish attack on the Suez Canal on March 14, 1917, the unit — while stationed at al-Arish — was recognized as an independent survey company within the British contingent and given the title Field Surveyors Company 7.

The mapping company made every effort to bring up to date the PEF maps, drawn 50 years earlier. Not detailed enough for battle purposes — such as the laying and locating of artillery — these maps served for general orientation and as a basis for planning the fieldwork of the surveyors, who were preparing tactical maps on a larger scale. Responding to the operational demands of headquarters, the mapping unit produced many sets of maps, among them topographic maps on a scale of 1:10,000 and 1:20,000, and maps of cities and their trenches. But the most important standard topographic series was on a scale of 1:40,000; by the end of the war it numbered 26 sheets and covered the center of the country.

German Military Map, 1:50,000, 1918

Ever since their first march on the Suez Canal in 1915, lacking their own mapping unit, the Germans had remained inferior in the cartography of the area under discussion. The Prussian Surveyors Company No. 27 only arrived in the country on 12 October 1917 and started work shortly before the fall of Beersheba at the end of August of the following year. The Germans, like the British, needed orientation maps as well as tactical maps, and for both types they used the PEF maps, brought up to date by field surveying and aerial photography. In addition, they decided on the preparation of a set of topographic maps for conducting the war, on a scale of 1:50,000, and by the end of the war had produced a series of 39 sheets, as well as seven sheets on a scale of 1:25,000 and one sheet of 1:100,000.

Ottoman Military Map, 1:200,000, 1918[6]

The General Staff of the Ottoman army set up in 1909 a Surveying and Mapping Department, under French professional guidance, and in 1910 began to map the empire. In 1917 the mapping unit worked on 12 sheets, five of them being of Palestine — Gaza, Jerusalem, Haifa, Jaffa and Nablus — on a scale of 1:200,000. In the spring of that year, the foundation of a network of triangulation points was measured and the topography surveyed, and during the autumn and winter the data were processed and the field sheets prepared for mapping. Work on the sheets of Jerusalem and Gaza was begun during the war, the work being completed with the Nablus sheet in 1918, on the eve of the retreat before the British.

The Turkish maps excel in describing the relief of the land surface, notably by drawing form lines similar to contour lines. The place names appear in Turkish in Arabic characters. A second version of these maps was published by the German mapping unit that served in Palestine during World War I.

The military cartographic efforts of the British and Germans during World War I were terminated on 19 September 1918, the day of the final attack by General Allenby, which completed the British conquest of the country, ending Ottoman rule.

Maps of the British Mandatory Period, 1920—1948[7]

The First Versions, on Scales of 1:20,000, 1:50,000, 1:100,000

The Survey Department of Palestine began its work in 1920, originally established for the purpose of surveying the country in order to create a framework for legal land settlement. The assumption was that the bone of contention among the residents of the country would be the issue of land ownership — a civilian matter that cannot be tackled without surveying and mapping.

A new geodetic control network was surveyed and established in the country and has since served as a basis for all surveys. The survey for the land settlement was made on a large scale — 1:2,000 or 1:2,500 — and this fact slowed its progress. To improve planning control, the maps were joined together and reduced in size, forming a key map on a scale of 1:20,000. The maps on this scale later made up the first topographic set of Mandatory Palestine.

The approach to topographic cartography changed in 1933 with the appointment of Colonel F. J. Salmon as director of the Survey Department, whose conception was that a topographic map in general must serve as a "national monument" of the scenery and, in Palestine in particular, must "distinguish the desert from the sown." He immediately stopped the production of the 1:20,000 map. Although intent on mapping the country on a scale of 1:50,000, Colonel Salmon feared that the large number of sheets and long production time this might entail would cause the whole mapping project to fail. He therefore ordered a standard topographic mapping of the country on a scale of 1:100,000.

The timing of the production of the 1:100,000 map is very important for understanding the connection between topographic and military maps. The first sheets of the map were published on the eve of the Arab uprising in 1936, when the army still had no detailed maps. The first set comprised 12 sheets not including the Negev, and the next 16 sheets. The army of course demanded maps that would provide a first-rate means of orientation and control. But the hurried production of the topographic maps was hardly a satisfactory solution, as a scale of 1:100,000 was too small for operational use. Hence the existing maps were enlarged to the scale of 1:50,000. However, to the disappointment of the director of the Survey Department, once the army started using the topographic maps for its own purposes, it also started to dictate its demands. The main demand was to simplify the legend of the maps by forgoing some of the colors in the printing, and to drop some of the conventional signs that made the maps difficult to read. The topographic map of Palestine was converted to a military map during World War II, with Military Survey Directorate intervention in the work of the Survey Department.

Maps of the State of Israel[8]

With the establishment of the State of Israel, the Mandatory Survey Department became the Israel Survey Department, and immediately set itself up to complete the Mandatory 16-sheet topographic series on a scale of 1:100,000 so that it would cover the entire country, to the Gulf of Aqaba in 24 sheets.

The maps in the enlarged Israeli set were temporarily updated by overlaying a print of violet color. The names of new settlements were inserted in Hebrew on the original maps, and the expanding road system was marked. Sixteen of the updated bilingual sheets were published in 1953, excluding topographic maps of the Negev, which remained privileged.

Concurrently, the preparation began of an updated topographic series using aerial photography; it was published in Hebrew in September 1960, in a format of 26 sheets. In 1975 a double topographic sheet of the center of the country — sheets 7–8 (keeping the original numeration) — was first published. Later, the series was complemented by additional sheets, for the convenience of the public.

With time, the need for a more detailed map increased. By 1957 a remapping was undertaken on a scale of 1:50,000, and this series was completed in the 1970s, with 88 sheets covering the whole country. However, the method of making the 1:50,000 map flawed its quality. The map was based on a combination of old and new maps created by different methods and only partially updated by means of aerial photographs, using a graphic method primarily based on handwork. It was therefore decided that instead of grappling with the defects of the old cartography, the country would be mapped anew. The transition from graphic production methods to mapmaking based on digital information opened new vistas for the use of the map series. With the establishment of the Geographic Information System at the Survey of Israel, it was decided that a map of 1:50,000 would serve in the creation of the computerized database as a basic library, and a new standard issue of 1:25,000 would take its place. That series is now beginning to be produced.

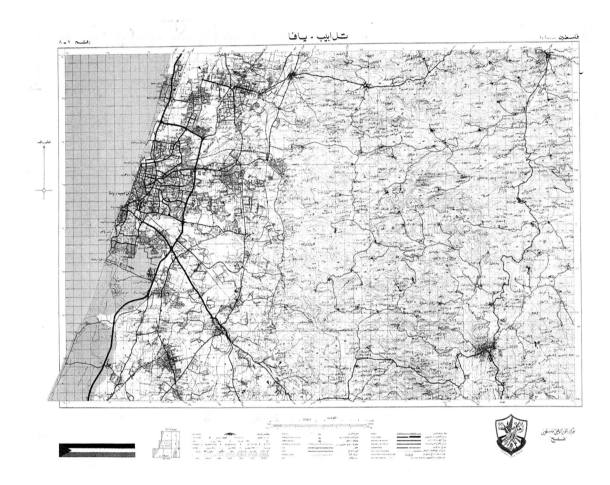

تل ابيب ـ يافا

PLO Map of Tel Aviv-Jaffa,
1:100,000, ca. 1980,
692x533 mm

The topographic map of Palestine on a scale of 1:100,000 (the whole set) was repeatedly copied by foreign armies[9] The Germans in World War II, the Egyptians in the Israeli War of Independence and again in 1955, the British in 1955 and 1957, and the PLO Map of Tel Aviv-Jaffa, ca. 1980 — all copied this set of maps for operational and intelligence use — without even attempting to mask the original form or hide the map's origins.

1. F. J. Salmon, "Topographic Maps," *Transactions of the Engineering Association of Ceylon* (1929?), pp. 1–9.

2. *Carte topographique de l'Egypte et de plusieurs parties des pays limitrophes levée pendant l'expédition de l'armée française* (Paris, 1810).

3. D. Gavish, "French Cartography of the Holy Land in the Nineteenth Century," *Palestine Exploration Fund Quarterly* 126 (1994), pp. 24–31.

4. C. R. Conder and H. H. Kitchener, *The Survey of Western Palestine: Memoirs of the Topography, Orography, Hydrography and Archaeology* (London, 1881–83).

5. H. H. Thomas, "Geographical Reconnaissance by Aeroplane Photography, with Special Reference to the Work Done on the Palestine Front," *Geographical Journal* 55 (May 1920), pp. 349–76.

6. E. Özkale and M. R. Senler, *Haritact Mehmet Sevki Pasa ve Türk Haritcılık Tarihi*, 1919 [an abridgment of *A Summary of Ten Years of Efforts Regarding Turkish Cartography*, by Mehmet Sevki Pasa] (Ankara, 1980), part 2 (in Turkish).

7. D. Gavish, *Land and Maps: The Survey of Palestine, 1920–1948* (Jerusalem, 1991) (in Hebrew).

8. R. Adler and D. Gavish, *50 Years of Mapping Israel, 1948–1999* (Tel Aviv, 1999) (in Hebrew).

9. D. Gavish, "Foreign Intelligence Maps: Offshoots of the 1:100,000 Topographic Map of Israel," *Imago Mundi* 48 (1996), pp. 174–84.

Maps after Commentaries by and on Rashi

Rabbi Mordecai ben Abraham
Yaffe, Polish, 1530–ca. 1612
The Delineation of the Borders
From *Levush Ha-Orah*,
Elucidation of Rashi's Biblical
Commentary, 1st ed. Prague,
1603, 2nd ed. 1860
315x200 mm (page),
184x144 mm (image)
The Israel Museum, Jerusalem

Rabbi Solomon ben Isaac, known by the acronym Rashi (1040–1105), is considered the leading Talmud commentator of all time, as well as an important Bible exegete. He lived and worked in Troyes in northern France, but studied in the most renowned yeshivas in Germany: first with Rabbi Jacob b. Rabbi Yakar in Mainz, then with Rabbi Isaac b. Rabbi Judah in the same city, and later with Rabbi Isaac b. Rabbi Eleazar Halevi in Worms. He founded a yeshiva that was soon to become the most important Torah center in Western Europe. His daughters married scholars of this center, and among his grandsons, who followed in his footsteps, were Jacob (Rabbenu Tam) and the Rashbam (Rabbi Samuel b. Meir), considered the leading scholars of their day. Rashi was known for his special combination of modesty and strength of character.

The sketches or diagrams appended to Rashi's commentaries, the earliest of which date back to his lifetime, were drawn to elucidate and illustrate various geographical issues. According to his grandson, the Rashbam, Rashi himself would make "boundary drawings." Two of the earliest sketches in a manuscript dated 1233 are preserved in the municipal library of Munich. Accompanying Rashi's commentary on Numbers 33–34, they delineate "the land of Canaan." In his commentary on the Babylonian Talmud he presents several diagrams of the land to clarify different *baraithas* ("external" Mishnah) pertaining to the geography of the Land of Israel. These are actually topological diagrams seeking to define graphically the location of settlements, sites, and major geographical reference points. This kind of diagram accompanies both manuscripts and printed books in various editions up to the second half of the 19th century. The basic scheme — also appearing in the elucidation of Rashi's biblical commentary by Elijah Mizrahi, a rabbi of the Ottoman Empire, in 1523, and by Rabbi Abraham Yaffe of Poland in 1603 — is explicitly founded on God's words to Moses in Numbers 34:2: "When ye come into the land of Canaan (this is the land that shall fall unto you for an inheritance, even the land of Canaan, with the coasts thereof) . . ." as well as in Deuteronomy 1–3.

The map seen here was made by Rabbi Mordecai Yaffe of Prague, who studied in Poland and was renowned for his knowledge of the Talmud and the Kabbalah, and was also well versed in astronomy and philosophy. He later headed yeshivas in Prague, in Grodno (Lithuania), and in Lublin.

The map is oriented to the east and, in addition to the boundaries, it delineates the route of the Exodus and some of the camps of the Children of Israel (Num. 20–21; Deut. 2–3). The country is described as an expanse of dry land. On its right side (to the south) the Red Sea is depicted as a strip of water; at the top (to the east) are the land of Sihon and Og, the Jordan, the Sea of Galilee, and the Dead Sea;

והא לך הציור תחומי ארץ ישראל על פי פירוש רש"י כאשר קבלתי והוא אמתי ונכון לפי כל דברי רש"י
ז"ל כאשר אבאר בע"ה וכאשר זכינו לצייר אותו כן נזכה לראותו בנוי ומיושב עין בעין בשוב ה' גדחי
ישראל ובא לציון גואל ויבנה אריאל אמן כן יאמר י"י האל:

ונכתב לכם הגדול מנגב למעלה עקרבים פרש"י כל מקום
של' ונסב או וינא מלמד שלא היה הגבר שוה אלא הולך
ויונא לחוק יונא המצר ועוקם לצד לפינו של עולם נאלכסין
למערב ועומד המצר בדרומה של מעלה עקרבים כו' מחוך
זפי' הזה חוכם הליור שציירתי לך שהרי אמר רש"י עוקם
לצד לפונו של עולם ולא אמר לצד לפון כחם אלא כונתו
לומר שהגבול של א"י נכנם חוך הלפון של רוחב כל העול'
שהוא נגד דרום של א"י שאותו הגד הסחוך לא"י הוא נד
לפינו של אותו חלק מן העולם ומחעקם המצר של א"י
וינא לחוק אותו אוחו הנגדול ולכך כיים רם"י דנדריו ואמר
נחלא מצלה עקרבים לפנים מן המצר כלומר שחלד דרום
של הרן ישראל יונא המצר ועוקם חוך לפונו של עולם
שנגד דרום של א"י כמלא מעלה עקרבים לפנים מן מיצר
א"י אבנלאם היה מיצר א"י שיה היה מעלה עקרבים מון
למיצר א"י ולפי ליור הנדפם בדפום המזרחי מחי ר"ל
רש"י נחלא מעלה עקרבים לפנים מן המצר דחשמע ע"י
העקחימות נחמלה בפנים דהא כ"ש הוא אם היה שוה שהיה
מעלה עקרבים בפנים וכן ת"ם רש"י נסחוך גני וינא חלר
הנד מחכפסט החילר ומרחיב לנד לפון כו' ר"כ לנד לפונו
של עולם אע' נסאמר לנפון סחם החך רש"י על מה שהסכאב
למעלה לפונו של עולם ולא הונדרך כאן לפרם ומה שאחר
נסתון וחסם והלאה וחחקןר המצר ונכתב לנד הגדרו' פירוסו
נ"כ לנד המיצר שנדרוס א"י וכן נגד לפון חה שציירחי לך
עוקם יונא מלנדרב זמלונה כו' שכן כתוב בפירום נקרא
וריא חולאות הגבול נגדר כלומר עד סם הולך שוה ואח"כ
וילא הגבול זפרונה כו'

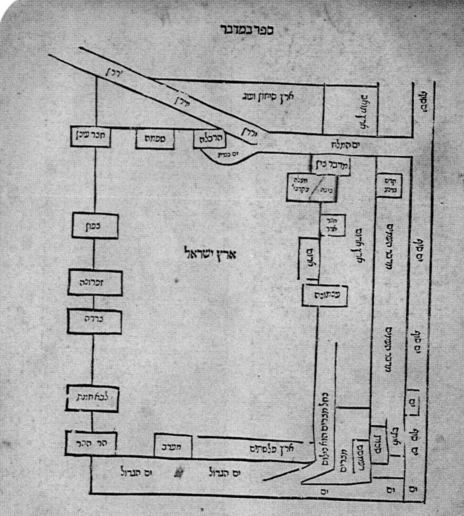

*Rabbi Elijah ben
Abraham Mizrachi,
Constantinople,
ca. 1450–1526*
The Land of Israel
*Woodcut (originally,
1523), copy, 18th
century (?)*
The Wajntraub Family
Collection, Jerusalem

and on the left is the northern border, according to the book of Numbers (34:7—9): "And this shall be your north border: from the great sea ye shall point out for you mount Hor: From mount Hor ye shall point out your border unto the entrance of Hamath; and the goings forth of the border shall be to Zedad. And the border shall go on to Ziphron, and the goings out of it shall be at Hazar-enan: this shall be your north border."

Below (to the west) is the Great Sea (the Mediterranean) scattered with ships and three "nissin" (islands). This Greek word is found in the Babylonian Talmud (Gittin 8:1): "The nissin in the sea seem as if a line extends from them from Turei Amnon to the stream of Egypt; inside the line is the Land of Israel, outside it — foreign lands." In the southwestern corner are "the Land of the Philistines," "the Land of Egypt," and "the River of Egypt" (the Nile). Inland of the Red Sea is "the wilderness of the people" (the Sinai Desert), according to Ezekiel 20:35: "And I will bring you into the wilderness of the people, and there will I plead with you face to face." Marking the southern land border are the desert of Tzin, Moab, Edom, Atzmon, Hazar-Addar, Tzin, and Maaleh Akrabbim.

Of interest from a geographical point of view is the erroneous delineation of the course of the Jordan as flowing across the Dead Sea before emptying into the Red Sea.

This map, in following "the Rashi Map," seems to ignore completely the cartographic achievements of the beginning of the 17th century. However, it is interesting to note that settlements, such as Levo-Hamat, are marked in a way similar to that of contemporary European (Christian) maps — by a European-style turreted structure. The camps on the itinerary, on the other hand, are depicted as a cluster of tents with pennants flying from the poles. The ships at sea are also similar to those in European maps, while the depiction of Mount Sinai, and especially of Mount Seir, is reminiscent of the stylized representation of mountains in Byzantine art. (A typical example of the latter may be seen in the Dionysius Map, the iconography of which apparently draws on medieval icons.)

The caption of the map also brings to mind the formula used in Christian maps, notably in its claim or aspiration to be a "true" representation that corrects former errors: "Here is a delineation of the boundaries of the Land of Israel according to the commentary of Rashi, as I received it and as is true and correct according to Rashi's words . . ." The caption ends with a sentence expressing the longing for Zion throughout the centuries of exile: "And as we were worthy of sketching it so will we be worthy, with our own eyes, of seeing it built up and settled, when the exiled [Children] of Israel shall return and the Redeemer will come to Israel and build up Ariel, Amen."

A. T.

Z. Vilnay, *The Hebrew Maps of the Holy Land: A Research in Hebrew Cartography* (Jerusalem, 1968), p. 7 (in Hebrew).

B. Narkiss, "Rashi and His Maps," in *Jubilee Book for Zev Vilnay*, vol. 2 (Jerusalem, 1984), pp. 435—39 (in Hebrew).

E. and G. Wajntraub, *Hebrew Maps of the Holy Land* (Vienna, 1992), pp. 39—41, W. 16, and *passim*.

Anonymous, Italian (?)

Anonymous, Italian (?),
16th century
"These are the journeys of the
children of Israel, which went
forth out of the land of Egypt"
(Num. 33:1)
Woodcut, Mantua, ca. 1560,
377x509 mm
Zentralbibliothek Zürich

Discovered and republished in 1991 by Hans Jakob Haag in Zurich, this is today considered to be the first printed Hebrew map of Palestine and Sinai. Drawn from a bird's-eye view, it is a unique and fascinating pictorial adaptation of the story of the Exodus and a description of the boundaries, according both to Rashi's interpretation and to a visual commentary on midrashic literature.

The map is oriented toward the east, with only about a third of it taken up by Palestine on both sides of the Jordan. The rest comprises the Sinai, the northern part of Egypt, the Red Sea, and, in the right-hand margin, a text and a large depiction of a Menorah — the seven-branched candelabra, as described in Exodus 25:31–2.

The lower right-hand corner depicts a dramatic depiction of the pursuit by Pharaoh and his troops, including chariots and horsemen, of the unarmed children of Israel headed by Moses and Aaron (Ex. 14). Moses raises his staff over the sea and the waters are divided, between Migdol and Pi-hahiroth. The pillar of smoke protects the Children of Israel from the arrows and spears.

Some of the central scenes in Sinai — "the wilderness of the people" (Ezek. 20:35) — are depicted in the upper left-hand corner, among them the revelation on Mount Sinai, the mourning for Aaron at Mount Hor, and the miracle of the brass serpent. Mount Seir, symbolizing the Edomite children of Esau around whom the Israelites were forced to make a detour, is depicted at the top; also shown there is an incident known only from rabbinical literature: the saving of the Israelites from the Emorites in Wadi Zered.

The land is depicted in relief, with the coastline raised above water level, the waves of the sea and the mountaintops, especially Mount Seir, being highly stylized. The country is strangely compressed, its boundaries drawn according to Numbers 34: the southern border passes through "the ascent of Akrabbim," Kadesh-barnea, Hazar-addar, and Atzmon, "unto the river of Egypt," with "the Great Sea" (Mediterranean) as the western border, appearing with its islands.

Mount Hor, constituting the northern coastal border, is rendered as a two-topped mountain, according to Rashi's somewhat vague formulation. The city of Hamath on the northern (left-hand) margin is identified as Antioch (according to Aramaic translations and other rabbinical sources), to which came the men sent by Moses (Num. 13:21). These twelve men are given great prominence; they face south and, again in line with Rashi's commentary, eight of them carry a giant cluster of grapes, one a fig, and one a pomegranate; Joshua and Caleb bring up the rear and are empty-handed.

Other points marking the northern border are Zreda, Ziphron, and Hazar-enan. The eastern border is drawn through Shepham and Riblah, reaching the Sea of Galilee. The representation of the sources of the Jordan, the Sea of Galilee, and the Dead Sea are very similar to that in the cartograms made according to Rashi, but in a perspective view. Moses stands spreading his arms atop Mount Nebo in Transjordan, opposite Jericho, which has the appearance of a geometric maze with its seven walls — an image recurring in early manuscripts and printed books.

The walled city of Jerusalem is prominently depicted with, at its center, the Temple — a structure resembling the Dome of the Rock, as often seen in contemporary Jewish literature such as illustrated Passover Haggadot or Tabernacle decorations (and also incidentally used as a "logo" by the Venetian printer Marco Antonio Giustiniani). Northeast of the city is Mount Zion, and to the south, outside the walls, the tombs of Eli the priest, Samuel the prophet, and Zechariah.

The depiction of Venice in the lower left-hand corner, with a gondola sailing alongside, as well as a number of fortified cities, seems to point to Italy as the source of this map. The text underneath the caption of the map includes some names: Jacob Qres (?), of whom it says, "The Lord... thanks and honor to him for he explained this form . . . .; Aaron bar Chaim Halevi Shalit; Joseph ben Jacob of Padua, a writer and publisher in 16th-century Mantua and

Venice; and Isaac ben Shmuel Bassan, who served in the synagogue at Mantua, and is believed to have published the Passover Haggadah of Mantua in 1560.

Above the Menorah is a quote from Psalms 36:9: "For with thee is the fountain of life: in thy light shall we see light." Some of the letters are marked, perhaps as a code indicating the date of the map's making.

Apart from calling to mind Jewish visual sources, this intriguing map is also reminiscent of early Christian maps, such as the Brandis de Schass woodcut (see p. 78).

A. T.

H. J. Haag, "Die vermutlich älteste bekannte hebräische Holzschnittkarte des heiligen Landes (um 1560)," *Cartographica Helvetica* 4 (July 1991), pp. 23—26.

Abraham Bar Jacob

Abraham Bar Jacob, German,
17th century
*Map of the Holy Land:
The Route of the Exodus*
Hand-colored engraving by
Moses Wiesel, 1695,
262x480 mm,
From *Haggadah shel Pessach*
(Passover Haggadah)
Amsterdam, 1695
The Israel Museum, Jerusalem
Gift of Dr. Silberstein, Geneva

Abraham Bar Jacob's map of the Land of Israel was printed in the Amsterdam Haggadah, one of the early printed Haggadot, published in several editions between 1695 and 1810. The map, using the common device of dividing the country into the Tribes of Israel, follows the pattern of the map by Christian van Adrichom (see p. 96).

The cartographer, presumably a proselyte, not only translated the map into Hebrew but turned it into a Jewish map by removing the references to Christianity and the New Testament found in Adrichom's Map, while keeping the general format of the original map.

The map, which faces east, represents the Land of Israel and the Sinai desert. In the lower part is "the Great Sea" (the Mediterranean), to the right the Nile Delta and Egypt. The farthest right portion of the sheet is devoted to the Sinai wanderings of the Children of Israel, their itinerary marked as a winding mountain path; the sequence of their encampments in the desert is indicated by the letters aleph to mem-aleph (i. e., the numbers 1—41) and a tent is drawn next to each camp. The order of the camps is further specified in an ornamental table at the bottom of the map. The country as a whole is divided into the inheritances of the tribes, from Naphtali and Asher in the north to Judah and Simeon in the south. We should note that the inheritance of Dan is indicated in the middle of the coastal plain and not in the north of the country, into which the tribe of Dan wandered according to the Book of Judges. All over the country, towns and

villages mentioned in the Bible are indicated, each portrayed as a structure or a group of structures with its name alongside. Between Hebron and the plain of Mamre we see Abraham's tent with the three angels; offshore are ships towing rafts of cedar trees from Lebanon that Hiram, king of Tyre, sent to Solomon for building the Temple.

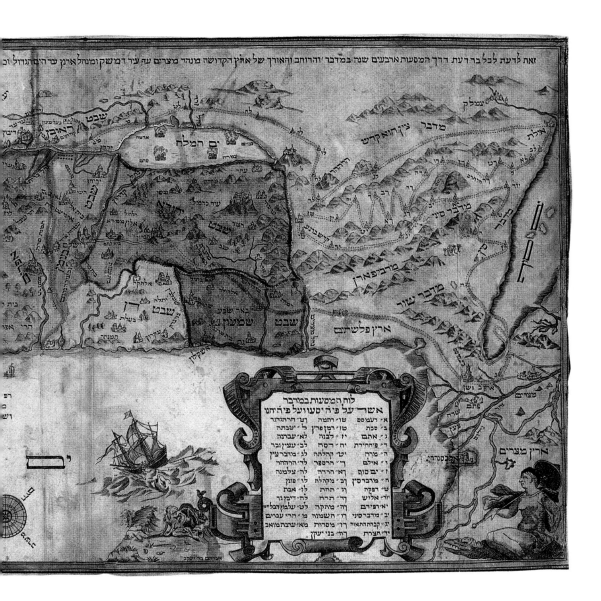

At the top of the sheet is a long sentence in which are written the Hebrew letters taf-nun-heh to indicate the year in which the map was printed (1695). In later editions additional letters were similarly marked to indicate their years of printing.

R. R.

Christian van Adrichom, *Situs Terra promissionis SS Bibliorum intelligentiam exacte aperiens* (Delft, 1590).

Passover Haggadah (Amsterdam, 1695) (in Hebrew).

K. Nebenzahl, *Maps of the Holy Land* (New York and Tel Aviv, 1986), pp. 138–39.

Rabbi Elijah ben Solomon Zalman

Rabbi Elijah ben Solomon
Zalman (The Vilna Gaon),
1720–1797
*The Division of the Land of
Israel According to Its
Boundaries*, ca. 1802
Ink, watercolor,
and gold-leaf on paper,
440x530 mm
The Jewish National and
University Library, Jerusalem
The Eran Laor
Cartographic Collection

Rabbi Elijah ben Solomon Zalman, known as "the Vilna Gaon [Genius]" or "Elijah Gaon," is considered one of the greatest of Jewish spiritual leaders. He established a large study center in Vilna and was one of the staunch opponents of Hassidism.

The Vilna Gaon was also proficient in algebra, geometry, astronomy, and geography. He evinced a special interest in the geography of the Land of Israel, which he fervently hoped to reach: "And I, thank God, am going to the Holy Land, which everyone hopes to see, the beloved of Israel and of the Blessed God. High and low yearn for her" (from his book *Alim Le-Trufa* [Leaves for healing], 1836). Alas, this blessing was granted only to those of his students who went to live there.

The Vilna Gaon wrote dozens of books, among them *The Shape of the Country and Its Boundaries*, first published in 1802, which included three maps of the Land of Israel. The map presented here was probably derived from this very book, having been (according to its caption): "copied from the great and famous and righteous Gaon . . ."

The map is oriented toward the east and depicts schematically and naively, with many geographical errors, the Land of Israel divided among the Twelve Tribes on both sides of the Jordan. Its design is rather original. Many quotes from the Bible are incorporated into the text alongside the various sites. The march of the Israelites is marked by a dotted line along the southern and eastern borders of the map, which is bounded on most sides by water. Below (to the west) is "the Great Sea" (the Mediterranean); to the east and northeast is the Red Sea, portrayed as a narrow strip. The Arnon is incorrectly depicted as running from the Dead Sea to the Red Sea (!) rather than westward to the Dead Sea. Wadi Zered, in the upper right-hand corner, also flows erroneously into the Red Sea rather than into the southern part of the Dead Sea. Along the northern (left-hand) edge of the map is the Euphrates, flowing into the Mediterranean! The sources of the Jordan are at Dan, after the Babylonian Talmud (Bekhorot 55:1): "Why is it called Jordan — because it descends from the Dan." Lastly, as in the maps following Rashi, the Jordan incongruently flows alongside the Sea of Galilee and only then continues to the Dead Sea.

Various indications on the map are of interest. The majority of the buildings marking settlements or camps along the course of the march of the Israelites have red roofs, most with chimneys. The European influence is quite obvious, the Temple in Jerusalem being shown as a medieval turreted citadel. Mount Moriah is pear-shaped, and next to it, in small letters, is the caption: "Zion is Jebus is Jerusalem." The cities of Heshbon (the seat of King Sihon of the Amorites), Jericho, and Gezer are enlarged and represented by palatial structures or late 18th-century castles. The Philistine cities, below right, are especially outstanding in their design — they look like matches. Other cities in the tribal patrimonies of Naphtali and Asher call to mind a row of cupboard drawers (rectangles with dots at the center) or the rungs of a ladder. The mountains

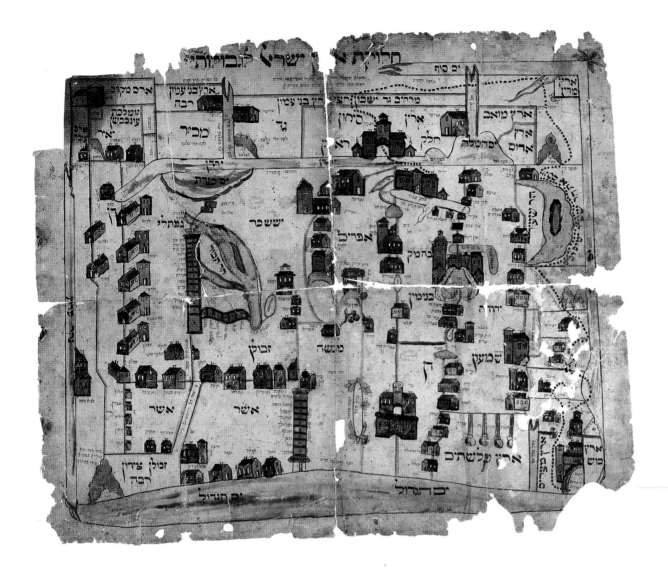

are rendered by decorative plant-like forms, recalling similar motifs in early Muslim maps. Mount Seir — which in the Bible represents the seat of the Edomites, descendants of Esau — stands out at upper right (the southeast), and around it is a large-lettered quote: " . . . and we compassed mount Seir many days" (Deut. 2:1). Mount Tabor is also prominent. Two mountains — at upper right and lower left — bear the name Mount Hor: one is on the border of Edom (Num. 20:23), Aaron's burial place; the other, seen in the northwest (Num. 34:7), "that is called in the Gemara Mount Amanus" (Babylonian Talmud, Bekhorot 55:1), is depicted

in the stylized mode described above. So too are Mount Sinai and Mount Horeb (which in the Bible are actually synonyms for the same mountain).

In spite of the fact that this map dates from the end of the 18th century, it clearly follows the style of medieval mapmaking.

A. T.

Z. Vilnay, *The Hebrew Maps of the Holy Land: A Research in Hebrew Cartography* (Jerusalem, 1968), pp. 22—23 (in Hebrew).

E. and G. Wajntraub, *Hebrew Maps of the Holy Land* (Vienna, 1992), pp. 124—26, W. 50.

Avigdor ben Rabbi Mordecai Malkov

Avigdor ben Rabbi
Mordecai Malkov, 19th century
Mapat Derekh Emet
(Map of the way of truth)
Colored lithograph,
530x790 mm
From *Derekh Emet*,
Warsaw, 1894
The Jewish National and
University Library, Jerusalem
The Eran Laor
Cartographic Collection

The caption of the map is written in Hebrew and in Russian (at the time of its creation, Warsaw was ruled by the Russians).

The author writes in the legend at upper right: "Look and see a new thing, a map of our Holy Land. . . . And the true way of the ascent of the Israelites from Egypt, their marches and camps: the deserts, the lands, and the seas that they passed till they came to Eretz Israel. . . . And you will find each in its place, seven-times refined according to *hazal* (our Sages of blessed memory) and the geniuses of the world. . . . And I also approximated their opinions to the study of surveying the land. The year 1894." In the accompanying booklet he describes the labor invested in preparing the map.

This map well illustrates that the Exodus story was a central motif in Jewish national consciousness, from biblical times until the renewal of Jewish settlement in the Land of Israel. It is a motif entwined in most Hebrew, as well as in many Christian maps. Old and new are here uniquely combined — both in the method of cartographic symbolization and in the historical and geographical data presented. On the one hand the route of the Israelites' wanderings, the encampments of the Israelites, and the division of the country among the Twelve Tribes are marked; the latter are indicated by numbers relating to the legend at lower left. The map also points out many biblical settlements, some derived from commentaries, others inaccurate or fictional. On the other hand it presents several innovations, notably in its depiction of the Suez Canal, the railroad from

Jaffa to Jerusalem, and the new Jewish settlements, uniquely portrayed by a slanting red roof with a chimney. Even if their location is not exact, this may be the first map indicating Beer Tuviah, Petah Tiqva, Mikveh Israel, and Zikhron Yaakov.

The map is oriented to the east, the heavily indented coastline stretching from Beirut in the north as far as Alexandria. The author adopted a special hachuring method for depicting mountains — always as circles or closed elliptic shapes. The sources serving Malkov in its creation are not clear, but he must have had before him some of the European maps included in this book.

It is difficult to overlook the deliberateness of integrating the texts in this map — they carry a clear message: "Thou shalt be a crown of glory in the hand of the Lord, and a royal diadem in the hand of thy God. Thou shalt no more be termed Forsaken . . . but thou shalt be called Hepsibah . . ., and thy land shall be married" (Isa. 62:3—4). And the lower left-hand corner bears the inscription: "The love of Zion and the affection for Jerusalem will never be forgotten." The first stirrings of Zionism are already clearly evident.

A. T.

E. Laor and S. Klein, *Maps of the Holy Land: Cartobibliography of Printed Maps, 1475—1900* (New York and Amsterdam, 1986), p. 121, no. 895.

Z. Vilnay, *The Hebrew Maps of the Holy Land: A Research in Hebrew Cartography* (Jerusalem, 1968) p. 34 (in Hebrew).

E. and G. Wajntraub, *Hebrew Maps of the Holy Land* (Vienna, 1992), pp. 197—99, W. 76.

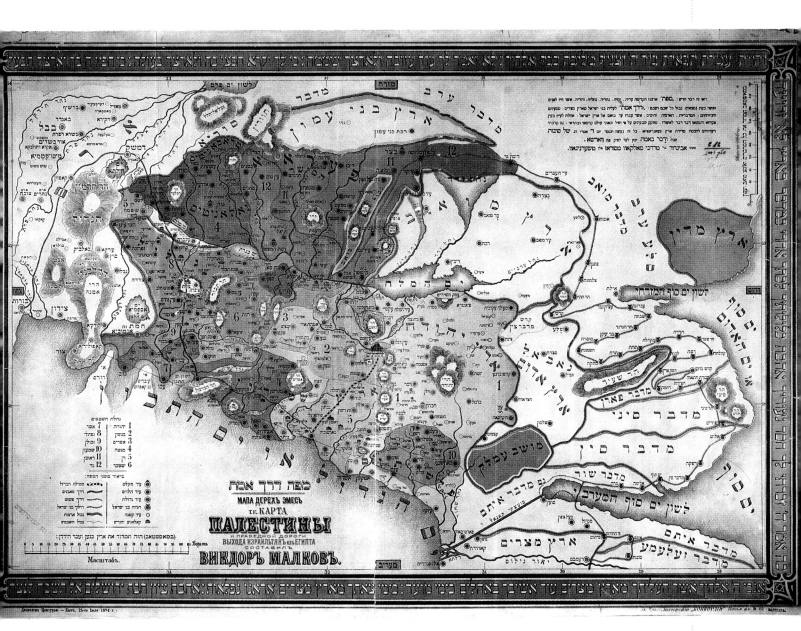

מפה דרך אמת
МАПА ДЕРЕХЪ ЭМЕСЪ
т.е. КАРТА
ПАЛЕСТИНЫ
И ПРАВЕДНОЙ ДОРОГИ
ВЫХОДА ИЗРАИЛЬТЯНЪ КЪ ЕГИПТА
СОСТАВИЛЪ
ВИКДОРЪ МАЛКОВЪ.

Масштабъ.

Mapmakers and Calligraphers: The Artistry of Muslim Cartography

Ariel Tishby

Historical Background

During the Middle Ages, while the power of the Christian church was reaching its height in Europe, a splendid cultural blossoming was under way in the Muslim world. It was evident in literature and art, in philosophy, in religious thought, and also in the sciences. In addition to its rapid spread, a crucial characteristic of Islamic culture was its assimilation of important elements from the cultures of conquered peoples, especially from the Persian and Hellenistic civilizations. Arabs, aided, *inter alia,* by Jewish scholars, played a vital role in conserving cultural and scientific values of ancient Greece and the East. These values were transferred to Europe just as the Renaissance, with its renewal of cultural and historic interest, was beginning. Though most of the Muslim philosophers and scientists were partly or even wholly non-Arab (e.g., the Persians), Arabic was the only language used in science and literature until the 13th century.

Already during the reign of the Umayyads — the first Islamic dynasty (661–750 CE) — an efficient postal service had been instituted along the extensive travel routes that criss-crossed the empire. The Muslims had built a navy capable of crushing the Byzantine Empire. The administrative demands of the state, as well as the needs of pilgrims to Mecca, triggered rapid advances in geographical science. These were additionally spurred on by the growth of trade from the 7th century onward, with the trade routes reaching as far as China in the east, the coast of Africa in the south, Russia in the north, and the Atlantic in the west. Against this backdrop a geographical literature flourished that included historical and topographic descriptions, astronomic research, geographical lexicons, etc. One of the common names for books on geography was *Kitab Al-Masalik Wal-Mamalik* (Book of the Roads and Countries).

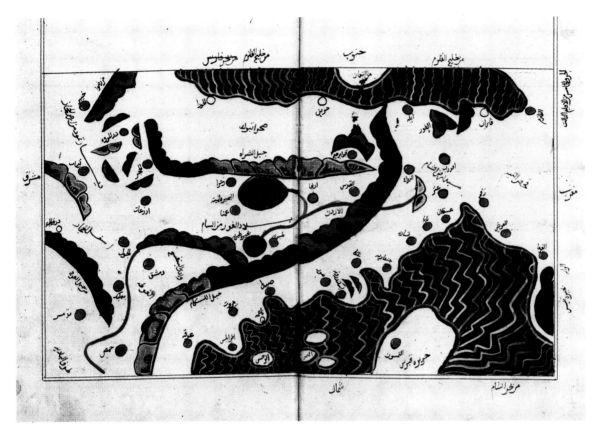

*Abu Ishak Ibrahim Al-Farisi
Al-Istakhri, active first half of
10th century*
Map of the Euphrates
and Tigris Rivers
*From a Persian manuscript
version of* Book of Roads and
Countries, *952*
*Gouache and manuscript on
paper, 18th century(?),
280x180 mm*
*The Israel Museum,
Jerusalem
Bequest of Y. Dawud,
London*

Important writers included the geographer Ibn Hawqal (d. 978), Al-Idrisi (12th century), and Iakut (13th century), as well as Ibn Battuta (14th century), a renowned author of travelogues, and, of course, Ptolemy of Alexandria (2nd century), a towering figure in astronomy (see p. 70). A primary motivation for astronomic research was the need to set the precise direction of prayer toward Mecca. The writings of Ptolemy were translated into Arabic from the Greek on the orders of the caliph al-Mamun in the early 9th century — a period almost forgotten in Europe but one that laid the cornerstone for the rise of astronomy and geography under Islamic culture.

For many years the study of Muslim cartography was all but ignored in the West. Lack of space here

precludes doing justice to the vastness and complexity of the subject; it is possible to present only a general outline and a few maps. However, it should be noted that the number of early Muslim maps focusing on Palestine is comparatively very low. Even more remarkable is the fact that although Jerusalem was under Arab rule for 460 years, from the fall of the Byzantine Empire in 638 until the Crusader invasion in 1099, not a single Muslim map of the city is known to us from this period.

In the mid-7th century, after about 150 years of Muslim rule over large areas of the Middle East, the translation of texts into Arabic went into high gear. By the beginning of the 10th century a large part of the surviving Greek philosophical writings on science had been translated. The writings of Ptolemy were the foundation of knowledge in the domains of astronomy and geography, and of subsequent mathematical and cartographic advances. The majority of the Islamic maps formed an integral part of textual manuscripts. Even in the era of printing there was an ongoing preference, right up to the 18th century, to carry on the manuscript tradition. The difficulty in deciphering and understanding these maps derives from problems pertaining to the texts. There is no doubt that most of the maps had a secondary purpose — didactic and illustrative — and were subordinated to the written material.

Early Muslim geography included various astromical instruments as the astrolabe and the globe, marine atlases, and a few maps of the world. When looking at the formal aspects of Islamic maps it is important to note that they are stylistically associated with Muslim illuminated manuscripts, and to bear in mind the Islamic prohibition against the visual representation of figures, which inclined artists toward geometric and abstract decoration. The basic geometric forms were seen as the building blocks of all shapes in the world, and symbolized the model of the world as conceived by the Creator — it is for this reason they play such a central role in Muslim art. Calligraphy was considered the highest form of art, for it involved the words of God and his Prophet. As with maps of the Christian Middle Ages, it is not possible to discuss these maps in terms of modern map design; they should rather be viewed in the context of the dominant aesthetic values and didactic goals of the society that created them.

The maps were drawn both on parchment and on paper. From the mid-8th century, when the secrets of paper making made their way from China to the West, the Arabs were for a few hundred years the main producers of paper in such centers as Damascus and Baghdad. The map outlines were drawn in ink with the coloring done by means of various mineral pigments. Al-Mukdasi (10th century) laid down certain rules for color usage: red for roads, yellow for desert sand dunes, green for seas, blue for rivers, and brown for mountain ranges. A huge gap existed between Arab astronomic and mathematical sophistication in the mapping of heavenly bodies on the one hand and the paucity of accurate cartographic representation of the Earth's surface on the other. (Nevertheless, Muslim seafarers' and traders' knowledge of such areas as North Africa, the Arabian Peninsula, Sudan, Ethiopia, and India was far more extensive than that of Europeans of their time.) This paucity was reflected in the lack of specialized cartographic terms. In Arabic, Persian, and early Turkish there was no specific word for map. The use of the word *sûrah* (Arabic for "form") is especially interesting, since this was the term used in Hebrew maps as well. Another similarity between early Hebrew and Muslim maps is the tendency to schematization, sometimes extending to the use of topological diagrams.

Two main schools of cartography developed during the period of early Islam: the Ptolemaic and the school after Balkhi. The former, based on Ptolemy's *Geographia*, was adopted by the caliph al-Mamun in the 9th century. The latter, based among other

Abu Abd Allah Muhammad Ibn Al-Idrisi, born Morocco,
active Sicily, ca. 1100–1165
Map of ash-Sham *(Syria and Palestine) (first edition,1154)*
From a Persian copy, 1533
Gouache and ink on vellum, 215x340 mm
Bodleian Library, Oxford

Abu Ishak Ibrahim Al-Farisi Al-Istakhri

Al-Istakhri was one of the foremost mapmakers of the 10th century — the golden age of Muslim science. His popular *Book of Roads and Countries*, which was translated into many languages, originally contained 21 maps. One of them is of the environs of the Euphrates and Tigris rivers. Oriented to the south, toward Mecca, it depicts *al-Jazirah* (the island), the northern half of the area between the great rivers. The straight river is the Tigris, the winding one the Euphrates. The artist has used a minimum of symbols: long- striped areas for rivers, circles for settlements, triangles for mountains. Very few sites on the map are named. Despite the unfamiliar cartographic language, the abstraction, and the minimal geometry, the map presents an actual geographic reality.

Abu Abd Allah Muhammad Ibn Al-Idrisi

Al-Idrisi, who lived in the 12th century, was of Moorish origin, born in Ceuta, Morocco, and educated in Cordoba, Spain. He undertook journeys to the centers of education in Asia Minor and in Africa, but his activities were concentrated in Sicily, a meeting point of Eastern and Western cultures then in the hands of the Normans, reflected in his unusual combination of Western and Arab cartography.

Al-Idrisi was commissioned by Roger II, the ruler of Sicily, to produce an atlas, of a type unknown in the Middle Ages. Entitled *Kitab nuzhat al-mushtaq* (The

things on the geographer Ibn Hawqal, concentrated on the Islamic empire, dividing it into 22 provinces or *aq-âlîm*. Unlike their Ptolemaic counterparts, these area maps did not have a mathematical basis of latitude and longitude.

The desire to fulfill the commandment of pilgrimage to Mecca is written in the Koran, and trade relations stretching from Morocco to India encouraged the creation of atlases, of portable dimensions, encompassing these regions.

book of pleasant journeys to faraway lands), it contained about 70 maps, including one of the entire known world — which shows an indirect Ptolemaic influence, both in the division according to *aq-âlîms* and in its relatively naturalistic imagery — one of Muslim settlement at the time, and the one before us here, of Syria and Palestine. This map, today housed in the Bodleian Library, Oxford, is from the Persian translation of a 1533 manuscript. Oriented to the southeast, it shows Syria and Lebanon (on the left) and Palestine between the Mediterranean and the Red seas. Both bodies of water are colored dark blue and embellished in a stylized mode with parallel wavy lines in a lighter shade. In the Ptolemaic tradition, the width of the Red Sea is greatly exaggerated. Cyprus is shown as a light area at lower right. The coastline reaches from Syria to Egypt, with most of the coastal towns demarcated by yellow-orange circles; they include Beirut, Tyre, Acre, Jaffa, Ashqelon, Rafiah, El Arish, and Alexandria. Jerusalem (Al-Quds) and Jericho are to the right, between two mountain ranges. At center, colored green, are the ball-shaped Sea of Galilee and the egg-shaped Dead Sea, connected very schematically by a winding Jordan, which has an additional long tributary heading southwest. The mountain ranges vary in color and are rendered in a style showing Western influence. The long range cutting diagonally through most of the area of the map represents the mountains of Lebanon, with the Judean Hills as their continuation all the way to the Red Sea, between Petra and Elath.

Al-Idrisi's attempt to describe different parts of the world on the same scale and in equal detail was unprecedented. His atlas includes more extensive and accurate data, and covers an area more extensive than that of any previous Muslim or Christian mapmaker, indicating settlements in southern and central Africa as well as the Far East, and even providing a detailed description of the Christian West. Al-Idrisi's maps influenced the way in which portolan cartographers depicted the coastlines of the Mediterranean basin and other areas. Among those who availed themselves of Al-Idrisi's knowledge were Petrus Vesconte (see p. 74), in his maps for Sanuto's book, and Abraham Yehudah Cresques, in the famous Catalan Atlas.

Piri Reis

Born in Gallipoli in the 1570s, Piri Reis is considered the father of modern Turkish cartography. He was a seaman who left to posterity three works that have kept his name alive: two maps of the world (1513 and 1529), of which only fragments remain, and *Kitab-i Bahriye* (Book of the seas). The latter, written in 1521 and enlarged in 1526, includes sea maps and sea routes and was written against a background of revolutionary and historical developments that led to the Ottomans becoming the dominant sea power in the Mediterranean. His uncle, Kemal Reis, a naval officer greatly feared by the Venetian navy, was the most famous seaman of his time.

Today, about 35 manuscript copies of *Kitab-i Bahriye* survive from different periods. The book deals in a methodical manner with the whole Mediterranean region, each chapter containing a descriptive text

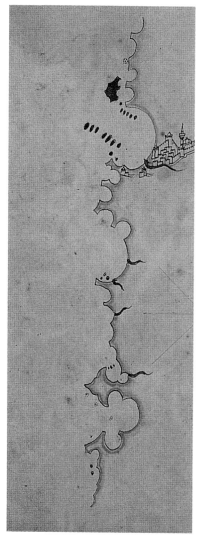

Piri Reis, Turkish, ca. 1470–1554
The Coast of Acre
From Kitab i-Bahriye, *1521–26*
Facsimile reproduction from the original book in the Nasser D. Khalili Collection

The manuscript, from the Nasser D. Khalili Collection, is neither signed nor dated, but its maps, including topographic views of Istanbul, Venice, and Cairo, among other cities, have been drawn after the first edition of the book. In addition there are impressive drawings of different types of ships. The copy from the Khalili Collection is comprehensive; it includes all the texts and seems to have been copied in the second half of the 17th century on Italian paper. Most maps have a descriptive title, this one being "The Contours of the Coasts of Acre, Ra's al-Khinzir and Payas . . . as Shown," Acre being at the time the most important coastal city in Palestine.

Although *Kitab-i-Bahriye* contains a wealth of information and is fairly accurate, its coastlines are still highly stylized and ornate, a relic of the decorative tendency of early Muslim maps.

A. T.

accompanied by a map or a number of charts. Even though European portolan atlases also included descriptive texts, there is no doubt that Reis excelled in the production of this book. The first edition included 130 chapters, the second 210, evidence of its exceptional range. Whereas in the Italian portolan atlases the role of the mapmaker is a modest one, here the author is especially prominent, having penned a personal foreword and an epilogue that includes some of his poems. His knowledge of cosmography and astronomy, including the global shape of the Earth, and pertaining to such issues as the geographic latitude, the equator, the poles, and the like — is woven into the text.

O. Grabar, *The Formation of Islamic Art* (New Haven, 1987), pp. 72–98.

Ahmet T. Karamustafa and Maqbul Ahmad, "Cartography in the Traditional Islamic and South Asian Societies," in *The History of Cartography*, vol. 2, book 1, ed. J. B. Harley and D. Woodward (Chicago, 1987).

H. Lazarus-Yafeh, ed., *Studies in the History of the Arabs and Islam* (Tel Aviv, 1970) (in Hebrew).

K. Miller, *Mappae Arabicae* (Stuttgart, 1926).

K. Nebenzahl, *Maps of the Holy Land* (New York and Tel Aviv, 1986) pp. 28–29, 34–35.

S. Soucek, *Piri Reis and Turkish Mapmaking after Colombus* (London, 1992).

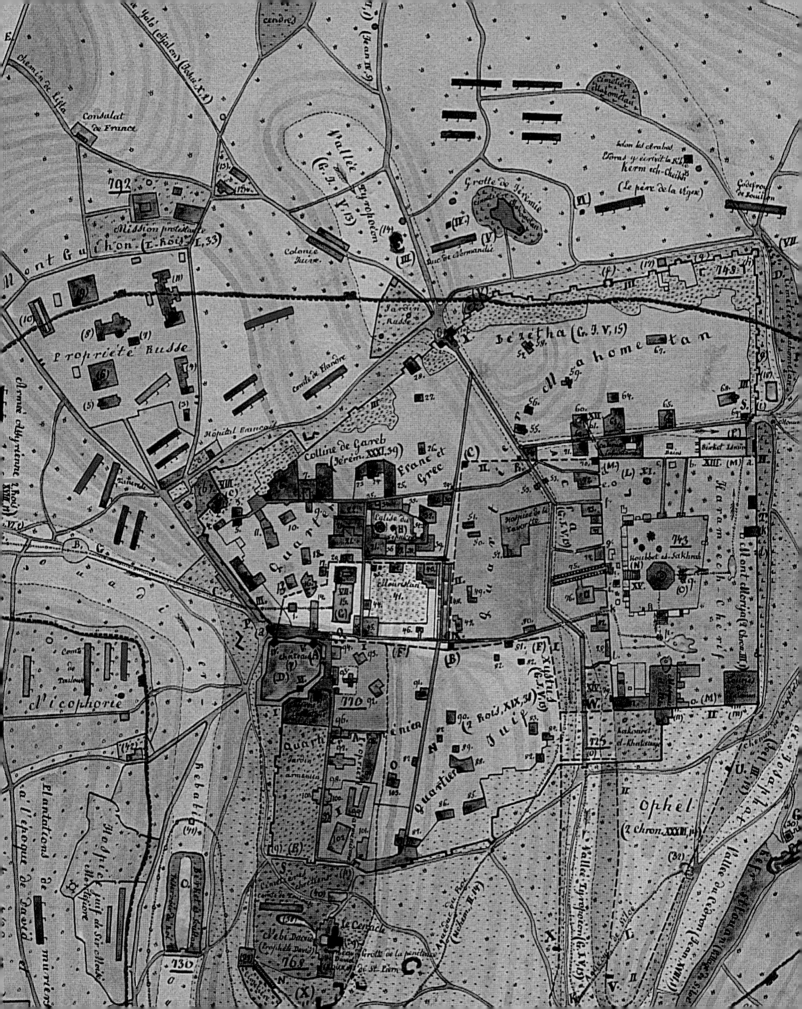

Jerusalem in Maps

"I lifted up mine eyes again, and looked, and behold,
a man with a measuring line in his hand.
Then said I, Whither goest thou?
And he said unto me, To measure Jerusalem,
to see what is the breadth thereof,
and what is the length thereof"

Zechariah 1:1—2

Crusader Maps of Jerusalem

Crusader Map of Jerusalem,
12th century
Manuscript on vellum
University Library, Uppsala
MS C.691, fol. F39

The conquest of Jerusalem by the Crusaders in 1099 placed Jerusalem at the center of interest of the Western Christian world. Traditional Christian holy sites gained renewed attention, and reports of events in Crusader Jerusalem proliferated. In addition to the written reports, maps of Crusader Jerusalem also started to appear. We are today familiar with some 15 maps depicting Jerusalem under the Crusaders. Some were drawn or copied during the 13th and 14th centuries, even though they no longer reflected the reality of the time, as Jerusalem was by then under Muslim rule.

Eleven of these 15 maps belong to one impressive group, known as "the round maps." The common characteristics of this group indicate that they derive from a single original that was apparently very popular. In these maps, all of which face east, the circle represents the city walls. It encloses the cruciform pattern of the major thoroughfares: the longitudinal street (Cardo) and the horizontal street (Decumanus) crossing it. This form, it seems, was influenced by the pattern of world maps common in the Middle Ages, called T-in-O. The city plan — with its gates, streets, the roads leading to it, and its main structures — is identical in all the round maps, with some personal additions or omissions by the copiers.

Characteristic of the round maps is the presentation — along with the plan of the city and its sites — of many Jerusalem traditions, based on the New and Old Testaments and on the apocryphal literature. We are in fact presented with a short visual history of the city in its different periods. It is obvious that the aim was not to map Jerusalem accurately, for use by pilgrims, but rather to present an inspiring image of the city with its wealth of Christian traditions, now renewed under Crusader rule. The viewer of these maps, rich in color and ornamentation, encounters a city wrapped in its past glory, its magnificent buildings dominated by the towers of the many churches. This view was probably meant to arouse pride in the hearts of Western Christians, and perhaps also to serve as an incentive to undertake pilgrimage and settle in the Crusader Kingdom.

The map presented here, the Uppsala Map, is one of the more impressive representatives of this group. Forming an integral part of a 12th-century manuscript, kept today in the university library of Uppsala, it appears between two works describing the First Crusade and the conquest of Jerusalem: Robertus Monachus's *Historia Hierosolymitana* and the *Gesta Francorum Expugnatium Hierusalem*.

As in all round maps, the city has five gates, the most prominent of them being the "Golden Gate," which is actually painted gold. Many of the maps indicate that this was the gate through which Jesus

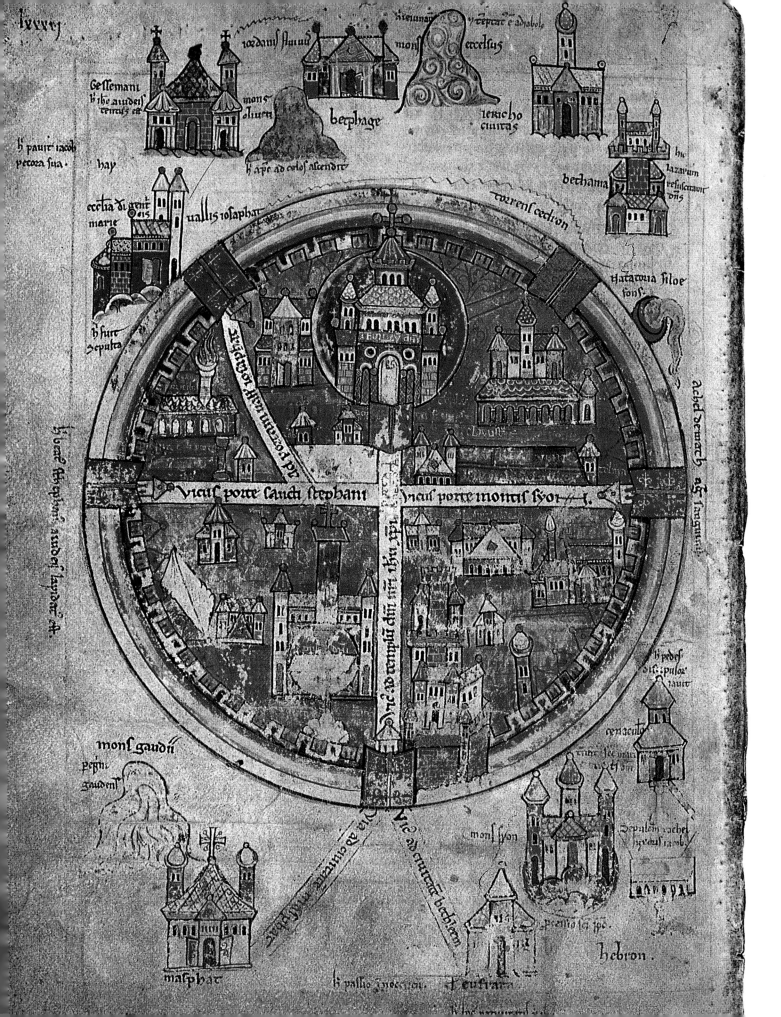

entered Jerusalem riding on an ass (Matthew 21:7–11, and parallel versions). The network of streets in this map is simple compared to the other maps, in which additional streets run parallel to the Cardo and Decumanus. In the lower part of the map we see two roads — one leading south to Bethlehem-Ephrata, the other north to Mizpeh, the town of the prophet Samuel. The use of the biblical names Ephrata and Mizpeh points to a desire to link the present with the past and to strengthen the Crusaders' roots in the country.

The eye is captured first of all by a structure called "the Temple of the Lord," at the top of the circle. This is the Dome of the Rock, which was used as a church in the Crusader period. A smaller circle, at lower left, contains the Holy Sepulchre. Under it the place where, according to Christian tradition, the Cross was found by Saint Helena, mother of Constantin, is designated. Next to the city wall, not far from the Holy Sepulchre, are depicted the rocks that rent at the crucifixion of Jesus (Matthew 27:51).

Adjacent to the Temple of the Lord we see "Solomon's Temple" — the al-Aqsa Mosque — which served as the residential quarters of the Knights Templar during the Crusader period. The complex where the Knights Hospitaller lived and worked is shown in the wrong place, in the lower right-hand side of the map. Other sites marked are St. Anne's Church, inside the city, and outside it, in the Jehoshaphat Valley, the Tomb of Mary and the Gethsemane Church (where the author notes: "Here Jesus was captured by the Jews"). On Mount Zion

three separate sites are highlighted: the Cenaculum, the room of the Last Supper; the chapel where, according to tradition, Jesus "washed the feet of the disciples"; and Zion Church, where the Holy Spirit descended upon the apostles. In the upper part we see the Mount of Olives, from whence Jesus "ascended into Heaven." Near the Golden Gate is the Gihon Spring, called by the Crusaders the Siloam. At center right is Hakel-dama (the field bought with Judas Iscariot's betrayal money) which was later used as a burial ground for pilgrims who died in Jerusalem. At the edge of the map and around it are sites in the environs of Jerusalem, such as Bethany, where Jesus raised Lazarus from the dead, Bethphage, and even Jericho and Mount Qarantena, where Jesus "fasted and was tried by Satan."

In the lower right-hand corner is "the Tomb of Rachel, Jacob's wife," and farther on Bethlehem — "the birthplace of Jesus Christ" and "the place of the slaughter of the innocents." In the lower left-hand corner is "the Mount of Joy of the joyous pilgrims," near Mizpeh (Nebi Samwil). This is the place from which, according to Crusader tradition, the Crusaders first saw Jerusalem and cried for joy. The list of sites and traditions ends with two interesting inscriptions: "Here Jacob shepherded his flocks" — most probably a reference to the tower of Edar (Gen. 35:21), identified in Christian tradition as being in the vicinity of Bethlehem; and "Hai," which is marked in the upper left-hand corner.

These two identifications, as well as the names Bethlehem, Ephrata, and Mizpeh, point to the fact that the Crusaders considered their roots to be not only in the Christian sites of the Holy Land but also in the Old Testament sites and traditions — a phenomenon familiar to us from the first centuries of Christianity. A short history of the city is included in some of the other maps, beginning with Jebus and continuing with David, Solomon, Ezra, and Nehemia. The Crusaders saw themselves, therefore, as heirs to the line of founders and builders of Jerusalem and the Land of Israel of the First and Second Temples, and not only as the saviors of the Holy Sepulchre.

Most important of the remaining four Crusader maps is the Cambrai Map. Made in the second half of the 12th century, this is also the most realistic of the maps known to us. It is rectangular in shape and around it are what seem to be topographic lines indicating the hills and valleys surrounding the city. It is obvious that the cartographer was well acquainted with the city. The Holy Sepulchre is depicted here after its renovation and inauguration by the Crusaders, complete with new bell tower, twin domes, and renovated square on the south side; under it, shown in great detail, is the complex of the Order of Hospitallers. The al-Aqsa Mosque appears as "the House of the Knights Templar," and inside it the inscription "the Stables of Solomon." The map also marks the site of the king's palace, near David's Tower, and the place in the northern wall where the Crusaders broke into the city. The cartographer was familiar also with the Eastern churches in the city. It is interesting to note that, in contrast to the round maps, this one describes only Crusader Jerusalem and depicts no traditions.

The final two maps are the square Montpellier Map, whose main aim is to describe the Crusader encampments around Jerusalem on the eve of the conquest, and the Harleian Map (extant in two versions), a very schematic description of Jerusalem and environs. The latter is a kind of pilgrim's road map, including the sites of pilgrimage and the main walking routes.

M. L.-R.

M. Levy, "Medieval Maps of Jerusalem," in *The History of Jerusalem: Crusaders and Ayyubids (1099—1250)*, ed. J. Prawer and H. Ben-Shammai (Jerusalem, 1991), pp. 418—507 (in Hebrew).

M. Levy-Rubin, "The Rediscovery of the Uppsala Map of Crusader Jerusalem," *Zeitschrift des Deutschen Palästina Vereins* 111 (1995), pp. 162—67.

M. Levy-Rubin and R. Rubin, "The Image of the Holy City in Maps and Mapping," in *City of the Great King*, ed. N. Rosovsky (Cambridge, Mass., 1996), pp. 352—79.

The Sanuto—Vesconte Map of Jerusalem

Marino Sanuto, Italian,
ca. 1260–1368, and
Petrus Vesconte, Italian,
d. ca. 1350
Map of Jerusalem
Manuscript on vellum,
350x255 mm
From *Liber Secretorum
Fidelium Crucis . . .*, ca. 1320
The British Library, London
Add. MS. 27378, fol. 189v

The map of Jerusalem drawn by Vesconte appears in his atlas, in the appendix to Sanuto's *Liber Secretorum*, and in the large Chronology by Paulino Venetto, published in 1323. Since each of these documents has survived in several manuscripts, a number of copies of the map are extant.

The Sanuto—Vesconte map is quite different from other known Jerusalem maps of the period. Though it faces east in the customary manner, an attempt was made here for the first time to depict realistically the outline of the city walls and the layout of the streets. The realistic representation of the point where the wall joins the Temple Mount is noteworthy, as is the effort to show the precise angle of the northwestern corner of the city wall. An intriguing detail is the depiction of the city wall as encompassing Mount Zion, which was not the case in the Crusader period. Such a detailed presentation of the wall's outline was no doubt achieved by exact and professional copying in the field; yet it is not clear whether the wall was actually so continuous and complete as shown here. It is possible that it had been broken through in some places and the cartographer completed the lines. In 1219 al-Malek al-Mu'azzamm 'Isa, the Ayyubid ruler of Jerusalem, destroyed portions of the wall for fear of a renewed Christian conquest of Jerusalem with the aid of a Crusader party that had landed the previous year in Egypt. He preferred to leave behind him a less strongly fortified city that would be more difficult for the Crusaders to defend. We have no evidence as to the rebuilding of the wall until the Ottoman period. Assuming that the wall's outline was filled in by the cartographer, the question remains whether

Mount Zion was enclosed within the walls at some point of time or whether this was not rather a figment of the cartographer's imagination.

The attempt to represent reality as precisely as possible is expressed also in the depiction of the churches and other holy places according to their true dimensions rather than their relative importance. Thus the Holy Sepulchre, as well as the Lord's Temple and Solomon's Temple on the Temple Mount, are not enlarged beyond their actual size. The area of the Hospitallers, with its churches, hospice, and hospital (known today as the Muristan, from the Turkish word for hospital: *beimuristan*) is also correctly positioned and accurately drawn, unlike in the round Crusader maps.

The map further attempts to delineate the water system of Jerusalem, including its springs and pools. Thus we find the Gihon and En-Rogel springs — the inner, upper, and lower pools — each identified with one of the pools mentioned in early sources. Information on the location of the city's water sources was obviously of value to those planning to reconquer the city from the Muslims. But the attempt to make the water sources and reservoirs correspond with their biblical names caused confusion and misapprehension, as exemplified by the Gihon being located in the map on the western instead of the eastern side of the city.

The author does not neglect Jerusalem's holy places, for the sake of which the city should be reconquered. The map clearly delineates the course of the Via Dolorosa in the northern part of the city, as it had by then crystallized. Thus clearly pinpointed are the home of Annas, High Priest of Jerusalem and father-in-law of Caiaphas, where according to tradition Jesus was tried; Pontius Pilate's house, where he was flogged, crowned with a wreath of thorns, and sentenced to death; and the [S]pasmus Virginis, where Mary fainted when she saw Jesus kneeling under weight of the cross.

On Mount Zion we find the house of Caiaphas, the room of the Last Supper, Mary's house whence she ascended to heaven, and the Kings' Tombs. Outside the city are the Church of the Ascension on the Mount of Olives and the Church of Agony — the Gethsemane Church — at the foot of the Mount of Olives.

Around the Mount of Olives the author identifies several traditions not mentioned in Crusader maps, among them the temples of Chemosh, Molech, and Asherah; the Valley of Hinnom and the Valley of the Ammonites; the Prophet Isaiah's tomb; and the fig tree cursed by Jesus (Mark 11:13—14). The Sanuto—Vesconte map is an interesting combination of a practical document almost completely lacking in illustrations and aspiring to precision and usefulness, on the one hand, and a tool for the transmission of traditions as well as religious and ideological messages, on the other.

M. L.-R.

D. Bahat, "Marino Sanuto's Map and Jerusalem's Walls in the 13th Century," *Eretz Israel* 19 (1947), pp. 295—98 (in Hebrew).

J. B. Harley and D. Woodward, ed., *The History of Cartography*, vol. 1 (1987), pp. 406—7.

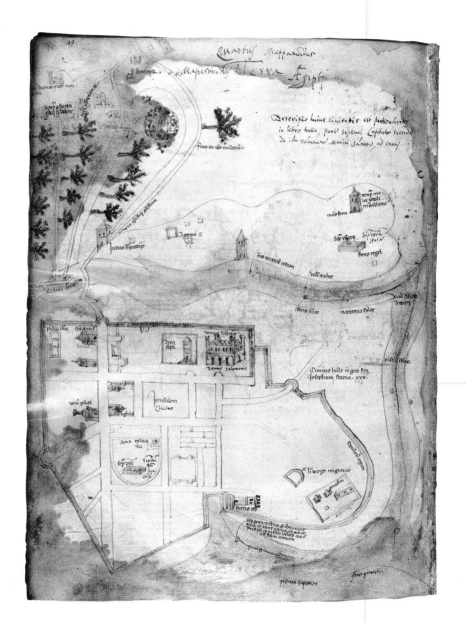

Imaginary Maps of Ancient Jerusalem According to Josephus Flavius

Anonymous, Czech,
16th century
Map of Jerusalem
280x410 mm
The Moldovan Family
Collection, New York

Among the many maps of Jerusalem, quite a few were prepared by historians and interpreters not familiar with the actual appearance of the city. As a rule, this phenomenon was rooted in humanistic education, which encouraged scholars to return to the ancient classical sources.

In his book *The Jewish War* (5, 4), Josephus begins his description of Jerusalem with the three walls surrounding the city and the course of these walls. A graphic analysis and non-realistic reconstruction based on this description were the basis of Adam Reissner's map, published in his book in 1563.

Jerusalem is depicted in this map as a rectangle divided into four parallel strips, each surrounded by a wall. The left-hand strip shows the southern part of the city — "the Upper City," according to Josephus. The central and largest strip includes the kernel of the city and the Temple. The two strips on the right represent the northern part of the city — "Bezetha" and "the New City." It should be noted that Reissner misinterpreted Josephus's description to mean that there were two separate units in the northern part of the city.

Reissner's map is quite detailed, although modest in comparison with the maps of its copiers. In it he depicted the Temple and its courtyards, the city gates with their names as mentioned in Josephus and other sources, and the hills surrounding the city. Reissner's graphic interpretation of Josephus's description was adopted by other authors, and similar depictions followed in two anonymous maps, one now in the Eran Laor Collection and one in the

Moldovan Collection. A similar map was also published in Bünting's book.

But it was Christian van Adrichom who took over this graphic depiction, improved upon it, and added numerous details. His map is dealt with separately (see p. 96).

Authors who followed Adrichom copied his map, rotated it — i.e., changed its orientation — and made it smaller or larger according to the formats of their books. One of these adaptations — that by Robert Sayer (1770) — deserves special attention, as it is not a mere copy but a complex adaptation.

Sayer adopted Adrichom's pattern, changing it only slightly; but in place of a relatively simple depiction of the Temple he had the structure held aloft on a set of arches and rising high above the city. Sayer's map is flanked by two sets of framed drawings, among them depictions of the Tower of Babylon, the Temple with its holy vessels, and the destruction of the Temple. At the foot of the map is a long text dealing with the history of Jerusalem and with various sites appearing in the map.

R. R.

A. Reissner, Ierusalem, vetustissima il la et celeberrima totius mundi, Francofurti [Frankfurt am Main] 1563, and there, a map entitled: "Geometrica urbis Ierosolymae delineatio"; the German edition: A. Reissner, *Jerusalem, Die alte Haubtstat der Juden* (Frankfurt am Main, 1563).

R. Rubin, "Original and Copied Maps: Carto-Genealogy of Ancient Maps of Jerusalem from the 15th–18th Centuries," *Eretz-Israel* 22 (Jerusalem, 1999), pp. 166–83 (in Hebrew).

R. Rubin, *Image and Reality: Jerusalem in Maps and Views* (Jerusalem, 1999), pp. 110–22.

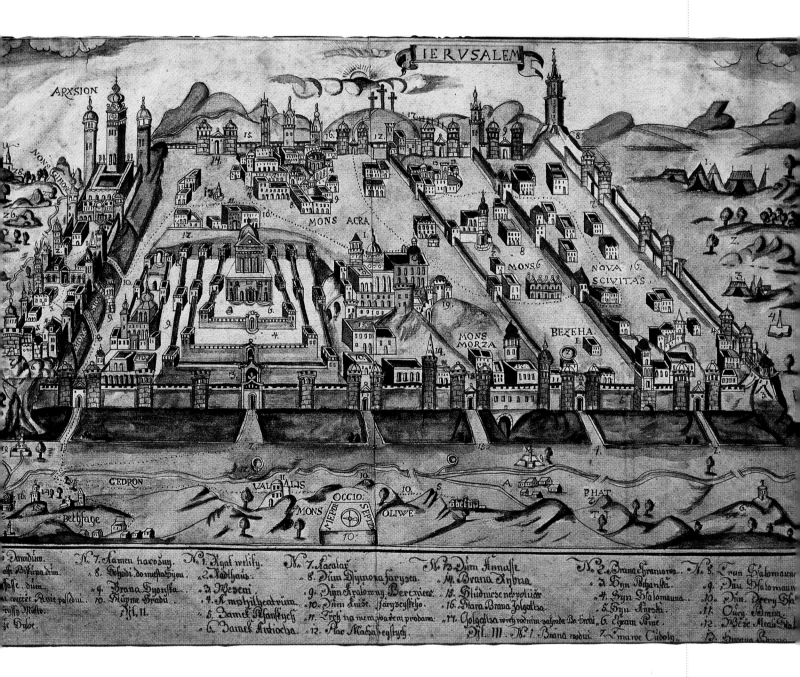

Giovanni Francesco Camocio

Giovanni Francesco Camocio,
Italian, 16th century
Civitas Hierusalem
(The City of Jerusalem)
Etching, ca. 1570,
290x420 mm
The Israel Museum, Jerusalem
Gift of Tamar and
Teddy Kollek, Jerusalem

Five Italian maps printed in the mid-16th century are found in different collections. They are so similar to one another they could well have been produced from the same printing block. The first was printed anonymously in 1543. Then followed the printing of maps by Ligorio, Camocio, Bertelli, and Ballino and Zaltieri. All were famed Italian printers active in Rome and Florence between 1559 and 1570.

Each of these maps depicts Jerusalem from the top of the Mount of Olives looking westward. In all, the Temple Mount and Lions Gate are prominent in the foreground, and the minarets of mosques, their height exaggerated, predominate. The northern wall of the city is a rounded line seen from the inner side of the city, and the structure of Nablus Gate, with the steps descending from it to the courtyard inside, is quite outstanding. Also prominent are the Church of the Holy Sepulchre and the towers of the Citadel near Jaffa Gate. In the courtyard of the Temple Mount, and in some maps also on the road descending to the city from the north, several figures can be seen drawn in fine schematic lines. But what seems specific to all these maps, and unifies them, are two framed structures, one on either side at the bottom of the sheet — the Cave of the Nativity in Bethlehem on the right, and the Church of the Holy Sepulchre with its monument on the left.

What was the source of these Italian maps or, more precisely, what was the source drawn on by the cartographer of the first, anonymous map of 1543? The two framed structures mentioned above seem to connect the Italian maps to the source: a map created in 1538 by Hermanus Borculus, a Dutch printer from Utrecht — presumably after his pilgrimage to Jerusalem.

In Borculus's map we see at top right the monument of the Holy Sepulchre, at top left the Cave of the Nativity, and in the center an ornamental ribbon bearing the inscription "Civitas Hierusalem 1538." The map is flanked by framed texts in Dutch and French, and a third text, in Latin, appears in the lower right-hand corner. The image of the city in this map strongly resembles the one described above and is likely to have been the source of the maps produced by the Italian printers, who had never seen the city.

In addition, in the lower part of the sheet, in front of the legend and to the east of the city itself, are two scenes with a religious connotation. One is the stoning of Saint Stephen outside the city gate, the other Jesus' entry into Jerusalem on Palm Sunday. A careful examination reveals two other figures, inside the Temple Mount, and next to them parts of a sentence giving the meaning of these figures. One is the adulterous woman, on trial (John 8), the other is Jesus chasing the money changers (Matt. 21:12). Atop the Dome of the Rock are two more figures, apparently meant to represent Jesus struggling with Satan (Luke 4:2–13). These figures seem to be the prototypes of the schematic figures peopling the Temple Mount in the Italian maps.

R. R.

R. Rubin, "The Map of Jerusalem (1538) by Harmannus Borculus and Its Copies: A Carto-Genealogical Study," *The Cartographic Journal* 27 (June 1990), pp. 31–39.

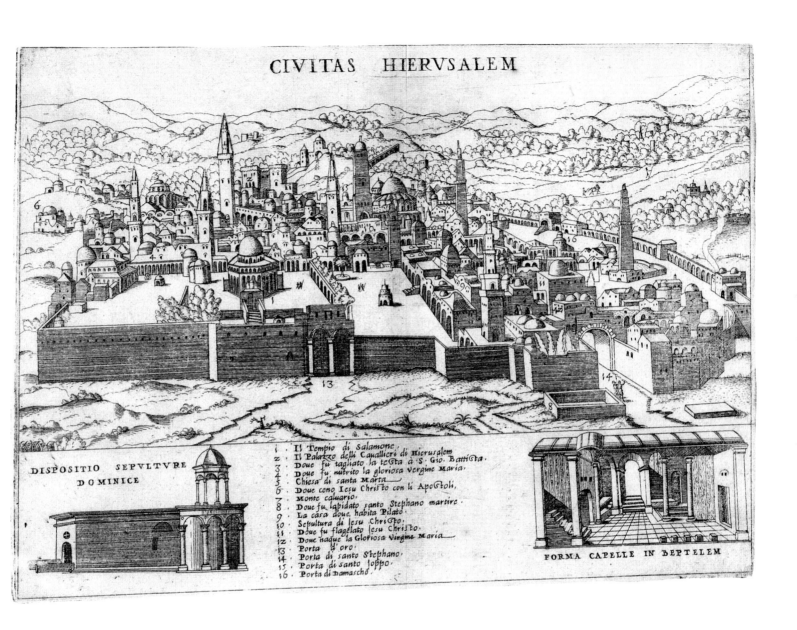

CIVITAS HIERVSALEM

DISPOSITIO SEPVLTVRE DOMINICE

1. Il Tempio di Salamone.
2. Il Palazzo delli Caualieri di Hierusalem
3. Doue fu tagliato la testa à S. Gio. Battista.
4. Doue fu nutrito la gloriosa Vergine Maria.
5. Chiesa di santa Marta.
6. Doue ceno Iesu Christo con li Apostoli.
7. Monte caluario.
8. Doue fu lapidato santo Stephano martire.
9. La casa doue habita Pilato.
10. Sepultura di Iesu Christo.
11. Doue fu flagelato Iesu Christo.
12. Doue naque la Gloriosa Vergine Maria
13. Porta d'oro.
14. Porta di santo Stephano.
15. Porta di santo Ioppo.
16. Porta di Damascho.

FORMA CAPELLE IN BEPTELEM

Frans Hogenberg

Frans Hogenberg, Flemish,
1535–1590
Jerusalem, the Holy City
Hand-colored etching,
330x418 mm
From Georg Braun and Frans
Hogenberg, *Civitates
Orbis Terrarum*,
Cologne, 1575
The Israel Museum, Jerusalem
Gift of Karl and
Li Handler, Vienna

Frans Hogenberg, a prominent Flemish engraver, cartographer, and publisher engraved many of the maps in the first editions of Ortelius's atlases. Together with Georg Braun, the German theologian (1541–1622), Hogenberg published in Cologne the monumental six-volume *Civitates Orbis Terrarum*, which included 363 views and city plans. After his death in 1590, his son Abraham continued this undertaking with Braun.

The present map, printed in the second volume as number 54, is a bird's-eye view of contemporary Jerusalem from the top of the Mount of Olives. This depiction combines the most comfortable angle for viewing the city, the place at which Jesus prophesied the destruction of the city (Luke 19: 41–44), and the site of his ascent to heaven. The caption of the map reads, "This is Jerusalem: I have set it in the midst of the nations and countries that are round about her" (Ezek. 5:5). This verse represents the Jewish, and later the Christian view of Jerusalem as the center of the world. Framed at lower left are the words: "The Holy City of Jerusalem, ever most famous in Judah and in the East in its size and greatness." At lower right is a detailed legend, thus defining this depiction as a map. In the foreground are turbaned and gowned Oriental figures. Above them is the Kidron Valley, and at lower left, above the cartouche, the Siloam pool.

Despite the relative reliability of the map, one must note its anachronistic and Christian aspects: The facade of the Holy Sepulchre is tilted 90° to the east to lend it greater prominence, as in Breydenbach's map of the late 15th century (see p. 80); and the sites listed in the legend are referred to by their Crusader names: the Citadel as "The Pisan Tower" (no. 29), the Dome of the Rock as "Templum Solomonis" (no. 14), and the al-Aqsa Mosque as "Sepulchrum Domini" (no. 15).

Hogenberg's map became one of the most popular depictions of Jerusalem. The source is not indicated, but research has revealed a great similarity with the map of Domenica dalle Greche of Venice, published in a travel account by Ulrich von Wilkenau, a Czech nobleman who toured the Holy Land in 1546.

Civitates Orbis Terrarum comprises two additional, completely imaginary-historical maps of Jerusalem. One was made after de Jode, copied from Petrus Laicstain; the other after Adrichom (see p. 32).

A. T.

R. Rubin, "Jerusalem in Braun and Hogenberg, Civitates," *The Cartographic Journal* 33, no,2 (December 1996), pp. 119–29.

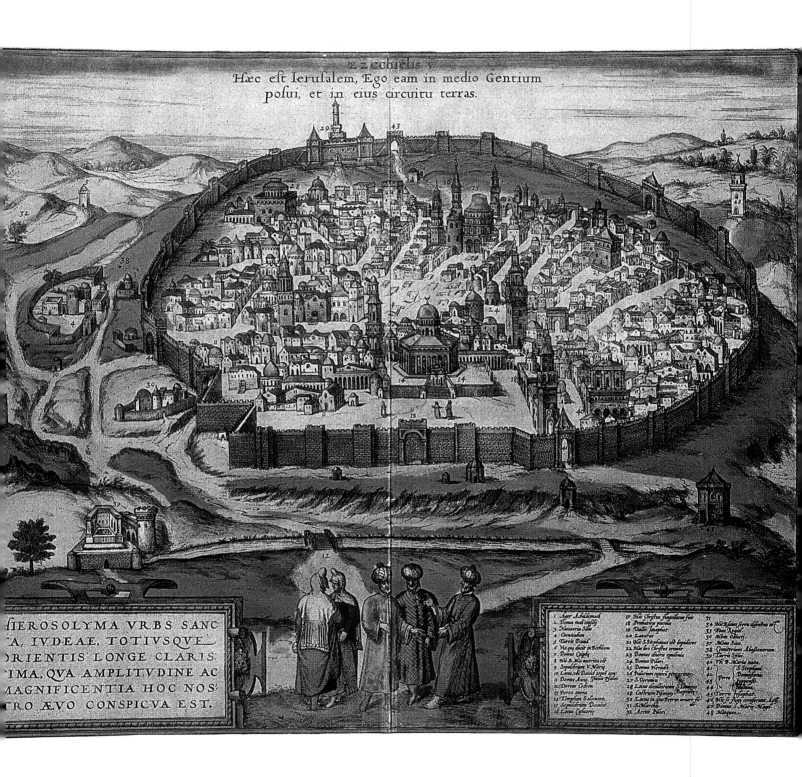

E. z echielis v.

Hæc est Ierusalem, Ego eam in medio Gentium posui, et in eius circuitu terras.

HIEROSOLYMA VRBS SANC
A, IVDEAE, TOTIVSQVE
ORIENTIS LONGE CLARIS:
IMA, QVA AMPLITVDINE AC
MAGNIFICENTIA HOC NOS
TRO AEVO CONSPICVA EST.

Antonio de Angelis de Lecce

Antonio de Angelis de Lecce,
Italian, 16th century
Hierusalem
Engraving, 1578,
550x810 mm (image)
The Moldovan Family
Collection, New York

Born in Italy, Antonio de Angelis de Lecce served as a monk of the Franciscan order, arriving in Jerusalem in 1570 and remaining there for eight years. During this time he amassed a wealth of knowledge about the city and the holy places in and around it. His map of Jerusalem, published after his return to Rome in 1578, was widely acclaimed and was repeatedly copied for several years, until it was lost. Only recently did it resurface, in a private collection in New York.

This very large map, printed from a brass engraving, presents a bird's-eye view of Jerusalem, from east to west. At the top a ribbon carried by two angels bears the caption "HIERUSALEM." In the lower left-hand corner is an oval decorated frame enclosing details about the printing of the map and dedicating it to Cardinal Alciati, "Protector of the Franciscan Order." The area encompassed by the map extends from the Kidron Valley in the east, the Kings' Tombs and the Muslim cemetery in the north, the Judean Hills up to Modi'in and Emmaus in the west, and Hebron and the Judean Desert in the south. The city itself is depicted in accuate detail. Surrounded by its wall and gates, it features prominently the Temple Mount, the Citadel, and the Holy Sepulchre, as well as a grid of streets and markets, affording the impression of a planned city. The numbers scattered across the map relate to the legend appearing on the right-hand side of the map; written in Italian, it provides information on nine sites. At the top of the frame appear the joined hands of Jesus and Saint Francis — the emblem of the Franciscan order — and below is the figure of an angel. The deployment of the map's biblical entries is mostly systematic, the sequence of the numbers conforming to the sequential location of the sites.

There is little reference in the map to the Muslim residents of the city (called "Turks" and "Moors"), and only two entries relate to its Jewish inhabitants. Most of the sites in the map refer to Christian traditions in and around Jerusalem. For some, the author quotes, in Latin, the specific reference from the Scriptures, these quotes apparently being popular among pilgrims. The map also presents a series of itineraries to the Christian holy sites in the vicinity of the city.

A one-day tour proceeds through the Monastery of the Cross to the spring where Philip baptized the eunuch (Acts 8, 36–38) — identified in those days as being southwest of Jerusalem — and from there to the village of Ein Kerem, the birthplace of John the Baptist. A second tour is longer — from Jerusalem to Bethlehem and thence to Hebron, including the holy sites along the way.

There is a notable contrast between the reliable and fairly exact description of the city and its buildings and the freely drawn depiction of the Judean Hills. Despite de Angelis's familiarity with the city's environs and the map's overall accuracy, a distortion occurs in several instances. Thus in order to highlight the Gihon spring and the Siloam pool, the area around them — known today as the City of David — does not follow the actual topography. Second, some buildings are fancifully depicted

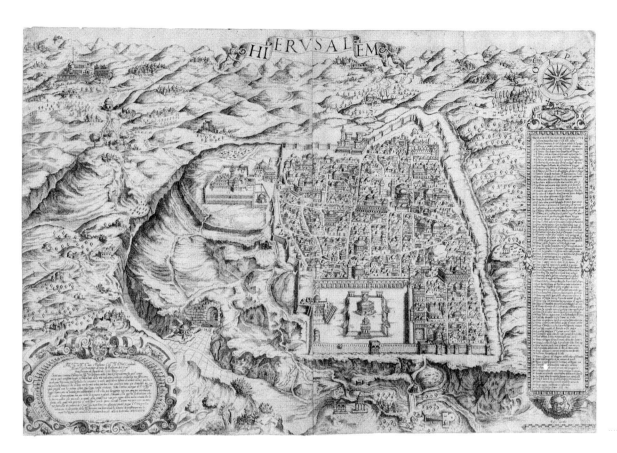

in the Italian style of the 16th century, the most outstanding examples being the (still extant) tombs of Absalom and Zechariah. Moreover, the palace of the Muslim kadi (site no. 6 on the map) and a similar building to the west of it in the Muslim Quarter both have the appearance of European palaces rather than Oriental edifices. An intriguing feature is the proportion of crosses to crescents in the map. In spite of being a Franciscan monk, de Angelis did place Muslim crescents on the tops of mosques, while omitting crosses from the churches. The only cross is in front of the al-Aqsa Mosque — a site known as "the place of the presentation of the Virgin Mary at the Temple" — this despite the fact that the mosque was in Muslim hands at the time and it is inconceivable that it would have been marked by a cross.

The map's unusually large dimensions, its vast detail, and the fact that it was based on firsthand familiarity with the city over an eight-year period greatly enhance its value as a source of information on Jerusalem at the time, particularly as regards religious traditions and the itineraries of Christian pilgrims in the city.

R. R.

A. Moldovan, "The Lost de Angelis Map of Jerusalem, 1578," *The Map Collector* 24 (September 1983), pp. 17–24.

R. Rubin, "The Map of Jerusalem by Antonio de Angelis — Original Map and Maps Derived from It," *Kathedra* 52 (1989), pp. 100–111 (in Hebrew).

R. Rubin and M. Levy, "The Legend of the de Angelis Map," *Kathedra* 52 (1989), pp. 112–19 (in Hebrew).

Juan Bautista Villalpando

Juan Bautista Villalpando,
Spanish, 1552–1608
*Vera Hierosolymae
veteris imago . . .*
(A true image of ancient
Jerusalem . . .)
Etching, 1604, 680x750 mm
From Hieronymus Prado and
Juan Bautista Villalpando,
*Explanationes in Ezechielis et
apparatus urbis ac templi
Hierosolymitani,* vol. 3,
Rome, 1604
The Gross Family Collection,
Tel Aviv

Juan Bautista Villalpando was a learned Spanish Jesuit monk and architect who lived and worked in Rome at the beginning of the 17th century. Together with another scholar he wrote an extensive commentary to the Book of Ezekiel. In the third volume of his book Villalpando analyzed the form of the Temple according to Ezekiel's vision, including a discussion from his point of view as an architect. Among the many illustrations in this book is a map entitled "A True View of Ancient Jerusalem."

The map does not relate to the actual topography of Jerusalem but creates an imaginary portrayal of the city, the hills on which it is built, and the streams around it — an image based on the Scriptures, the writings of Josephus Flavius, and other historical sources. The city is surrounded by an irregular wall, and its streets are delineated in a grid pattern. In contrast to Adrichom's map, the city area is not filled in; only major structures appear, identified by inscriptions. An inner wall divides the map into two main sections that in turn are subdivided. The right-hand (northern) section includes in its upper part "Mount Acra," "The City of Shalem of Melchizedek," and the Temple Mount with the Temple; in the lower part is the "Bezetha" quarter surrounded by its own wall, and next to it another quarter defined as the "New City." Several monuments are shown in this part of the city, among them a theater, the house of Pilate, and the Acra of Antiochus. The entire left-hand (southern) part is referred to as "Mount Zion"; a hilltop at its center, surrounded by a wall, represents the "City of David," with the king's palace in the middle. Other sites appearing in this part, are the hippodrome, the upper market, the courtyard of the water gate, and Agrippa's palace.

The Temple Mount, in the center of the map, was the focus of Villalpando's interest. Surrounded by walls, it is raised by a series of very tall supporting arches. The Temple court is divided into nine square-shaped courts, a plan based on Villalpando's interpretation of the description of the Temple in Ezekiel (40—42). This plan of the Temple Mount — especially the subdivision into nine courts and the high supporting walls — appeared in a second map in the same volume and was widely copied by others as a whole or in part.

As in other maps, the camps of the various armies that had besieged Jerusalem in the course of its history are depicted at various points around the city, along with other sites. Among the latter are Absalom's Tomb, the holy sites of Gethsemane and the Mount of Olives in the east; the Tombs of the Kings in the north; the site of the Crucifixion, identified by the inscription "Mons Calvaria," in the west; and Ager Fulloni, the cliffs of the Hinnom Valley, and Hakel-dama in the south.

Like other maps, Villalpando's is diachronic in character; it depicts, side by side, structures and sites of different ages, without chronological differentiation. Many authors used this map as a model. Some copied it fully, others appropriated selective elements, among them the massive supporting walls on which the Temple was built and the ninefold subdivision of the Temple court.

VERA HIEROSOLYMAE VETERIS IMAGO
A IOANNE BAPTISTA VILLALPANDO CORDVBENSI E SOCIETATE IESV ELABORATA PRO SVO VRBIS AC TEMPLI HIEROSOLYMITANI APPARATV COLLATO STVDIO CVM P. HIERONYMO PRADO EX EADEM SOCIETATE
Romae Superiorum permissu cum Priuilegio summi Pontificis Imperatoris Regis Catholici ac Senatus Veneti.

Villalpando's book, like other treatises on this topic, epitomizes the tendency of scholars of the time to return to ancient historical sources, as part of the enlightenment and humanism that emerged in Europe in the early 17th century.

R. R.

H. Pradus and J. B. Villalpando, *Ezechielem explanationes et apparatus urbis, ad templi Hierosolimitani*, vols. 1–3 (Rome, 1596–1604).

J. B. Villalpando, "Vera Hierololymae veteris imago," in *Ezechielem explanationes*, vol. 3 (1604), following fol. 68.

R. Rubin, *Image and Reality: Jerusalem in Maps and Views* (Jerusalem, 1999), pp. 123–35.

De Pierre

De Pierre, Austrian,
18th century
*Wahrer und gründlicher Abriss
der welt-berühmten und
hochheiligen
Stadt Jerusalem*
(A true and thorough draft of
the world-famous and most
Holy City of Jerusalem)
Etching, 1728, 633x870 mm
(plate), 540x852 mm (image)
The Jewish National and
University Library, Jerusalem
The Eran Laor
Cartographic Collection

The map of Jerusalem by De Pierre is a large detailed map of Jerusalem and environs, unusual in its rich detail, its reliability, the many illustrations of sites and figures, and the large area it encompasses. This is a rare map, known in only two copies: one in the Eran Laor Collection at the Jewish National and University Library, Jerusalem, the other in the Library of Congress, Washington, D.C.

A three-line legend in German appears at the top. The first two lines describe the map as "a precise and reliable drawing of the most famous and holiest city in the world, with all the sites and holy places in its environs, and all the noteworthy things sanctified in the life, miracles, agony, death and resurrection of Our Lord Jesus Christ." The third line dedicates the map to "The Queen Empress Elizabetha Christina V, presented to her by her humble servant, who sketched it very carefully." The printing date of the map — 1728 — is encoded in this line in the Latin letters I, V, L, C, M, used as Roman numerals.

The identity of the author is unclear, the only clue being the title "Knight of the Holy Sepulchre" (De Pierre Eques S.S. Sepulchri), which appears along the lower edge of the map. This title was bestowed by the Franciscan order in Jerusalem upon European Catholic noblemen who had completed a pilgrimage.

The center of the map is taken up by the walled city of Jerusalem, around it the area from Hebron in the south; east to Jericho, the Jordan, and the Dead Sea; west to Emmaus, Ein Kerem, and the graves of the Maccabees; and north to the line joining Jericho and Gibeon. Below, 71 items are listed in detail, referring by letters and numbers to the sites and buildings within the city and adjoining it. Outside the walls are scattered some 100 additional descriptions of sites. The combined number of sites marked in this map is far greater than that of any other map from the 15th to 18th centuries. Accompanying each inscription is a miniature drawing, artistically rendered, relating to the site or the tradition described. For instance, next to Hebron we see Cain, Abel, Abraham, and the angels; next to Bethlehem, we see the star seen by the wise men "of the East" at the birth of Christ, as well as Rachel's Tomb; and near Jerusalem, David's triumph over Goliath. Interesting is the representation of the four cities of the plain — Sodom, Gomorrah, Adamah, and Zeboim — as bonfires burning in the Dead Sea (a representation appearing also in other maps of the period).

The representation of Jerusalem is detailed and reliable; one can identify many of its buildings. The majority of sites refer to holy Christian traditions, only a few to daily life in Jerusalem. Against a realistic background the map emphasizes especially the historical recollections and religious sentiments awakened during a pilgrimage to the holy city. Various scenes are depicted from the time of Adam to that of the map's author. Thus we see Cain and Abel, Abraham and the three angels, David and Goliath, Peter weeping after his denial of Jesus, and Judas Iscariot hanging from a tree branch — alongside Greek monks, Arab horsemen, and camel caravans of the time of the author.

De Pierre paid special attention to Christian Orthodox monasteries in Jerusalem as well as in

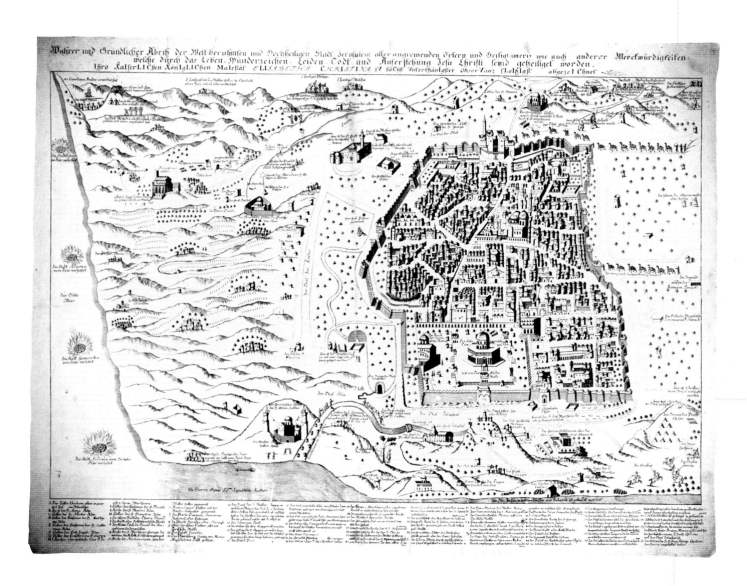

the Judean Desert. The reason may be that he copied a Greek Orthodox map included in the book by the Greek Orthodox Patriarch Chrysanthos printed that same year.

R. R.

R. Rubin, "A Chronogram-Dated Map of Jerusalem," *The Map Collector* 55 (Summer 1991), pp. 30—31.

Franz Wilhelm Sieber

Franz Wilhelm Sieber, German,
1789–1844
Karte von Jerusalem
(Map of Jerusalem)
Etching and engraving, 1823,
440x590 mm (image),
470x620 mm (sheet)
From Franz Wilhelm Sieber,
Reise von Cairo nach Jerusalem,
Prague and Leipzig, 1823
The Jewish National and
University Library, Jerusalem
The Eran Laor
Cartographic Collection

Franz Wilhelm Sieber, a physician, traveler, and naturalist from Prague, switched to the natural sciences after first studying engineering. Becoming a traveler at an early age, he brought back a whole herbarium already from his first trip, to the Alps.

In December 1816 he set off on a journey to the East. For one year he explored, collected, and mapped in Crete; then he went on to Egypt and Palestine. In April 1819 he returned to Prague laden with collections from his travels. From Egypt he brought sarcophagi, mummies, and hundreds of other items, including coins, ethnographic exhibits, and items of daily life. From Palestine he brought a collection of religious souvenirs, bird skins, amphibia, insects, and rock samples. His herbarium included plants from Egypt and Palestine as well as a collection of seeds. The Bavarian Academy of Science in Munich bought the collection, and Sieber was thus able to defray most of his travel costs. A member of several scientific societies and in contact with naturalists all over Europe, Sieber wrote prolifically about his journeys and gained world renown, in particular for the twenty-three herbaria collected on his travels in Europe, Asia, and Africa. Sadly, however, having been committed to a mental hospital in 1827, he spent the last fifteen years of his life in institutions.

After a six-week visit to Jerusalem in 1818, Sieber published the first map of the city ever to be based on exact geographic and topographic data. When asked his reasons for making this map, he mentioned his awe of the Holy City and the urgent need he felt to study it thoroughly — this apparently despite several attempts upon his life from the local population. Sieber's map met with high praise, both for its relative accuracy, given the conditions under which he had made the survey, and for its originality.

Sieber's map faces east. Outside the frame the four directions are indicated, in their Arabic versions: "evening," "sunrise," "noon," and "midnight." In the east the map encompasses the area to the top of the Mount of Olives and depicts, among other sites, the Church of the Ascension and the Tombs of the Judges; in the west the Mamilla pool; and in the south the Hill of Evil Counsel. In the north it reaches slightly beyond the northeastern corner of the wall. It also includes four sub-maps: the Holy Sepulchre, ancient Jerusalem according to the 18th-century French cartographer Bourguignon d'Anville, Jerusalem according to Richard Pococke, and "Jerusalem in 1806" according to François René de Chateaubriand. The topography is indicated by hachuring and shading; the street pattern (which omits the lanes) and main buildings are well marked and detailed. The built-up area is presented in gray, so that the undeveloped open areas inside the walls are easily discernible. Outside the city are broad spaces of tilled fields — apparently exaggerated.

The map marks a transition in the mapping of Jerusalem, from maps based on early sources and eye-witness accounts to those drawn according to actual surveys.

H. G.

F. W. Sieber, *Reise von Cairo nach Jerusalem und wieder zurück, nebst Beleuchtung einiger heiligen Orte* (Prague, 1823).

F. W. Sieber and C. von Würzbach, ed., *Biographisches Lexicon des Kaiserthums Oesterreich*, vol. 34 (Vienna, 1877), pp. 177–79.

R. Rubin, *Image and Reality: Jerusalem in Maps and Views* (Jerusalem, 1999), pp. 161–62.

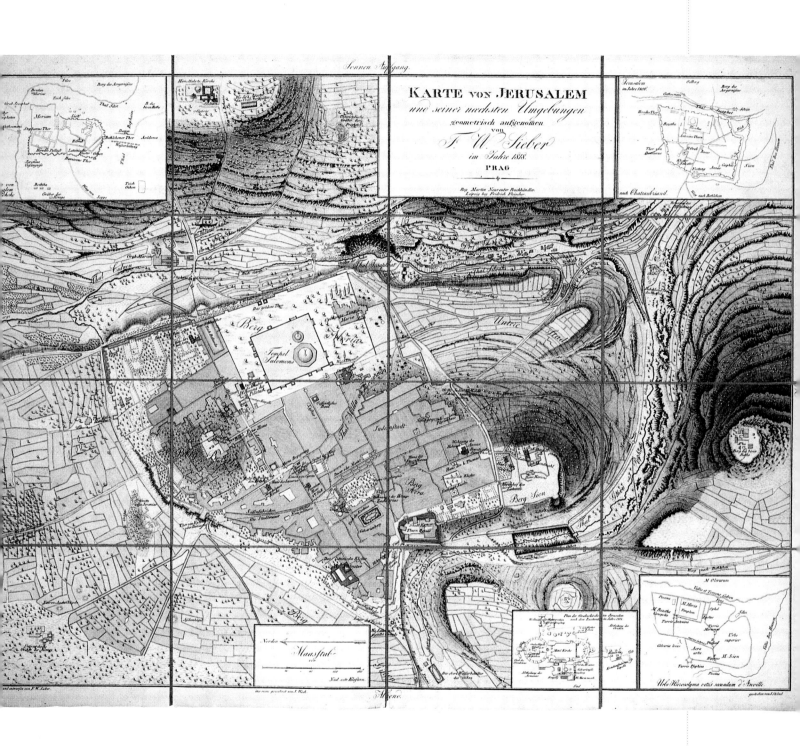

KARTE von JERUSALEM
und seiner nächsten Umgebungen
geometrisch aufgenomen
von
F. W. Sieber
im Jahre 1818.
PRAG

Carel William Meredith Van de Velde

Carel William Meredith Van de
Velde, Dutch, 1818–1898
*Plan of the Town and Environs
of Jerusalem . . .*
Lithograph, 1858,
630x800 mm
From *Memoir by Titus Tobler,*
Justus Perthes, Gotha, 1858
The Jewish and National
University Library, Jerusalem
The Eran Laor
Cartographic Collection

Carel William Meredith Van de Velde, a Dutch naval officer, acquired his expertise in surveying and mapping while working for the Royal Dutch Hydrographic Office in Batavia (the island of Java) between 1839 and 1841. Being a pious Protestant, he was keen on using his skills to explore the Holy Land. His single-handed achievements, both in cartography and in drawing, were remarkable. He made two explorations to Palestine, the first in 1851–52 and the second ten years later. These explorations yielded a travelogue in book format, an album of a hundred admirable water colors, and a map of Palestine on a scale of 1:315,000 in eight sheets. The book, which was published in several editions, in German and in English, included a memorandum detailing its preparation, a map of the environs of Jerusalem on a scale of 1:125,000, and the map exhibited here on a scale of 1:10,000.

Van de Velde was well aware that one man alone could not survey and map the whole of Palestine. He therefore made use of the earlier maps available to him as well as putting together information discerningly gleaned from other maps and travel descriptions. To these he added the results of his own surveys, carried out with minimal portable equipment.

Two previous sources served him when preparing the map of Jerusalem. The first was a trigonometric survey carried out by a group of British officers, mostly surveyors of the Royal Engineers' Corps, who had accompanied the forces sent to Syria in the summer of 1840 under Admiral Sir Robert Stopford,

as part of the effort to terminate Egyptian hegemony in Palestine and reestablish Ottoman rule. In the winter of 1841 they had surveyed Jerusalem and drawn a map on a scale of 1:4,800, using various equipment — such as instruments for astronomic calculations and for measuring heights — that was not available to Van de Velde. Yehoshua Ben-Arieh praises the team's proficient mapping of the environs of the city; however, it seems that the measurements taken inside the city were insufficient, and the description of the network of streets is therefore incomplete and often inaccurate.

Van de Velde's second source was the city map drawn by Titus Tobler (1806–1877), a Swiss physician who became one of the foremost 19th-century European scholars of Palestine and Jerusalem. Tobler made four expeditions to the country and wrote dozens of books and articles that still serve as an invaluable source for cartographic research. His second visit was devoted specifically to the study of Jerusalem, and one of its outcomes was a city map, published in 1849, which was also based on previous maps but gave for the first time a full picture of the streets and alleys of the entire city.

The map featured here was published in 1858 by the Geographic Institute of the Perthes Brothers publishing house in Gotha, Germany. Prepared by Van de Velde on the basis of the maps compiled by the British officers and by Tobler, as well as on the data he himself had collected in the early 1850s, it is accompanied by a memorandum by Tobler.

The map, measuring 700x800 mm, does full justice to Van de Velde's skill. The hachuring artistically portrays the topography of the environs: the streams encircling the city and the hills surrounding it. The many graveyards outside the walls are prominently marked, as is the network of paths leading to the gates. The description of the area within the walls is largely based on the information Van de Velde derived from the two aforementioned maps. An important document for the study of Jerusalem at that period, the map details, for example, the few buildings that existed outside the walls before the process of building neighborhoods beyond the walls began in the later part of the century.

H. G.

C. W. M. Van de Velde, *Memoir to Accompany the Map of the Holy Land* (Gotha, 1858).

Y. Ben-Arieh, "The First Survey Maps of Jerusalem," *Eretz Israel* 11 (I. Dunayevsky Book) (1984), pp. 64–74 (in Hebrew).

H. Goren, *"Go Spy Out the Land": German Exploration of Palestine in the 19th Century* (Jerusalem, 1999) (in Hebrew).

Y. Jones, "British Military Surveys of Palestine and Syria, 1840–1841," *The Cartographic Journal* 10, no. 2 (1973), pp. 29–41.

The Ordnance Survey and the Palestine Exploration Fund

Sir Charles William Wilson,
English, 1836–1905
Ordnance Survey of Jerusalem,
·1:10,000, 1864–65,
1005x710 mm
From Charles W. Wilson,
Ordnance Survey of Jerusalem,
George E. Lyre and
William Spottiswoode
for Her Majesty's
Stationery Office,
London, 1865
The Wajntraub Family
Collection, Jerusalem

The 1865 map of the Old City of Jerusalem prepared by the British Ordnance Survey was the first accurate map of the city. Previous attempts to produce a detailed and precise map of the city met with varying degrees of success. The most noteworthy were the landmark maps made in the course of the 19th century by the physician and natural historian F. W. Sieber (1818), the architect F. Catherwood (1833), the soldiers Lieutenant E. Aldrich, and Lieutenant J. F. A. Symonds, R.E. (1841), the Swiss physician T. Tobler (1845), and the Dutch explorer C. W. M. Van de Velde (1858) — the latter being the best available map until publication of the Ordnance Survey of Jerusalem. Each of the above-mentioned mapmakers relied on and tried to surpass his predecessors, until Captain Wilson started the process of scientifically mapping Jerusalem from the beginning, even though he knew the previous maps.

The survey of Jerusalem originated in a petition from Dean Stanley of Westminster to Lord de Grey and Ripon, British Secretary of State for War, indicating that the city sorely needed an improved water supply and sewerage system, and that this could not be achieved without a proper mapping expedition first being undertaken. Notwithstanding the stated aim of the survey, it was actually of a broader scientific nature. The work was funded by a donation from the philanthropist Angela Georgina (later Baroness) Burdett-Coutts. The expedition was organized by Colonel Sir Henry James, Director General of the Ordnance Survey, and led by Captain Charles W. Wilson of the Royal Engineers.

The survey party reached Jerusalem in October 1864, and surveying proceeded until May 1865, with the use of local laborers. The baseline was half a mile to three quarters of a mile long, measured three times with a standard chain that was checked between reference marks laid down on the ground with a leveling staff. The surveying of the angles of triangulation was done with the use of a 7-inch theodolite, whereas the longer and more difficult lines were laid down and a traverse survey of the city and the Haram al-Sharif (Temple Mount) was done with a 5-inch theodolite. The map of the city (scale 1:2,500) was contoured at 10 feet vertical intervals and showed details of all the streets and important buildings. Benchmarks were cut at the corners of the city walls, at the city gates, and on churches and other public buildings. Another smaller map (scale 1:10,000) was prepared of the environs of the city, covering an area about 3 miles square, showing the principal valleys and elevated areas, as well as various features and buildings located outside the Old City. In addition, Wilson drew detailed plans of the Citadel structures, the Haram al-Sharif, and the Church of the Holy Sepulchre. Accompanying the survey team was a professional photographer, Sergeant James McDonald, R.E., who prepared an extremely valuable pictorial record of the city's buildings. The activities of the survey led to local fears that it was the harbinger of increased taxation, and some residents of the Jewish Quarter refused Wilson entry to their houses. The architectural historian James Fergusson visited Jerusalem toward the end of October and together with Wilson examined

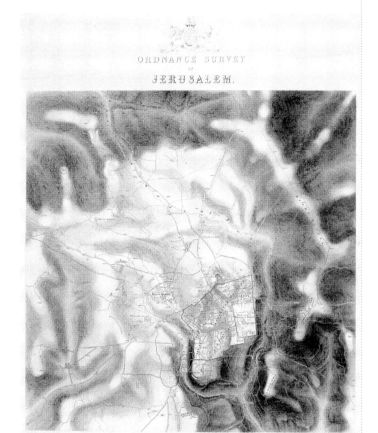

many of its subterranean antiquities, particularly in the area of the Haram al-Sharif.

In his preface to the published survey Sir Henry James asserted that its success was one of the reasons for the founding of the Palestine Exploration Fund in 1865. Charles Warren, who succeeded Wilson in the task of exploring Jerusalem, supervised Corporal Hancock in March–June 1867 in the completion of the contouring around Jerusalem and the plumbing of the city walls.

In 1868 relief maps of the city and its environs were produced by the Ordnance Survey and offered for sale to educational establishments and museums. The Ordnance Survey map of Jerusalem continued to be used by the PEF's explorers, notably by C. F. T. Drake, C. R. Conder, Conrad Schick, J. E. Hanauer, and others; a new edition incorporating their discoveries and corrections was printed in 1876. This updated version was subsequently used by all visiting explorers and resident antiquarians of Jerusalem, and when a new map was prepared by the Palestine Survey in 1937 only minor revisions were deemed necessary. The revision survey was conducted in 1935–36 by J. H. Mankin, Superintendent of Surveys in the British Mandate government, who proudly noted: "It must be recorded that the great work carried out under difficult conditions during the Turkish regime by the 1865 Sapper Surveyors stood the test of time and was — in fact — a monumental survey."

S. G.

Y. Ben-Arieh, "The First Surveyed Maps of Jerusalem," *Eretz-Israel* 11 (1973), pp. 64–74 (in Hebrew).

Y. Ben-Arieh, "The Catherwood Map of Jerusalem," *The Quarterly Journal of the Library of Congress* (July 1974), pp. 150–60.

S. Gibson, "The Holy Land in the Sights of Explorers' Cameras," in *Jerusalem in the Mind of the Western World, 1800–1948, With Eyes to Zion*, vol. 5, ed. Y. Ben-Arieh and M. Davis (Westport, 1997), pp. 235–48.

I. D. Hart, "The Surveys of Palestine," *The Royal Engineers Journal* (September 1965), pp. 214–25.

Y. Jones, "British Military Surveys of Palestine and Syria 1840–41," *The Cartographic Journal* 10 (1973), pp. 29–41.

J. H. Mankin, "Survey of the Old City of Jerusalem, 1865 and 1935," *Palestine Exploration Journey* (January–June, 1969), pp. 37–39.

H. E. M. Newman, "The Ordnance Survey in the Near East," *The Royal Engineers Journal* (March–June 1949), pp. 64–77, 168–81.

G. Webster, "Portrait: Baroness Angela Georgina Burdett-Coutts," *Biblical Archaeologist* 48 (1985), pp. 186–89.

Hermann Bollmann

Hermann Bollmann, German,
1911–1971
Map of Jerusalem, 1:5,000
Colored offset print, 1969
605x942 mm
Published by Wim van Leer
Publications Co. Ltd.,
commissioned by
Carta Ltd., Jerusalem

This map of Jerusalem, drawn by Hermann Bollmann, was commissioned by Wim Van Leer, an industrialist and filmmaker. Following the Six-Day War and the reunification of Jerusalem, Van Leer decided he would like to produce a three-dimensional map of Jerusalem like the map of Amsterdam he had in his possession. The only person capable of making such a map was Hermann Bollmann, a native of the city of Braunschweig in Germany. Bollmann spent five weeks photographing 187,000 ground and aerial views of the city from different angles and then spent twelve months making the seven sketches that constitute the 20x6 m map of the city. His draftsmanship was amazingly precise — every window and balcony, every floor and special building, and even such things as construction cranes were blended into the map as part of the panorama at that particular point in time. The map was delimited in such a way as to incorporate on the one hand the Old City, including the Kidron Valley, and on the other the more recently built areas, including the Givat Ram university campus, the Knesset, the government offices, and in the center the old neighborhoods such as Mea Shearim, Geula, and Nahlaot and the newer ones such as Rehavia and Talbieh.

This colored map was first printed in 1969 in two versions: one on a scale of 1:5,000, the other, just of the Old City, on a scale of 1:3,000. In addition, a black-and-white version of the original was prepared and made available to decorators and architects, but there did not prove to be much demand for it.

The map's draftsmanship is supremely elegant and shows outstanding attention to detail. The height of the buildings has been cropped in order to emphasize the facades, creating the vantage point of a passerby, in contrast to an aerial perspective, which emphasizes the roofs. Occasionally, narrow streets have been widened for the sake of sketching in details of buildings. Bollmann's choice of colors was felt by him to reflect the nature of the city: shades of light blue-gray were used for buildings and landscapes, with shades of brownish-red for tiled roofs and a yellowish hue for others. An exclusive version of the map that had some of the items as well as the decorative border embossed in gold came to be known as "Jerusalem of Gold." Worthy of note is the map's illuminated border, executed in the style of ancient maps and featuring the word "Jerusalem" in 16 languages — in fact, a work of art in itself. The map's orientation is tilted slightly to the northeast to provide the ideal angle for a three-dimensional portrayal of the buildings. The shading assumed the source of light to be from the northwest.

Hermann Bollmann, cartographer and artist, was born in 1911 in Braunschweig, Germany. He studied graphics and woodcutting, and after World War II was appointed to document the restoration of the war-scarred city. He gained additional experience preparing a detailed map of Amsterdam, which he did by walking the streets with an easel and making detailed drawings of all the buildings. Bollmann developed a graphic style all his own. In 1948 he conducted a field survey of 24 European (mainly

German) cities, from which he produced three-dimensional maps. He then perfected his work methods. Using an automatic camera with a wide-angled lens mounted on the roof of a commercial vehicle and connected to a distance gauge, he could in one short drive take thousands of photos of a city's layout. He also installed a network of eight cameras on an airplane, which made it possible for him to survey a large city in less than an hour, taking 7,000 photographs. Bollmann's series includes 120 maps of cities in Germany, Switzerland, Holland, and Denmark, as well as of New York City; he has also published maps of Nazareth, Bethlehem, and Acre. Bollmann published part of his maps — some representing two or more points in time — in a book entitled *Städte* (Cities), but Jerusalem was not included. Since 1978 his son-in-law, Friedrich Bollmann, has directed the publishing company, taking care to update the maps every 10—15 years on the basis of meticulous fieldwork in the spirit of Hermann Bollmann.

T. S.

Aerial Photography in Palestine

Aerial photography is a direct tool for documenting the landscape and studying the appearance of the land surface. The photograph preserves the changes occurring over time and records the physical and cultural imprint of natural phenomena and man's way of life on the landscape. Many layers of raw data are captured in an aerial photograph, and these aid us in describing and analyzing the history of the land, its development, its physical planning, its reconstruction — in cases where destruction has occurred — and its preservation.

The first aerial photography of Palestine was of Acre, on 31 December 1913, from a French airplane on its way from Paris to Jerusalem and Cairo. Since then, the country has been photographed by people of various nationalities involved in aerial activity over Palestine, both civilian and military.

World War I provided the impetus for the first wave of aerial photography, the battle over this country being accompanied by a great deal of activity on the part of air squadrons — British (including one Australian) as well as German. The pilots photographed for a variety of purposes: intelligence, mapping, the recording of ancient sites. These were the first photographs of the country, and they numbered in the thousands.

During the British Mandate the Royal Air Force, at the government's request, made aerial photographs of the country for purposes of security, city planning, archaeological surveys, and mapping. Civilians too now joined in the aerial photography, largely for Zionist purposes and for journalistic documentation of public events. During World War II the scope of aerial photography grew significantly. Allied air squadrons stationed in the area provided aerial photographs of the country and its surroundings needed by the military. But it was only at the end of the war, in December 1944, when the need for photographic missions in Europe declined, that a British air squadron was seconded to systematically photograph the entire country — for the first time in its history.

Prior to the 1947–1948 War of Independence, several strategic sites had been surreptitiously photographed from the air, at great risk, by a Palmach air squadron, and during the war, too, targets were photographed by the "Air Services" — the budding Israeli Air Force. In 1949 civilian aerial photography was launched by the Institute of Photogrammetry, and in 1956 the Israel Survey Department started regular and systematic aerial photography for mapping, planning, and development purposes.

The historical aerial photographs of Palestine were in black and white. Today most photographs are in color, adding rich information about the landscape, as well as making for pleasant viewing.

Since World War I topographic mapping has availed itself of aerial photography, and this includes a small number of maps produced by the Mandatory government. During World War II, this so-called photogrammetric mapping was much improved and

became the main tool for surveying and creating topographic maps.

An aerial photograph differs from a map. The former represents the landscape through a lens and thus not vertically, as does a map. Moreover, its scale is not uniform. Information in a photograph is raw — i.e, topically undifferentiated — unlike that found in maps meant for various purposes. Reading a map and interpreting an aerial photograph are therefore entirely different processes. A map will usually carry a legend that simplifies its reading, whereas the information in an aerial photograph requires deciphering by a trained eye.

D. G.

D. Gavish, "Aerial Perspective of Past Landscapes," in *The Land That Became Israel*, ed. Ruth Kark (Jerusalem, 1989), pp. 308—19.

Satellite images represent the technologically most advanced stage in mapmaking. In a sense, for the first time in the history of humanity the "instantaneous God's-eye view" is laid before us, enabling us to gauge the extent to which maps made throughout history, most measured with minimal and simple tools, were faithful to reality. A number of central dates stand out in the saga of satellite imagery: 1829 — the first photograph is taken by two Frenchmen; 1858 — the first aerial photograph is taken from a balloon; 1909 — the first photograph from an aircraft is taken by an American pilot; 1957 — the first satellite, the Russian *Sputnik*, is launched; 1961 — the first cosmonaut is sent into space; 1972 — the first satellite, NASA's *Landsat*, is employed for mapmaking; 1986 — the French satellite *Spot 1* is launched via the missile *Ariane*; 1988 — the first Israeli satellite, *Ofek 1*, is launched.

These images are not photographs in the traditional sense of the word — light exposed on photographic film. It is a blend of spectral (i. e., light and radiation of different wave lenghts) sensors or sensory channels transmitted in images made up of a large number of pixels, to stations on the Earth's surface, which receive the data and process it. The *Spot* satellite greatly improved the resolution of the data, allowing for transmission back to Earth of images of a stereoscopic nature: when viewed with special glasses they can be seen in 3-D. The satellite, weighing 1,750 kg, floats at an average height of 832 km above the sea, attaining a complete coverage of the Earth's surface in a series of orbits around it for the duration of 26 days. A single orbit takes 101 minutes, with every image covering an area of 60x60 km.

Apart from mapping, satellite data have many uses, such as land and water, agriculture and forestry, urban development research, etc. Such information can then be used in subject maps as well.

The unusual image shown here — a diagonal view from northeast to southwest encompassing a large part of the historical Land of Israel — is the brainchild of Richard Cleave, aided by his son Adrian, and published by RØHR Productions Ltd. The project is the result of intensive cooperation with John K. Hall of the Israel Geological Institute, and Gennady Agranov and Craig Gotsman, computer scientists at the Technion, Haifa. The image combines color information from the *Landsat* and high-resolution gray-scale information from *Spot*, merged by the computer scientists with topographic data from a digital terrain model. This combination of a bird's-eye view with information regarding surface elevations provides a 3-D effect and makes for the simulation of the view as if recorded from space.

Another version of the image, using layer tints representing differences in elevation on the surface, gives the sense of a relief map, strengthening the 3-D impression of the area's rich and varied topography. One can clearly see the snowy Hermon range at the bottom of the image, the Jordan Valley, the Sea of Galilee, the Dead Sea, and the Arava down to Eilat. The hilly Galilee terrain, the Jezreel Valley, the Carmel range, the mountains of Judea and Samaria, the Judean and Negev deserts, and of course the curved coastline, are instantly recognizable.

The shading on the map is the result of information received from *Landsat* at 9.30 a.m. on a day in the month of January, when the sun is low in the south and creates a shadow toward the northwest. Cleave claims that geographical relief is best achieved when shadows fall across the picture, and hence the preference for a southwestern orientation. Obviously, this diagonal perspective does not allow for a uniform scale, and the foreshortening of the Arava Valley as opposed to the lengthening of the Jordan Valley stand out.

An additional aspect of satellite mapping is its use in navigation. A technological revolution has occurred in this field, and today, using GPS (global positioning systems), it is possible to pinpoint, in seconds, a location that is accurate to the centimeter.

A. T.

R. L. W. Cleave (et al.), *The Holy Land Satellite Atlas*, vols. 1 and 2 (RØHR Productions Ltd, Nicosia, 1999).

Biblical Archaeologist 60, no. 3 (September 1997).

Index

Photographic Credits: